OUTSTANDING PRAISE FOR

SNAPSHOTS FROM HELL

"Perceptive, instructive, and always entertaining, this is the one book that should be read by anyone thinking of going to business school."
—Laurence Tisch, chairman, president, and CEO, CBS Inc.

"An engaging, critical look at his year at Stanford's Graduate School of Business."
—San Jose Mercury News

"For anyone contemplating business school, SNAPSHOTS is as useful as a 'Let's Go' guide in the backpack of the budget traveler."
—Chicago Tribune

"Robinson's primer covers it all. . . . Gives readers a thorough look at the rigors involved in getting an MBA."
—Christian Science Monitor

"A funny and frenetic account. . . . An education in itself as well as a cautionary tale."
—Kirkus Reviews

"Robinson is a graceful writer and sharp observer."
—Boston Globe

more . . .

more . . .

Snapshots from Hell

The Making of an MBA

Peter Robinson

WARNER BOOKS

A Time Warner Company

Warner Books Edition
Copyright © 1994 by Peter Robinson
All rights reserved.

Warner Books, Inc., 1271 Avenue of the Americas, New York, NY 10020

Ⓦ A Time Warner Company

Printed in the United States of America
First Trade Printing: August 1995
10 9 8 7 6 5 4 3 2 1

Originally published in hardcover by Warner Books, Inc.

Library of Congress Cataloging-in-Publication Data
Robinson, Peter
  Snapshots from hell: the making of an MBA / Peter Robinson.
    p. cm
  ISBN 0-446-67117-7
    1. Robinson, Peter, 1957– 2. Business students—California—Stanford—
Biography. 3. Stanford University. Graduate School of Business. I. Title.
HF1134.S77R63 1994
650'.092—dc20
[B]   93-47682
                                              CIP

Cover design by Diane Luger and Tori Nelson
Cover type by Nicholas Brealey Publishing

ATTENTION: SCHOOLS AND CORPORATIONS

WARNER books are available at quantity discounts with bulk purchase for educational, business, or sales promotional use. For information, please write to: SPECIAL SALES DEPARTMENT, WARNER BOOKS, 1271 AVENUE OF THE AMERICAS, NEW YORK, N.Y. 10020

ARE THERE WARNER BOOKS
YOU WANT BUT CANNOT FIND IN YOUR LOCAL STORES?

You can get any WARNER BOOKS title in print. Simply send title and retail price, plus 95¢ per order and 95¢ per copy to cover mailing and handling costs for each book desired. New York State and California residents add applicable sales tax. Enclose check or money order only, no cash please, to: WARNER BOOKS, P.O. BOX 690, NEW YORK, N.Y. 10019

For Edita

Recibe estas arras

CONTENTS

Snapshots from Hell

October 13

It is one o'clock in the morning, I have at least two more hours of studying to do, and I am struggling to stay alert by gulping coffee that was cold at midnight.

My friend Steven warned me before I came here that most of my classmates would be former engineers, consultants, and financial analysts, people who knew how to work with numbers. "Then there'll be a few students with flaky backgrounds like yours," he said. "Poets. You know, people who've never done anything real for a living."

Today this poet sat through all three of his classes feeling utterly lost, then went to the library and studied "utility maximization" models for two hours but still couldn't do the problems. Finally I gave up and went to the campus bookstore. When I picked up a book I recognized, the Divine Comedy, I flipped to the canto in which Dante finds himself standing at the gates of the inferno, looking up at the inscription:

ABANDON ALL HOPE, YE WHO ENTER HERE.

That's me all right, I thought. A poet in hell.

AUTHOR'S NOTE

I owe this book to Scott Turow, for two reasons. *One L,* Turow's book about his first year as a student at Harvard Law School, helped persuade me not to go to law school. Turow writes vividly. He presents detail. Had I been of the proper temperament to become a lawyer, *One L* would have kindled a little flame within my breast. As it was, the book poured cold water on an idea that deserved to be doused.

One L also prompted me to believe that a similar book, about business school, could prove useful.

Each year, tens of thousands of young Americans consider going to business school. Each year, these Americans are joined by thousands abroad. My class at Stanford business school included students from Japan, Ghana, New Zealand, Mexico, Argentina, and most of the nations of Western Europe. (Current Stanford classes include students from Russia and China.) All these thousands find themselves beset by an itch to make something of themselves. All want, to be crass, to make money.

They begin to investigate the business school proposition as I did, by requesting catalogues from the array of business schools that interest them. But when the catalogues arrive, they turn out to contain only glossy photographs, scant facts about the curriculum, and, typically, seductive sales pitches—business schools, after all, know something about marketing.

No matter how much information these catalogues convey, they fail to answer the prospective student's paramount question, the only question that really matters. What is business school like?

What will the other students be like? Number-crunchers? Hustlers? What about the professors? The workload? The cost? Can you have a social life?

To repeat: What is business school *like?*

In the following pages, I attempt to answer that question.

I attended the Stanford University Graduate School of Business in Stanford, California, some thirty miles south of San Francisco, from 1988 to 1990. Like all my classmates, I went to business school to acquire a credential—a Master of Business Administration, or MBA, degree—that I believed would launch me into a stimulating and lucrative business career. Unlike the majority of my classmates, who arrived at business school with two or three years of business experience, I also went to business school to learn the basic disciplines. Within just a couple of days of my arrival, I discovered that business school was going to be a far more turbulent and, as they say in California, awesome experience than I had expected, and I began keeping a journal and making notes for this account. Soon I came to see writing this book as a simple act of decency, like going back to the last calm bend in the river and nailing up a sign that reads, "Waterfall Ahead."

I graduated in 1990, as I've said, just when the long boom of the eighties was coming to an end. Yet even in the recession that followed, business schools remained a remarkable phenomenon.

Right through the depths of the recession, more than 250,000 young men and women a year paid $40 apiece to take the GMAT, the Graduate Management Admissions Test, the scores that most business schools require, while some 75,000 a year actually went on to enroll in business schools. (Contrast this with the somewhat more than 200,000 a year who took the LSAT, the Law School Admissions Test, and the fewer than 50,000 a year who entered law schools.) And right through the depths of the recession, the marketplace went on rewarding students for getting MBAs. The median starting salary for the Stanford business school Class of 1991, the class that graduated into the worst economy in a decade, was more than $65,000.

Business school, as we shall see, is not a sure ticket to riches. Yet during recessions as in boom times, MBAs remain in many ways a special class of people, who lead exceptional lives.

In writing about my experience at Stanford, I confine myself to the first year of the two-year MBA program. At any business school the first year is the year of drama. It is the year of new faces and new surroundings. It is also the year of loneliness, self-doubt, and constant, unyielding pressure. For a great many students there come moments during the first year when, often for the first time in their lives, they wonder, quite seriously, whether they will fail. By the second year the pressure, along with the self-doubt, has abated. Nobody thinking about going to business school needs to worry about getting through the second year, any more than he needs to worry about being able to endure springtime after a bitter winter. It is the first year he had better ponder.

Everything I write about happened. But in the interest of a readable narrative I have compressed the action to some extent, taking liberties with dates and chronology. In order to protect the privacy of my classmates and the business school faculty, I have peopled the book almost entirely with composite characters, each made up of traits, experiences, and backgrounds drawn from several others. The professors in the pages that follow are not the professors whose classes I took. My roommates, although based on students I knew, are not my true roommates. The very few characters who appear under their own names either gave me their permission to portray them or are public figures whose identity it would have been silly to disguise.

Although I try to convey the feel of the business school curriculum without being technical, there are a few passages in the book some readers will find heavy going. If you do, skip them. I often wished I could skip some material myself.

One final note.

I am proud to be a graduate of Stanford business school. The faculty and administrators are men and women of unusual intelligence and ability, constantly striving to adapt and improve an already remarkable institution. If some of what follows sounds critical, it is based on notes that were written *in extremis*. Now that business school is well behind me, I find myself looking back on Stanford with a kind of awe at all that it taught me.

Sometimes these days I even see Stanford through such a golden haze of affection that I wish for a moment that I could go back. Then I ask myself, *What would you do if somebody actually told you that you had to repeat the first year?*

The answer is always the same. *Drop to my knees and beg for mercy.*

PROLOGUE

Farewell
to the Chief

One Friday evening in the summer of 1988, I said goodbye to the President of the United States.

I stood for a moment on the colonnade that runs in the shape of an L along two sides of the Rose Garden, waiting. The broad rectangle of lawn in the middle of the garden, so exquisitely fertilized, reseeded, aerated, watered, and mown that in the midday glare it could look like a putting green, had taken on a rich, stately hue. Among the shrubs and flowers of the garden borders, shadows had gathered, making dark accents. The whiteness of the White House itself had faded to cream.

Jim Kuhn, President Reagan's personal aide, opened the door to the Oval Office. "He's finishing his paperwork," Jim said. "It'll be just another minute."

Jim met the President every morning in the family quarters on the second floor of the Residence, rode down with him in the elevator, and walked with him along this colonnade, from the Residence at the long end of the L to the Oval Office at the other end. Then, in the evening, Jim walked the President back. Sometimes Jim arranged for a departing member of the staff to make this evening walk with the President, too. It gave the staffer a moment to say farewell.

The door to the Oval Office swung open. Jim Kuhn stepped out.

A photographer followed, then a Secret Service agent, and then, after a moment, the President.

The President wore a brown suit. His face looked ruddy, soft, and friendly. He looked at me and winked. "Well, Peter," he said, "I want to thank you for all you've done."

The photographer snapped a few standard handshake shots, and for a moment I thought that would be all. Then President Reagan, his actor's eye ever alert, turned to the photographer and said, "This is a pretty sunset. What about a few walking shots?" So the President and I strolled along the colonnade, chatting, while the photographer scuttled along in front of us, the motor drive on his camera whirring away. When we reached the door to the Residence, the President paused.

"Now, just where is it that you're going?"

"Stanford business school, Mr. President."

"Stanford? Well, you be careful. The faculty out there is a little . . ."

His eyes pooled up with mirth and he put his head to one side and gave it that famous little Reagan shake. I knew what he was recalling, of course. Stanford had once been suggested as the site for the Reagan Library, a complex to house the President's papers after he left the White House. But the Stanford faculty and students had protested. There had been marches, placards, and ugly speeches—a brief reeffulgence of the sixties. The proposal for putting the Reagan Library at Stanford had been dropped.

The President held his pause for an actor's beat, a perfect, rounded moment. "The faculty out there is a little . . . left-leaning." He chuckled. "But you get in touch with my friend Milton Friedman. Milton will keep you on the straight-and-narrow."

Jim Kuhn handed the President a small box, gift-wrapped in gold foil. Inside, I knew, lay a pair of cufflinks embossed with the presidential seal.

"Well, thank you again for all you've done," the President said, handing me the box. "Especially that speech at the Berlin Wall." He gave me another wink. "I was very eloquent in Berlin."

The Secret Service agent opened the Residence door. The President shook my hand once again.

"Good luck," he said.

Then the President, Jim Kuhn, and the agent stepped through the door and were gone.

The photographer turned to walk back to his office in the West Wing. I dawdled, taking in the scene around me before leaving the White House for the last time.

The last time. Only now, as I lingered before walking back to gather the few remaining possessions in my office in the Old Executive Office Building, did the finality of what I had chosen to do begin to sink in. The past week had simply been too hectic, a blur. It wasn't until the day before, Thursday, that I'd shipped the last of more than twenty boxes of books, kitchen utensils, and winter clothes (no need for my heaviest coats and sweaters in California) home to my parents, who would hire a kid from the neighborhood to stack them in their cellar. I'd spent untold hours disposing of furniture, closing out accounts, and attending to last-minute paperwork from Stanford. Every night for more than a week I'd had to go out for drinks or dinner as friends had said goodbye and wished me well.

Now I thought of all I was giving up. It had been fun to work at the White House, the nerve center of global and national affairs but also an island of small comforts, even outright luxuries. When I traveled with the Chief, a government car would drive me to Andrews Air Force Base and Air Force One, which would fly us directly to our destination and the waiting motorcade. No ticket lines—no tickets. Calling from the White House, I never, *ever* had to wonder whether or not a phone call would be returned. Even my office (which had once belonged to John Dean, of Watergate fame) carried with it comforts known by few other thirty-year-olds—fourteen-foot ceilings, handsome hardwood furniture, a marble fireplace. I could get to work in the morning, have a cup of coffee and read the newspapers in the White House mess, then stroll out to the South Lawn to listen to the Marine Band play anthems as the limousines of heads of state pulled up to the Portico and howitzers on the Ellipse boomed salutes. I was giving all of this up . . . to go to business school? To become, once again, a student?

Was I doing the right thing?

I was not alone in asking. For weeks, my boss, Tony, the Chief
Speechwriter, had tried to talk me out of leaving. "Peter," he would
say, "this is the center of things. You can make a difference here. You
want to give this up to become just another Wall Street prissy in an
$800 suit?" Sure, MBAs made a lot of money. But they ended up
spending it all so they could live in Connecticut and send their kids
to effete boarding schools. They barely knew their kids anyway,
because they all worked about a hundred hours a week and burned out
at the age of forty-five. "That's what you want? Are you *crazy*?"

Even casual acquaintances looked at me as if they must be missing
something when I told them of my plans. "You're at the White
House," one said, "you're writing speeches for the President, and
you're leaving to go to business school? Isn't that a step backward?"

Was I doing the right thing?

Was I crazy?

Was this a step backward?

I had worked my way through these questions during the long
winter months as the Reagan administration entered its final year.
I had been at the White House for six years since arriving, directly from graduate school, at the age of twenty-five. I came from a
small town called Vestal, just outside Binghamton, in upstate
New York. I had gone to a public high school. My family was
modestly middle class, and my parents had limited their involve-
ment in politics to voting. I had no conceivable claim on a job at
the White House, and when I presented myself to Vice President
Bush's speechwriter, showing him a letter of recommendation
from a journalist friend, I would have been grateful if he had
directed me to a middle-level position in Department of the
Interior or the Post Office. Instead he told me he had an idea.
Since he was about to leave the White House, since his replacement had just fallen through, and since no one on the Vice
President's staff wanted to give up what he was doing to work on
speeches, why didn't I just take his job?

A year and a half later I benefited from a second fluke. Three
Reagan writers left within months of each other, cutting the

President's speechwriting staff in half. The Director of Communications needed at least one replacement fast. He took me.

Not until the administration had less than a year to run had I begun to consider what I would do next. Politics, law, and journalism were the fields in which I supposed my experience promised the best opportunities. Yet there had been problems with each.

Politics? The obvious move was from the Reagan White House to the Bush campaign. Bush's Press Secretary talked to me about joining the campaign. The excitement, the adrenaline rush, of a presidential campaign appealed to me. But if George Bush won? Back to the White House and more of the same. I detected a lack of progress.

Law? I felt I had a fitness or aptitude for law, and some years earlier, as a result of one of my temporary spells of frustration at the White House, I had applied to one or two leading law schools and been accepted. But most of the lawyers I knew who were actually practicing law were bored. At age thirty, I doubted the wisdom of devoting three years and considerable expense to getting a degree I was uncertain I would ever want to use.

"Forget it," an editor at a national newsmagazine said when I asked about journalism. "You'd have to train alongside completely green kids straight out of college. And the pay would stink."

Politics, law, and journalism got me nowhere.

I doubt I would have pursued them, anyway. During my years in government I had grown curious about and then fascinated by a field that had never interested me during college or grad school—business. I had spent six years writing speeches about how the private sector was creating new jobs at the rate of more than 100,000 a month, far more than any government program could attempt, and about how blacks and other minorities were benefiting from among the most dramatic gains in income that they had experienced in American history. I had become convinced that free markets represented an enormous force for good.

I had also witnessed—all too plainly, and increasingly over time—the good that free markets were doing for my friends. When I joined Vice President Bush's staff and began drawing a government salary, most of my college friends were making somewhat more in the private sector, but not dramatically more. Charles, a former roommate who had just started at an investment bank in New York, represented the extreme. He was making about two and a half times my salary, not more.

But in subsequent years my friends' incomes rose steeply while my own remained relatively flat. By the time three years had passed, Steven, another former roommate, had graduated from Stanford business school, started work with a management consulting firm, and begun making more than twice as much as I. And after I had spent a full six years on a government paycheck, Steven was making close to three times as much as I, Charles more than five times as much.

None of this had mattered much when I was in my middle twenties. But by the time I was thirty, the situation had grown irksome. I had fallen in love. I suspected that within four or five years I would want to marry, start a family, and buy big, expensive things, like furniture, a second car, and a home. Steven, Charles, and other friends in the private sector all owned their own homes and drove new European cars. I was basically broke, still saddled with student loans, still renting a small apartment, and still driving a used Ford Escort.

"Listen, pal," I told Steven in one conversation, "you owe me. It's like the house that Jack built. I wrote the speeches that Reagan delivered that enacted the program that caused the boom that's making you rich."

"Right," Steven answered, "and next time I'm in Washington dinner's on me. You want more than that, you're going to have to get off the public payroll and into the private sector where things are happening."

Inspirited by the way the public good coincided with my own, private good (which I had decided was, after all, one of the points of free markets), I grew determined to make a clean break from the public sector and start out fresh in the private. I wrote to business schools for brochures, filled out applications, waited anxiously for decisions—and in the end decided to make my way across the continent to Stanford.

Despite my friends' incredulity and my own lingering doubts, as I left the Rose Garden and trudged back to the office, I managed to convince myself, at least for the moment, that I *was* doing the right thing.

FALL TERM

Inferno

ONE

Math Camp

It was the first morning of math camp. Professor George Cooper, a trim, cheerful man in corduroys and a baggy sweater, stood at the front of the classroom, beaming. "Welcome to the math preenrollment course," he said. "My purpose over the next two weeks will be to encourage crisp, quantitative thinking. I also want to reduce the revulsion at numbers that some of you may feel when you see notation that looks like—what example shall I use?—let's say this." He turned to the board and wrote:

$$\lim_{x \to c} f(x)$$

"Very simply," Cooper said, still beaming, "this means 'the limit of the function of x as x approaches c.' "

I felt revulsion.

This was in the middle of August, still almost three weeks before the beginning of the MBA program. Yet scattered among the seats in the amphitheater-like classroom were some fifty students, present because Stanford had more or less commanded us to be there.

My notice had arrived in late June. For two months I had been basking in the glow of my acceptance (Stanford admits about one candidate in ten), feeling optimistic about my future, imagining myself as a future Financial Wizard or Captain of Industry, and giddily looking forward to two years in California. "Hey, dude," I'd say to my secretary, "I've got those rewrites here for that President dude."

The notice spoiled all that. It stated that for students with weak backgrounds in mathematics, or, in the business school vernacular, "poets," Stanford would be presenting two remedial courses at the end of the summer, a ten-day class on quantitative skills followed by a three-day course on computers. "Based on our review of your academic record, we strongly encourage you to attend these special sessions."

I couldn't fault Stanford's review of my academic record. I'd had trouble with math since at least sixth grade. The last math course I'd taken was tenth-grade algebra, and that was only to satisfy the minimum requirements of the New York State Board of Regents. At Dartmouth I'd managed to go all four years without a course in mathematics, meeting the sciences requirement by taking introductory courses in geology, astronomy, meteorology, and oceanography (or, as we called them, Rocks, Stars, Clouds, and Oceans). Only after deciding to apply to business school had I even attempted to balance my checkbook, a task, as I discovered month after month, that lay beyond me.

The notice went on to explain how to send a check to the Stanford Bookstore to order two textbooks, *College Mathematics* and *Essentials of Accounting*. "It is very important for you to achieve a thorough understanding of the concepts in these two books *before* you begin the Stanford MBA program."

I was appalled. I'd known, of course, in a vague sort of way, that I'd probably have to work fairly hard once I got to Stanford. But this? Toiling over the summer, on subjects I had ignored for fifteen years, in order to prepare for a remedial course in those same subjects, all before I would be deemed competent even to *start* the MBA program?

What was I getting myself into? I called my friend Steven, who had graduated from Stanford business school a few years before, at his Boston office.

"Lighten up," Steven said. "A lot of this is just scare tactics. They want you to know you're supposed to hit the ground running."

"So I should ignore all this stuff?"

"No, not entirely," Steven answered, "but it's nothing to get worked up about." He admitted that students who lacked a grounding in mathematics—the poets—would have to work harder than other students, especially during the fall term. The use of graphs, charts, and mathematical notation would take getting used to. "But frankly," he added, "this isn't rocket science." The math in business school would be mostly addition, subtraction, multiplication, and division. "You should take the remedial math course, just to get warmed up. And buy the books if you want to, but I wouldn't waste a lot of time on them this summer. Once you get started, you'll do fine."

I desperately wanted to believe Steven, largely because I didn't have much choice. I'd arranged to hold my job until the day before I left for California (Stanford would be expensive, after all), and I still faced the tasks of selling furniture, packing my belongings, closing my bank accounts, and saying goodbye to friends. I did order the books. But when that long summer of packing and farewells came to an end and I got in my car to drive west, *College Mathematics* and *Essentials of Accounting* lay at the bottom of the trunk, unread.

"By way of encouragement," Professor Cooper continued on that first morning, "I want to tell you about a student I once had."

Cooper described a young man who had emotional problems whenever he looked at something mathematical. He would see an equation on the board and freeze, unable to think or speak, his breathing reduced to a wheeze. The business school had to get him psychiatric help. Eventually he got over it, managing to graduate and become an advertising executive.

"So never give up!" Cooper said. He began bounding around the teaching well like a cheerleader. "Never despair! *It can be done!*"

A psychiatrist? I saw myself being carried from the room in a straitjacket.

Professor Cooper explained that during the first week he would be "course-specific," covering the techniques that we would need for our fall classes, and that he would devote the second week to calculus. "The ideas of differential calculus," he said, "underlie virtually every aspect of the core curriculum." Then he distributed the syllabus.

I cast my eye down the first page. As soon as Professor Cooper finished his "Introductory Remarks," to which he had alotted fifteen minutes, he would begin a twenty-five-minute segment on "The Fundamental Building Blocks of Algebra." Cooper would spend half an hour on "The Associative, Commutative, and Distributive Laws," twenty minutes on "The Algebra of Inequalities and Absolute Values," and ninety minutes on eight more aspects of algebra. Then he would turn to a new field, closing the morning session with half an hour on "Factorial Notation, Permutations, and Combinations." Cooper would thus present, explain, summarize, and dismiss the basics of algebra, the most advanced mathematics I had ever studied, in the first three hours of this, the very first morning of a two-week course, so that, with half an hour still left before lunchtime, he could move on to mathematics at a level I had never encountered in my life.

Turning to the second page of the syllabus, I found that tomorrow morning we would begin on "Exponents" and "Logarithms," concluding, tomorrow afternoon, with "Quadratic Equations." I flipped through several more pages, noticing that on Friday of this first week we would cover "The Concept of Continuity" and "Some Useful Derivative Theorems for Finding Derivative Functions Associated with Complicated Original Functions."

I was still experiencing waves of disbelief and panic when, becoming conscious once again of the classroom, I realized that Professor Cooper had already begun to lecture. Once I got my notebook out of my book bag, I was a page of notes behind.

During the lunchtime break, the poets mingled in the courtyard in the middle of the main business school building, breaking into groups of three and four. Conversation tended to fall into a simple formula. "Where are you from? What did you do before coming to Stanford?" I decided to look for company, which I here defined as someone as miserable as myself.

I tried talking to a pert woman from Boston, but it turned out that she had spent the summer getting ready for this math course by taking a math course. "My husband went to business school himself before getting his teaching job at Harvard," she said. " 'Anne,' he told me, 'you've got to be able to solve linear equations in your head.' So I made sure that I could."

I struck up a conversation with a classmate who looked as though he was barely out of his teens. "This?" he said. "Just a refresher. I took a lot of math as an undergraduate at Yale."

Several tanned, muscular men were circulating in the courtyard to put together a business school volleyball team to take on the students at the law school. "Lawyers are wussies," one explained, asking me to join the team. "We'll crush 'em." When I demurred, mentioning the demands of Cooper's math class, all three just looked at me for a moment before turning the conversation back to sports.

Then I found Conor O'Flaherty.

Conor was sandy-haired and slight. An Irishman, he had taken his undergraduate degree back in Dublin in philosophy, and he knew no more about mathematics than I did. Conor stood in the courtyard blinking, pushing his glasses back up the bridge of his nose, and wondering about the adjustments he would need to make at business school in order to fit in.

"I don't know how I'll be able to study for this course," he said. "My wife works at the consulate, and we're living in Pacific Heights, right in the middle of San Francisco. The commute to business school's an hour to and an hour from. And since we have a little boy, when I get home in the evening, I have to spend time being a dad."

Conor and I had lunch together, and when we returned to the classroom I moved my books and name card from my old seat to sit next to him. Clinging to Conor made me feel better. He was in even deeper trouble than I was.

*　*　*

"Many of you still see mathematics as foreign and difficult," Cooper said, beginning the afternoon session. "So I'd like to depart from the syllabus for a few minutes to give you a practical demonstration of the way mathematics can help you to think." He put his chin in his hand and peered at us. "If you took a single piece of paper," he said, "folded it in half, folded it in half again, and kept on folding it in half a total of thirty-two times, how thick would the sheet be?" He called on a woman in the front row.

"Maybe two inches?" she said.

"Wrong!" Cooper said, looking gleeful. He called on a man in the back of the room.

"A foot thick?" the man said.

"Wrong!" Cooper called on others.

"Two feet thick?" "Three feet?"

Cooper shook his head. "The correct answer, ladies and gentlemen, is that the sheet of paper will achieve a thickness of just over 271 miles. Observe."

Turning to the chalkboard, Cooper took us through the mathematics. A ream of paper of 500 sheets was about two inches thick, and each individual sheet was therefore about 2/500 or .004 of an inch thick. After one fold, a sheet of paper took on the thickness of two sheets, after two folds, of four sheets, and after three folds, of eight sheets. Two, four, and eight could also be expressed as two to the power of one, two to the power of two, and two to the power of three.

"After 32 folds," Cooper said, "the sheet has the thickness of two to the power of 32, or 4,294,967,296 sheets. That number times .004 inch equals 17,179,869 inches. Seventeen million one hundred seventy-nine thousand eight hundred and sixty-nine inches equals 1,431,655 feet. And one million four hundred thirty-one thousand six hundred and fifty-five feet equals approximately 271 miles.

"Ladies and gentlemen, there is no way intuition gets you there. But math gets you there in just a brief series of calculations."

Even I had to admit that Cooper had made his point: Math could provide a compact, powerful tool of analysis. For a moment I was even struck with a kind of wonderment, a poet glimpsing the poetry of math. Then Cooper turned back to the syllabus, started a discussion of simultaneous linear equations, and lost me, as it were, simultaneously.

Drudgery broken by brief, surpassing moments of understanding proved the pattern during Math Camp. We'd slog through linear equations drawn in the X and Y coordinates of Cartesian graphs, vectors involving the mathematics of magnitude and direction, and probability theory, "defined," as Cooper emphasized, "strictly in terms of sets," and therefore illustrated by way of the overlapping circles of Venn diagrams. Then Cooper would offer a particular example or insight, and for at least a moment I would see something of the usefulness and beauty of mathematics.

One afternoon Cooper told us to write our birthdays on slips of paper, then fold the slips of paper in half and pass them to the front of the room. He held up a five-dollar bill. "This says at least two of you have the same birthday. Who's a taker?"

"I'll see that five," one of the volleyball players said. Seven or eight others slapped five bucks apiece down on their desks. I figured that with 365 days in a year but only about 50 students in the class, Cooper was offering us a pretty safe bet. But after spending the past few days watching all my answers turn out to be wrong, I left my wallet in my back pocket. Cooper unfolded the first slip of paper and read the date. *Three* hands went up. The students who had put their money down groaned while everyone around them laughed.

Taking us through the mathematics, Cooper demonstrated that in a group of our size the probability of two birthdays falling on the same date exceeded 90 percent.* Then he set down his stick of chalk and strolled through the room picking up one five-dollar bill after another. "One of the lessons we attempt to teach here at the business school," he said cheerfully, "is that rigorous, mathematical reasoning can lead to big profits."

---

*As Cooper led us through the mathematics of this birthday bet, I took careful notes. I still can't understand them for more than about thirty seconds before feeling baffled all over again, but I present the mathematics here for readers with an appetite for numbers.

"The easiest way to approach the problem," Cooper said, "is backward, calculating the probability that no two people in a group of 50 will have the same birthday." As of the first person in the group, Cooper explained, the probability that there was "no match" was $365/365$ or I, since there was no

At the end of each afternoon session I would go for a quick jog on the campus to clear my mind. Then I would buy a slab of pizza and a Diet Pepsi at the campus snack bar and head back to Wilbur Hall, the undergraduate dorm I'd been assigned to until the beginning of the term.

My room held two army-style metal bunks with stained mattresses, two big, dented metal desks, and two battered wooden closets. Since the room smelled, I would shove my desk next to an open window. Then I would bend a rusted gooseneck lamp over my books and start on the problems.

I would read a problem like this:

> If the relationship between total cost and the number of units produced is linear, and if cost increases \$5 for every unit produced, and if the total cost of producing 100

---

one else with whom to match. As of the second person, the probability that his birthday did not fall on the same date as that of the first person was 364/365. That is, there were 364 days that met the desired condition of not falling on the birthday of the first person. As of the third person, there were only 363 non-matching days left. In other words, only if the second person's birthday fell on one of the 364 non-matching days, and the third person's birthday fell on one of the 363 remaining non-matching days, would there have been a non-match.

"We can carry this through," Cooper said. "Only if each of the 50 had a birthday that didn't fall on any of the other 49 birthdays would we have gotten no match. Since the probability of multiple independent events is simply the multiplication of their individual probabilities, we can describe the probability of no match as follows."

Cooper wrote:

$$\frac{(365)}{(365)} \times \frac{(364)}{(365)} \times \frac{(363)}{(365)} \times \ldots \times \frac{(365 - 50 + 1)}{(365)}$$

"Or," he said, still writing, "more succinctly":

$$\frac{(365)\,(364)\,(363)\,(\ldots)\,(365 - 50 + 1)}{(365)^{50}}$$

If you worked these numbers out on a calculator, Cooper explained, you could reduce the series to a single term, .03, or 3 percent. And if the probability of no match equaled 3 percent, then the probability of a match—that is, that at least two people would have the same birthday—was 97 percent, or better than nine chances in ten.

units is $600, what is the equation that describes the relationship between total cost and units of production?

Or I would read a problem like this:

What values of x will satisfy the following equation?

$$x^2 - 8x + 15 = 0$$

Or a problem like this:

Let the term

$$y = p(x) = a_n x^n + a_{n-1} x^{n-1} + \ldots + a_1 x + a_0$$

represent any polynomial function. Then, using the theorems we discussed in class, solve the following equation:

$$\lim_{x \to b} p(x) = a_n b^n + a_{n-1} b^{n-1} + \ldots + a_1 b + a_0 = ?^*$$

When after two or three hours I could take no more, I would go down the hall to the pay phone, pull out my credit card, and dial my girlfriend, Edita, in Phoenix.

Edita had worked down the hall from me at the White House, in the Scheduling and Appointments office. We had dated for two years, but since neither of us had felt ready to get married we had decided to test our feelings for each other by submitting ourselves to a separation. While I was at Stanford, Edita was giving business school a try herself at the American Graduate School of International Management. She had left Washington for Arizona a couple of weeks before I had left for California.

"I hate it here," Edita would say.

"You hate it there?" I would answer. "*I* hate it *here*."

"Cheer me up."

---

*The solution to the first problem: *Total cost = 5 times the number of units produced + 100*. The solution to the second problem: *5 and 3*. And the solution to the third problem: *p(b)*. (If certain of my Stanford classmates had written this book, they'd have printed a 900 number in this space and charged a dollar an answer.)

"You cheer *me* up."

"You cheer me up *first*."

These calls offered an early, bewildering instance of a phenomenon that we would eventually come to recognize quite clearly. Business school is the enemy of romance.

Then I would call my parents.

"It reminds me of your first weeks during graduate school at Oxford," Mom would say. "Don't you remember how much trouble you had, getting used to England?"

"This is different," I would answer. "I'm older. Don't you think it's kind of strange for a thirty-one-year-old man to be calling his parents for comfort?"

"Goodness, no. Your parents are always your parents. Just persevere."

Then my father would get on the line.

"What do you think, Dad? Maybe I should just go back to Washington and look for something in public relations, right?"

"You thought it through before you went out there," my father would say. "Now you owe it to yourself to stick with it, at least until Christmas."

Next I would call Conor. "How's the studying going?" I would ask.

"Studying?" Conor would answer. "Our little boy spent the last half hour throwing up. Stomach flu. If I can get him to sleep I'll be able to start Cooper's assignment, but I know I won't understand it and I'll be half asleep myself by then."

Even though talking to my girlfriend and parents would afford me little comfort, these conversations with Conor would always make me feel a lot better. Conor was going through the same thing I was, and he was doing even worse.

I would study every night until one or two in the morning, marking the readings in yellow highlighter, then working the problems. While reading and rereading the texts proved slow and painful, by the second or third day I was beginning to understand a good portion of the material. Even when I got the answers wrong, as I did constantly, I started to be able to figure out where I had made my mistakes. Maybe I can handle math after all, I thought.

Then we got to calculus.

"Be prepared to walk away today feeling that there was more than you could easily digest," Cooper said as he began the second week of the course. "Every time I teach calculus," he continued, "I gain a deeper insight into the material. Calculus is very, very subtle and very, very beautiful. But you must be prepared to stay with it."

Halfway through the first night of studying I found that when I took each concept or equation by itself I seemed able to understand it. But by the time I reached the bottom of a page, all that I thought I understood at the top had entirely evaporated, leaving me without so much as the merest trace of knowledge or comprehension.

Calculus involved rates of change—that much I could grasp. In a business context, calculus might be applied to rates of change in inflation or in the prices of raw materials. But sooner or later every reading would do something that would strike me as simply surreal, like defining the derivative of a function as:

$$\lim_{\Delta x \to 0} \frac{f(x + \Delta x) - f(x)}{\Delta x}$$

I would look at that at one or two in the morning and simply cease cognition. If I had been attached to a monitor my brain waves would have read flat. Even if I had had more time, I felt forced to conclude, calculus would have lain beyond me as surely as conducting an orchestra or achieving a respectable point total in the decathlon.

Cooper assigned sixty pages of difficult mathematical readings that second week. He set dozens of problems. I was able to hobble along, but only by leaning on a crutch. On Tuesday morning Cooper put on the board four complicated but brief differentiation formulas, telling us that among them these four formulas would solve every problem he assigned. "Memorize the formulas if you want to," he said. "But for your own sakes make sure you understand them first." I could not understand the four formulas. Nor, I found, was I even able to memorize them, since the notation of calculus kept confusing me with all its little f's and x's and arrows. But I could and did copy the formulas onto a three-by-five card, secrete them in the flap at the front of my notebook, and, back in my dank, smelly room in Wilbur Hall that night, teach myself how to manipulate the formulas well enough to get mostly correct answers to the next day's problems.

Was I learning? Clearly not. I was going through motions. Yet I was able to tell myself quite convincingly that I had no choice. By the end of the week Cooper was lecturing on topics that included "The Geometric Interpretation of a Set of First Partial Derivatives as a Gradient Vector" and "Using First and Second Partial Derivatives to Find Maximum and Minimum Points of a Continuous Function of Several Variables."

As one mathematical concept after another went past me, I found myself picturing the episode of "I Love Lucy" that, as I recalled, was set in a chocolate factory. A bell rang. A door popped open and bite-size pieces of chocolate rode out on a conveyor belt. Lucy topped each chocolate with a cherry and placed it in a box. When one box was full, she turned to place the box, just so, on a shelf, and then picked up a new box. The bell rang again. Then again. The chocolates rolled toward Lucy faster and faster. Cherries flew. Stacks of boxes toppled. When chocolates began falling off the end of the conveyor Lucy started to stuff them in her mouth, in her hat, down her dress. The audience howled.

I understood what Lucy was going through.

On the day Math Camp ended Cooper dismissed us at noon. "Take the rest of the day off and get some rest," he said. "Some of you look as though you need it."

The next day, Saturday, I slept until one o'clock in the afternoon before rising for pizza. After lunch I considered going for a run, then thought about something less taxing, like shaving. Then I stopped thinking and climbed back into bed for the rest of the day. On

Sunday I did go for a run, trying to forget about calculus by touring the campus.

The two business school buildings lie on the northern end of the campus. The main building is a rectangle four stories high around a central courtyard. A product of the 1960s, the building has big plate-glass windows and a series of outdoor stairways and balconies that break up its squat mass and make it seem airy. It houses the library, the classrooms, Bishop Auditorium, and the deans' offices. The cafeteria in the basement is called the Arbuckle Lounge.

Behind the main building stands the new Littlefield Building. Three stories high, the Littlefield Building is shaped like a U, with the wings or arms embracing a broad lawn. In the middle of the central part of the building stands a big, open arch that gives the whole structure some flair, like a miniature Arc de Triomphe stuck into a blocky edifice. Littlefield houses professors' offices. Like almost all Stanford buildings, both Littlefield and the main business school building have red-tile roofs.

Across the street from the business school rises the Hoover Tower, while to the west of the tower lies the oldest part of the university, the Main Quadrangle, a series of buildings and courtyards built at the turn of the century. To the southeast lie playing fields, a baseball diamond, a basketball arena, tennis courts, swimming pools. At the far edge of the campus stands the huge, half-sunken oval of the football stadium. That night, I wrote about the stadium in my journal:

September 18

The Stanford stadium is a big, oval-shaped bowl that looks a lot like Memorial Stadium at Dartmouth, Soldiers' Field at Harvard, or the Yale Bowl. But the landscaping is different. This is not the Ivy League. This is the azalea league. The entire exterior of the stadium had been planted with azaleas, rhododendron, oleander, and a dozen plants I couldn't identify—huge bushes, five and six feet tall, hundreds of them. As I jogged around the sta-

dium looking at all those plants, I thought of Dad. He used to struggle through every upstate New York winter to keep the two scraggly rhododendron bushes in front of our house alive. Every year he employed more elaborate devices to protect the plants, until during the last winters before he and Mom retired to North Carolina he was erecting a shack over each bush that was more weatherproof than most doghouses. But by springtime the result was always the same: At least half of each rhododendron plant would have turned black and died.

But here in California it is different. California has never known the white death of a Northeastern winter. It is as if God has protected this state, decreeing that California shall be unto all men a foretaste of paradise. And as I jogged around the stadium, agog at the Stanford azaleas and rhododendron, big, silent, glossy beings, gently rustling in the sun and breeze, that is what it felt like: paradise.

Once I got back to Wilbur Hall, it took me fifteen minutes to shower, change, and seat myself at my desk in front of College Mathematics *to try to learn some of the calculus that had escaped me the week before. Calculus. From paradise back to hell in a quarter of an hour.*

On Monday morning Computer Camp began. The three-day course was taught by Associate Dean Stanley Slowacki, a big, friendly, shy man, each day beginning with lectures in the auditorium, then ending with practice periods downstairs in the computer lab after lunch. We learned how to send electronic messages to each other, then how to use a software program called Kermit to permit our modest desktop machines in the computer lab to talk to the university's gigantic mainframe computer. By the second day these preliminaries gave way to the main aim of the computer preenrollment course, teaching poets how to use spreadsheets.

Dean Slowacki told us that for the next two years we would be using spreadsheets "constantly," and that in business analysis spreadsheets were "absolutely basic, the most important tool in modern business practice." So help me, I had never heard of spreadsheets. But since we did use spreadsheets over and over again during the next two years, just as Dean Slowacki told us we would, it is worth taking a moment to describe the first spreadsheet I managed to construct. It turned out to be simple, even fun. On the afternoon of the second day I went downstairs to the computer lab, opened the manual that Slowacki handed out, and followed the instructions.

First the manual set the scene, instructing me to imagine a company that made and sold "units" (I was free to imagine units of dog food or units of processed plutonium: it didn't matter). Each year, the manual continued, the company incurred certain costs, sold a certain number of units, and received certain revenues. It needed to construct a spreadsheet that would provide a month-by-month display of these data.

Following the manual, I hit a series of keys on the computer keyboard, loading the spreadsheet software, a program named Lotus 1-2-3. An empty spreadsheet materialized on the screen. A series of vertical lines lying on a series of horizontal lines to form little boxes, the spreadsheet looked like a grid or chess board. The letters of the alphabet ran across the top of the screen and numbers down the left side, making it possible to identify each box or "cell." Cell B5, for instance, was the second cell to the right, five rows down.

The manual told me how to create, in effect, a twelve-month calendar, entering the names of the months as column headings across the top of the screen, then how to enter "unit sales," "price," and other business terms as row headings down the left-hand side of the screen. Next the manual instructed me in entering formulas that described the mathematical relationships between the row headings. "Revenue," for example, was equal to "price" multiplied by "unit sales." After an hour of reading the manual and pecking the computer keys I found my first spreadsheet glowing on the screen.

Of course I knew that this was baby stuff, a spreadsheet so elementary as to prove useless in the business world. But for someone like me, so used to thinking in words rather than numbers, the tightness of this spreadsheet, the compactness with which it presented so much information, proved something of a revelation. If January unit sales were, say, 100, then revenue would be *precisely* $5,000, and you knew *precisely* why.

"Suppose," the manual said next, "that January sales were to be 120 rather than the 100 originally estimated." Following the instruc-

	A	B	C	D	E	F
1						
2						
3		January	February	March	April	
4						
5	Unit Sales	100	105	110.25	115.7625	
6	Price	50	50	50	50	
7						
8	Revenue	5000	5250	5512.5	5788.125	
9	Total Cost	3000	3100	3205	3315.25	
10						
11	Net Profit	2000	2150	2307.5	2472.875	
12						
13						
14						
15						
16						
17						
18						

tions, I changed the January "unit sales" from 100 to 120. When I hit "Enter" an astonishing little event took place. January "revenue," "total cost," and "net profit" all changed to higher numbers. I had entered one pesky change—and the mind of the computer had instantaneously performed all the calculations and recomposed the spreadsheet.

The manual called this "What If?" analysis, and even I saw how useful "What if?" analysis could be. What if a business decided to charge another dollar for very unit it sold? Enter one change. A spreadsheet would show you the rest. What if costs rose? Or sales slumped? With a spreadsheet it was easy to play with the numbers. In the next day and a half Slowacki had us build much bigger, more elaborate spreadsheets, but all our work only involved more complicated variations on the theme of constructing a model and playing "What if?"

By the afternoon of the third day I had become quite proficient with Computer Camp spreadsheets. I had even started working on the optional problems at the back of the manual. After so miserably failing at calculus, it felt good to find something I could do. Conor felt the same way. "I do believe that I am enjoying myself," he said, tapping away at the computer keyboard next to mine. But then, a moment later, his face clouded. "We've been practicing with spreadsheets for two days," Conor said, pushing his glasses back up his nose as he swiveled in his chair to look at me. "But I just realized that when the bankers and consultants get here next week, a lot of them will have worked with spreadsheets for two or three *years*." Conor and I managed to go back to our tapping. But now we weren't having fun, just dreading the year ahead.

That evening Professor Cooper invited the poets to his house for a barbecue. He lived on one end of the Stanford campus in what he called "the faculty ghetto." It didn't look like much of a ghetto. The houses were big split-levels, with swimming pools and landscaped, well-tended lawns. In his big backyard Cooper had set up a couple of grills, and the poets brought hot dogs, hamburger meat, soda, and chips. Conor and I chatted. As the party ended one of the women in our class gave a little speech thanking Professor Cooper on the poets' behalf. "The real business school program hasn't even begun yet," she said, "but we want you to know how grateful we are that you've already gotten us this far." When we finished applauding, Professor Cooper replied.

"Teaching the math preenrollment class every year, I always end with the feeling that the poets have a great advantage over the other students at this business school." Professor Cooper thought of the poets as the most interesting students in each class. "Denise," he said, gesturing toward the woman who had just spoken, "worked in Calcutta for Mother Teresa. Conor was in the Irish civil service." He named me for working at the White House.

"Among your classmates who'll be arriving in the next few days," Cooper continued, "there'll be a lot of management consultants and investment bankers. That's certainly interesting and lucrative work. But there's not a lot of variety there.

"And because you poets come here knowing so much less about the material, you'll get far more from your Stanford experience than your classmates. They'll be going for a two-year hike. You poets will be scaling the Himalayas."

There was something appealing about the way Professor Cooper had put it, I confess. Climb every mountain, ford every stream, that sort of appeal. However, this was not a movie musical. This was life. *My* life. And once you looked beneath the sentimental appeal of Professor Cooper's remarks, what he was saying came to this. We here at Stanford have admitted you poets to add some variety and interest to our institution. But we don't intend to thank you. Oh, no. We intend to make you slave.

TWO

Orientation: Woe Is Me in a Hot Tub

Over the weekend I moved from Wilbur Hall to the house in Portola Valley, a town in the foothills a few miles from campus, that I would be sharing with a couple of classmates whose names I had found on a business school bulletin board. The house, a redwood A-frame, felt big and airy. It had lots of tall windows, a front porch, a side porch, and a back porch, and tucked under the eaves of the garage stood a hot tub.

A hot tub.

I had written on my business school application that I wanted to attend Stanford instead of an East Coast school, since Stanford was on the West Coast and therefore "open to Japan, Korea, and the whole Pacific Rim—open, indeed, to the future itself." I don't know whether the admissions committee fell for any of that, but the truth was I couldn't have cared less about Asia or the future of international trade. I wanted to go to Stanford so I could try living in California. Just as even primitive peoples often believe in a golden age before discord or pain entered the world, I as an Easterner believed in the Golden State, the land of never-winter-again, and I viewed the hot tub as the totem of the California way of life. Neither of my roommates had arrived yet, so as soon as I hauled my bags in from the car I changed into my swimsuit, slid the cover off the hot tub, and climbed in.

The motor growled and the water bubbled and boiled. I leaned my head back against the side of the tub, at peace. Then it occurred to me that the water was really very hot. I fumbled for the floating thermometer, saw that it read 122 degrees and recalled a warning I had seen posted in a Washington health club about the dangers of lingering too long in the sauna. Sauna, hot tub, they seemed a lot alike. Maybe sitting in this tub alone was not a good idea. I could see how someone could pass out and parboil to death. Maybe I would faint, slip under the surface, and drown without a bubble. I clambered out. As I toweled myself I noticed that my limbs had already turned bright red.

What was the matter with me? California living was supposed to induce a sense of robustness. I felt like a wimp. Math Camp had already taught me that I probably wouldn't be able to handle the business school workload. Now it looked as though I wouldn't be able to handle business school pleasures, either.

Returning to the house with groceries on Sunday afternoon, I found that the first of my roommates had arrived. Joe Toscana was upstairs in the bathtub. Joe wasn't bathing. He was scrubbing.

"The guys who lived here last year must have been pigs," Joe said. The tub was encrusted with rust, dirt, and mildew. The sink was filthy. Even so, my own attitude had been, Who cares? It's only a rented house. But Joe could not abide the grime.

Joe was twenty-six, five-nine, and muscular. He had grown up in New Jersey, majored in economics at Rutgers, then gone to work as a financial analyst at Salomon Brothers, a big investment bank. He had spent a year with Salomon in New York, two years in San Francisco, then a fourth year back in New York. San Francisco had dazzled him.

"I just really fell in love with Northern California when I was out here," Joe said, still standing in the tub. "For a guy who grew up in Jersey, it was heaven." He had applied to many business schools, but

Stanford was at the top of his list. "Now that I'm in, it feels like the best thing that's ever happened to me, you know?"

But it was an awkward time for us to talk.

"I bought a bucket and some cleaning supplies," he said. "Figured we'd just split the cost three ways." And with that, Joe turned his attention back to spraying Tilex foam over every surface in the bathroom. I noticed later that in places Joe had taken the bathtub right down to the zinc.

While Joe scrubbed, I finished carrying my groceries in from the car. Suddenly, from down the road there came the sound of a car engine—a loud, loose sound, not the purring of a powerful German sports car, nor the tight, balanced whir of a Japanese car, nor even the nondescript, uninteresting rumble of a present-day American sedan. This was a sound from the past, almost the throaty roar of a jalopy. It created the impression that if you listened closely you could hear each piston firing individually.

As the roar grew louder an enormous, rusted-out, forest green Buick convertible, its canvas top in tatters, appeared around the corner and pulled into the driveway. The driver applied the brakes and turned off the ignition. The car lurched and coughed before falling silent.

" 'Ello," the driver said, getting out. "I am Philippe Rougemont. The car, she is wonderful, no? Buick Le Sabre"—he pronounced this in French, so that Buick sounded like Boo-eek—"1973. How could it be that you Americans 'ave stopped making such automobiles?"

Philippe, my second roommate, was twenty-eight, trim, six feet tall, blond, blue-eyed. He turned to reach into the backseat, picking up a bottle of wine with each hand.

"Napa Valley," he said. "I am eager to compare the California wines to the French."

Inside the house, I set down my groceries, he his wine.

Philippe had grown up in Switzerland, near Geneva. "My family are bankers. I broke with the family tradition by becoming a lawyer. But the law is too dull. In truth, Geneva is dull—Switzerland is dull. So I 'ave broken tradition again to study in America."

Before returning to his car to bring in his bags, Philippe gestured toward one of the bottles, a Chablis. "I believe this wine will go well in our 'ot tub, no?"

On Monday morning, the more than 300 members of the Class of 1990 came together for the first time. We milled for a few minutes in brilliant sunshine in the business school courtyard, then entered, blinking, into the dark, wood-paneled auditorium. At nine o'clock promptly, Orientation began. We listened for most of the morning as Esther Simon, the woman who served as Director of the Office of Student Affairs, introduced one speaker after another—the Dean of the Business School, the President of the University, the associate deans of this and that, the librarian, the Director of the Office of Financial Aid.

Orientation proved in most regards just about what you would expect of an institutional, first-day welcome. The speakers offered encouragement, inspiration, a batch of humorous anecdotes, and their genial best wishes. The Dean assured us that we were one of the brightest, most accomplished classes ever to be admitted to the business school, as no doubt he had assured every other entering class during his tenure. An associate dean strove to impress us with the caliber of the faculty. To join the business school, he said, an academic had to be gifted as *both* a researcher and teacher. "We only hire faculty," the associate dean said, "who are the best in their field at one and truly outstanding at the other."

Only two speakers departed from this happy air of welcome. Neither talked for more than a couple of minutes, but they sounded ominous. "The core can be tough on people," Esther Simon said. She was a short, friendly woman who spoke in soft tones, clearly intending to soothe and reassure us. She wanted us to know we could visit her office anytime. She and her staff were good listeners. They could refer us to support groups. If the need arose, they could even send us to trained counselors. Simon was so soothing that she unnerved me. Stanford business school knew quite well, she seemed to be saying, that many of us would soon be requiring professional help.

Sonia Jensen, the Director of Administration, was a tall, handsome woman who spoke with a Swedish accent. Uff course we must eat properly and get our rest, she said. But abuff all, we must manage our time, planning our days from the moment we awoke to the moment we climbed back into bed, setting aside big blocks of time for studying all seven days a week.

"Do not vaste eeffen *ten minutes*."

Ten minutes? I thought that at least to some extent she must be putting us on, and I waited for her to crack a joke or break into a smile. She only turned from the microphone and strode grimly back to her seat.

When Orientation ended, my classmates and I filed back out into the sunshine of the courtyard. Tables had been set up and laden with chips, tostadas, pretzels, soft drinks, and beer, and the courtyard sounded with the din of conversation as we performed little jigs of introduction, shaking hands, then taking a step or two back, swigging our beers and sodas, and asking each other what had led us here to Stanford.

The Director of Admissions had provided us with a brief set of statistics, telling us during his remarks that the 333 members of the class had graduated from 127 undergraduate institutions and come from 21 countries. The oldest member of the class was, at forty-two, nearly twice as old as the youngest, who was twenty-two, while the average age was twenty-seven and a half. One sixth of the students were thirty years old or older; another third would be thirty by the time we graduated. Women numbered eighty-three, just under a quarter of the class.

But the statistics failed to provide any sense of the students' attainments. In the first quarter of an hour in the courtyard, I met a Navy pilot who had landed fighter planes on carriers, three medical doctors, a former Cleveland Browns fullback, and a Coast Guard helicopter pilot who while on duty in South Florida had routinely flown several drug interdiction missions each month. For two or three minutes I joined a group that included a professional rock musician, an Exxon engineer, and a young man, just returned from graduate studies in Leningrad, who described his hobby as "capitalist encirclement." Later I introduced myself to a twenty-five-year-old recently returned from a sailing trip across the Pacific. He had paid for the trip with money he had made by selling his design for a lighter, more comfortable, more attractive wheelchair to a manufacturer of medical equipment. Among the women in our class I met a classical pianist, a neurosurgeon, and the finance director of a presidential campaign.

It was clear at once that my classmates had self-confidence, intelligence, talent. Although I had worked with gifted people at the White House I had never seen a group like this, in which every member proved so articulate and conveyed such vitality. These young men and women even looked perfect, almost without exception tanned and fit.

Were they children of affluence? Or had they acquired their self-confidence in rising up from obscurity and poverty? I would learn later that the class contained elements of each. One of my classmates was the son of a billionaire, another the son of one of the most prominent executives in Hollywood. At the other end of the scale, one student had grown up in a Los Angeles barrio, another in a tough Puerto Rican section of Brooklyn. But mingling in the courtyard on the first day, it was impossible to say. In England, where I had done my graduate work, class distinctions would have lain on the surface, in accents, modes of dress, even posture. But here accents said nothing. Clothes? Rich, poor, middle class, everyone was attired in California hip: shorts, brightly colored T-shirts or polo shirts, and running shoes or sandals.

I was certainly a member of the middle class myself. My entry into the working world by way of the White House may have sounded impressive, but it had neither made me rich nor equipped me with skills that I could readily market, the call for presidential speechwriters being limited. I had come to Stanford for a new start, following the American logic: If the land on the old homestead is played out, pick up and move west.

Now I found that many of my classmates had done the same. "I just realized I didn't want to spend the rest of my life as an accountant," the student from the tough neighborhood in Brooklyn told me. "I watched the guys who were out there on the edge, doing the big deals that I was just working the numbers on. And I said, 'Hey, I'm as good as they are. But my life right now is in a rut. I've gotta get out.' "

A tall brunette who had been an actress had grown up in the Midwest, majored in drama at Indiana University, then spent five years in New York trying to make it. "I just got sick of it. Agents tell you you're too fat or too thin or you need to dye your hair or get tinted contacts. The best jobs I got were gigs singing on cruise ships. They paid pretty well, and once the bookers got to know you, you could work pretty steadily all winter. But spend my life singing to a bunch of widows? No way."

Even those who had come to Stanford to advance careers they had already begun were hoping that business school would give them the chance to do something new. "I'd done my two years as an analyst at Goldman," one investment banker told me. "After that, it's just expected that you'll leave to go to business school, then go back to Goldman. But what I really want to do is get into something more entrepreneurial, maybe start a business of my own."

The Americanness of the scene in the courtyard seemed its defining characteristic, at least to the MBA candidate who had just spent several years writing presidential addresses. People were here to make something of themselves. Even foreign students like Conor appeared to be possessed of the can-do, pioneering American spirit. "It was time to move on," Conor said. "I came here for a new start." Background, status—none of this mattered; at business school, we would remake ourselves.

Since Joe and Philippe both had plans for dinner, that evening I found myself alone in our house, and while just a few hours earlier I had felt exhilarated, now, at twilight, anticipating my first business school classes the next day, I felt despondent. I poured myself a glass of wine and slid into the hot tub, which was cooler now that Joe had located the controls. As the motor growled and the water bubbled and boiled, I reviewed my situation.

In the morning I would begin the core. The core, short for core curriculum, was the set of thirteen courses in which every candidate for a Stanford MBA had to achieve a passing grade or flunk out of the institution. Since first-year students took five courses a term for each of the three, ten-week terms, we could all look forward to choosing two electives for the spring term. But the first thirteen courses—the core—were a matter of diktat.

The core filled me with the same dread that calculus had. I was certain the material would prove too quantitative and move too fast. And I found no comfort at all in the way those who knew the core described it. "It's like boot camp," Steven had said. "You know, basic training. Crawling through mud." During Orientation one associate dean had quipped that we would find taking the core "like trying to drink from a fire hose."

My classes tomorrow, a Tuesday, would be the first meetings of my three Tuesday-Thursday core courses, Decision Making Under Uncertainty, Computer Modeling and Optimization, and Microeconomics. Wednesdays would ordinarily be free, but since orientation had taken place on a Monday, my two Monday-Friday courses, Financial Accounting and Organizational Behavior, would hold their first meetings on Wednesday, the day after tomorrow.

The course titles conveyed nothing to me. Studying for an MA in English instead of an MBA, I reflected, I might have found myself taking a course entitled the Later Novels of Jane Austen. This string of words would reliably have informed me that the course would deal with the novels that a writer named Jane Austen had composed in the final years of her life. Decision Making Under Uncertainty? What did *that* mean? The only image that came to mind was of Monty Hall on "Let's Make a Deal." "Do you want door number one, door number two, or whatever is inside the envelope I'm holding in my hand?" Computer Modeling brought to mind no image at all. In twelve hours I would thus begin a course of study that was now a void.

I did know that Stanford straddles two basic forms or methods of instruction, the case method and the lecture-and-textbook method, each championed by one well-known school. At Harvard Business School, most instruction takes place by the case method. Students read histories of business problems, often quite long and detailed histories, then discuss them in the classroom, attempting to find in the particularities of each case lessons of fundamental importance and wide applicability. At the University of Chicago, most instruction takes place by way of the contrasting method of lectures and textbooks. Stanford employs both. The readings assigned for my first class in Decision Making Under Uncertainty, for example, included both a brief case and a chapter from a textbook.

Under either method of instruction the professor at Stanford enjoys total power, notably the right to cold call, roughly the classroom equivalent of the right to launch tactical nuclear weapons on unprotected populations. The cold call means simply that the professor can call on any student at all, at any time, whether or not the student has raised his hand. Typically, cold calls take place at the beginning of a class, the professor using one student to summarize a case or, perhaps, the principal points in a reading. Then the professor begins cold-calling other students, asking them to correct or supplement the first student's answer. Once a student is cold-called, either he is able to speak intelligently about the material or he is not.

I knew, of course, that I would not.

I recognized, even then, that few would have pitied me, sitting, as I was, in a hot tub, sipping Napa Valley wine under the stars. But no matter. I felt quite sorry enough for myself.

THREE

Inside the Classroom: Snapshots from Hell

I say it now. The entire term felt like a punishment. Especially among the poets there was much gnashing of teeth (here I am being figurative) and weeping (here literal). I cannot provide a detailed account of all the material my five core courses covered during fall term, but by offering brief descriptions of the first meeting of each class, perhaps I can at least provide snapshots, as it were, from hell.

In Decision Making Under Uncertainty, or Trees as it quickly became known, the instructor, Omar Kemal, entered the classroom a few minutes after 8:00 in loose khakis and a cardigan, his hair a mop, looking like Albert Einstein at the age of perhaps sixteen. (Later I'd look Kemal up in the business school catalogue. He had been born in Lebanon but educated here in the United States, graduating from M.I.T. at nineteen. He was now in his twenties.) "After the midterm," Kemal said, "we'll be examining probability theory and techniques for the spreading of risk. But for the next ten sessions, we'll be concentrating on decision trees." He thunked a stack of handouts on the front row desktop. As students distributed the handouts, he added, "Trees will become your life."

I had made sure to get to school a quarter of an hour early so that I could have my pick of seats. All the classrooms in the business school were little amphitheaters. In the center lay a sunken stage or teaching well. Behind the well rose a backdrop of blackboards. Facing the well rose four horseshoe-shaped tiers, each with twenty or so swivel seats bolted behind a single long table or desktop. On the front edge of each table ran a groove into which students inserted their big, block-letter name tags at the start of each class.

I'd learned during Math Camp that the row you sat in said a lot about you. To sit in the front row, on the same level as the teaching well, you had to be a teacher's pet or a class clown, while to sit in the fourth and highest row, the skydeck, you had to be cool, in such command of the subject that you could afford to hunker in the back of the room and pay attention only when you wanted to. The second and third rows, in the middle of the classroom, were for students who wanted to pay attention but not stand out. Good news. When I got to school there were still several seats left in the center of the third row. Bad news. Despite my choice vantage point, within the first ten minutes of class I was lost.

Probably the best way to introduce decision trees is to mention two insights, even though neither came to me until much later. The first is that trees were actually very simple, just diagrams that helped you to think about decisions you might have to make. The second is that it was the method of our young professor to take the essential simplicity of trees and obscure it.

The case we were dealing with that morning was entitled "Leslie Electronics." A contractor, about to begin construction of a recording studio, had gotten in touch with Robert Leslie, the owner of Leslie Electronics. The contractor needed to know whether Leslie could provide 100 portasols for $1,000 each. (Reading the case the night before I assumed a "portasol" was some sort of electrical device, but I was unable to find the word in my dictionary and kept picturing port-a-johns.)

Leslie and his engineer, Hans, talked over the contractor's request. Because this was a slow period at their plant they wanted to accept the contract. To make portasols, however, they needed to obtain portasol housings, and here, the case stressed, they faced a choice. They could either buy the housings or, after purchasing a new piece of equipment called a housing mold, make their own.

Hans, the engineer, argued that they should buy the mold and make their own. This would both save them money on the current contract and provide them with a mold to keep on hand in case any more portasol contracts came their way.

But Leslie, the owner, was worried. The casting of portasol housings was tricky work. Any mold he purchased might produce only defective, unusable housings. And if that happened, Leslie would have spent thousands of dollars for nothing.

What should Leslie do?

Professor Kemal's handout presented this dilemma in the form of the first decision tree I had ever seen.

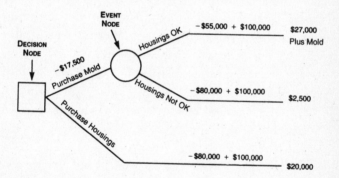

For a good fifteen minutes Kemal discussed this tree in detail, explaining the significance of the square, the circle, the numbers, and the branches. I struggled, but failed, to follow him.*

---

*After poring over my notes that night, I was able, if dimly, to grasp the main points.

The square was a "decision node," a symbol that meant Leslie either had to buy the mold or purchase the housings, a choice that was up to him. If he did buy the mold, Leslie would have to spend $17,500, the figure above the line to the right of the square. The circle stood for an "event." "Events" did not involve decisions. They just happened, like the weather. In this case the mold would either produce acceptable housings or defective housings, and there was nothing Leslie could do but wait and see.

The three lines or branches on the right-hand side of the tree each represented one of the three possible outcomes in the case. If Leslie bought the mold and the housings proved acceptable, the top

"So, friends," Kemal said at last, "how does Leslie use this tree to make a decision?"

Silence.

"Friends, friends," Kemal said, "you have to help me here."

Joe, my roommate, raised his hand.

"This may be too obvious," Joe said.

"Go ahead," Kemal responded. "The answer here is not complicated."

"Okay," Joe said. "It depends on a couple of things. One, how big a chance is there that the mold will make good housings? And two, how much chance is there that Leslie will be able to use the mold on other jobs in the future?"

"Exactly," Kemal said. "Leslie needs to evaluate those two events, then make some decisions about the likelihood of the outcomes from those events. This will get us talking in at least an elementary way about probabilities. Let us begin with the first event, whether or not the mold will produce acceptable housings."

The handout that Kemal distributed next presented further dialogue between Leslie and Hans. Under close examination from Leslie, Hans estimated that there was about an eight in ten chance that a mold would produce housings that they could use.

"So now we know," Kemal said. "The mold will produce acceptable housings with a probability of 80 percent or .8."

Kemal began adding numbers to the tree, multiplying these numbers by dollar amounts, and talking about Expected Monetary Values, or EMVs. Soon we were more than an hour into the class

---

branch would apply. Here Leslie would be out the $17,500 for the mold, plus $55,000 for materials and labor. But since the contractor had offered to pay $1,000 for each of the 100 portasols, Leslie would receive $100,000, thereby netting $27,500.

If Leslie bought the mold but the housings proved defective, the middle branch would apply. Here Leslie would be out the $17,500 for the mold, plus another $80,000, the price of buying the housings, which he would now have to do. So Leslie would net only $2,500.

If Leslie simply purchased the housings to begin with, the bottom branch would apply, and he would net $20,000.

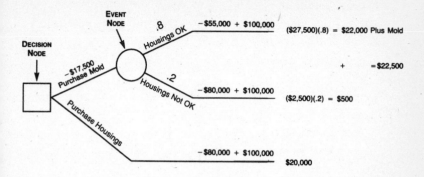

period. It is difficult to find a phrase for the way I felt, although profoundly mystified comes close.*

"What should Leslie do?" Kemal, summing up, finally said. "Why, friends, it is a matter of elementary observation that the top two branches have a higher EMV than the bottom branch. Leslie should purchase the mold without delay."

Kemal devoted the rest of the class to evaluating the second "event," the likelihood that Leslie would be able to use the mold on jobs in the future. He distributed yet another handout, then began festooning the tree with more branches, probabilities, and Expected Monetary Values. At one point he apologized for repeating techniques he had already demonstrated. "It is not my intention, friends, for you to be bored." My own emotions were running closer to panic.

---

*Kemal added .8 over the "housings okay" branch of the tree and the reverse, .2, over "housings not okay." Next he multiplied these probabilities by the dollar amounts on each of the top two branches. Not until late that night was I able to make sense of what Kemal explained next.

If Leslie bought the mold and it produced acceptable housings, Kemal said, Leslie would net $27,500, as indicated by the top branch. Yet since he would have only a .8 chance of netting that $27,500, the correct Expected Monetary Value, or EMV, of the top branch was not the full $27,500, but only $27,500 multiplied by .8, or $22,000.

In just the same way, the correct EMV of the middle branch, the branch that applied if the mold produced defective housings, was actually only $500.

Since the Expected Monetary Value of a decision with different possible outcomes is the sum of the EMVs of each of the possible outcomes, the EMV of the decision "purchase mold" was $22,000 plus $500, or $22,500.

This number, $22,500, was the figure Leslie needed to compare with the $20,000 he would net, as shown on the bottom branch, if he simply purchased the housings to begin with.

Near the end of the class I raised my hand.

"There's something basic about this case I still don't understand," I said.

Kemal looked puzzled. "I am here to be of service."

"What's a portasol?"

Kemal smiled. "Is there anyone here who can help Mr. Robinson?"

No one answered.

"Do we have an audio expert among us?" Kemal continued. "An electrical engineer?"

He paused.

"Because, friends," he said, looking bemused, "I myself have never taken the trouble to find out."

My classmates were still chuckling about that one as they packed their book bags and strolled out into the hall. The joke was on me, clearly. Only a poet could have failed to see that this course was about numbers, not words.*

Professor Seungjin Park, a short, stocky man, entered the classroom at precisely 10:00 to march down the stairs, slap his notes on the desk in the teaching well, then rip off his jacket and fling it over a chair. He loosened his tie with a jerk, stepped in front of the desk to face the class, cracked an enormous smile, and said, "Welcome! I'm Professor Park. Call me Jin. I'm gonna teach this course, Computer Modeling. And this is gonna be some kind of fun course. Ya!"

In this course we would be spending lots of time downstairs in the computer lab, Jin warned us, but we were not to worry. We were to

---

*While writing this book, I decided to make a final effort to learn the definition of "portasol." I got in touch with the National Academy of Recording Arts and Sciences, the Electronics Industry Association, the Audio Engineering Society, the Recording Industry Association, and the Society of Professional Recording Studios. Not a soul had ever heard the word, although one woman called back a day later to let me know that a friend of hers thought "portasol" might be the brand name of a gasoline-fueled space heater.

It finally dawned on me that "portasol" is a nonsense word, just like "widget." It must have been invented by the person who wrote "Leslie Electronics," a case that dates from before either Kemal or I ever got to Stanford.

be happy. Jin did not let students fail. "Life is too short! You get worried, you talk to Jin, ya!"

Then Jin began the first case, "Benson Appliance."

Mr. Maximilian Benson, president of the Benson Appliance Corporation, was putting together his budget and operating plan for the coming year. Benson Appliance manufactured two products, electric knives and electric can openers. The company could expand production of either item on short notice. But the "unit variable manufacturing cost" would rise by 25 percent when annual production of the item exceeded 400,000 units.

The corporation incurred fixed manufacturing costs, which it allocated equally to the two products. It also incurred variable manufacturing costs, made up mostly of materials and labor, and variable marketing costs, including sales commissions and freight expenses.

Mr. Benson asked his marketing manager, Clare Voyance (pun intended, I suppose), to report on price and advertising experiments she had conducted the year before. "At every level of advertising expenditure," she responded,

> our unit knife sales appear to vary approximately linearly with knife price, so long as we keep the price between $12 and $23. . . . Within this range, an extra 100,000 units are sold every time we cut the knife price by an extra dollar. . . .
>
> To see the effect of advertising on sales, I plotted unit knife sales . . . against price charged per knife. . . . Then, if we advertise, the effect of advertising is to shift the unit sales line upward at every price by an amount directly proportional to how much we spend. . . . At every level of advertising expenditure, our unit can opener sales also vary approximately linearly with opener price. . . .

Mr. Benson also consulted Truman Hardy, the director of manufacturing, whose dialogue made that of Clare Voyance look sprightly and concise.

The case concluded by assigning students to form study groups, then write a report advising Mr. Benson. The reports were to include a computer model that, accepting different advertising budgets and prices as "inputs," would "project automatically," for both knives and can openers, the resulting unit sales, average unit manufacturing costs, sales revenues, and profits. We were furthermore to name the specific pair of prices and pair of advertising expenses that would "maximize" the company's profits. Finally, we were to tell Mr. Benson how to structure the bonus package for Clare Voyance and Truman Hardy to win their support for the pricing and advertising policies we chose to recommend.

"Let me just give you a couple of hints. Ya!" Jin said.

In the next ninety minutes Jin covered all three boards with diagrams and formulas. He listed unit prices and advertising as the central "decision variables," and, as the crucial "performance measures," profit maximization for Mr. Benson, revenue maximization for Clare Voyance, and cost minimization for Truman Hardy. Over one entire board, Jin spread a huge "influence diagram," demonstrating what variable depended upon what.

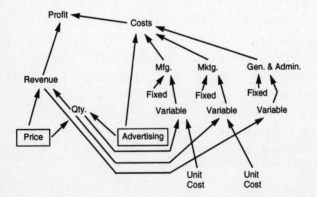

Influence Diagram for "Benson"

I understood none of this, of course, the incomprehensibility of the "influence diagram" in particular unnerving me. When Jin finished he turned from the board, spotted me and one or two others who were lost, and announced, "Nobody gonna leave here today with long face. So Jin gonna tell you a little story about this case, make you feer maybe a little better."

When he assigned "Benson Appliance" last year, Jin told us, he went downstairs to the computer lab one evening to see how his students were doing. "And, ya! There they all were, working hard on the computers. Oh, I was so proud, ya!" At one computer, Jin noticed an empty chair where a student had stepped out to run an errand or get a bite to eat. Jin looked at the screen.

"I was hoping to see real sophisticated formulas. But on the screen I see only two words. These two words are in big capital letters, ya. They are followed by exclamation mark. These two words are, 'BENSON SUCKS!' "

I joined the laughter, but uncomfortably. It felt somehow wrong to experience both terror and hilarity at once.

I'd been warned about Yeager. "A good teacher," a second-year student had told me, "but a real hard-ass." Other students had heard the same, and as we took our seats for the first class there was an almost preternatural decorum in the classroom, with students speaking in whispers rather than engaging in the usual preclass din.

When Yeager entered and walked down the stairs to the teaching well, he looked tight-lipped and humorless. His hair was gray. His trousers were gray. His shirt was a pale, steel blue that tended toward gray. He showed no sign of warmth. "Good afternoon," he began, setting his papers on the podium and squaring the edges meticulously. "Welcome to Microeconomics for Poets."

There were, Yeager said, three languages in which the subject matter of microeconomics could be developed, the languages of words, graphs, and mathematics. "What makes this a course for poets," he said, "is that I will teach primarily in the first two languages—not that I will somehow teach less." We would cover all the concepts that our more mathematically inclined classmates would cover in their own classes, but because there were certain concepts that could be dealt with more easily in mathematical terms than in words or graphs, our own workload would prove, if anything, heavier.

"I do not teach easy courses. And I do not teach less microeconomics because I am teaching it to poets."

Yeager glared at us briefly, then began to lecture. His subject was "opportunity cost."

Resources are scarce, Yeager stated. No one, for example, ever feels he has enough money. Individuals and enterprises thus face a persistent problem in deciding how much time, money, effort, and so forth to devote to various undertakings. The discipline of microeconomics summarized this problem in the notion of "opportunity cost."

"Many of you were bankers or consultants before coming here," Yeager said. "The salary and bonuses you've given up to attend Stanford represent your opportunity cost." For a student who had been earning $50,000 to $60,000 in his old job, the opportunity cost of two years of business school lay in the range of $100,000 to $120,000. "Add to that the price of tuition, food, and lodging, and for some of you the full cost of attending this business school will come to $160,000, a fact that the school cleverly omits from the application materials we send out."

Yeager smiled. Obviously, he enjoyed being obnoxious. On the other hand, he had made his point in a vivid, memorable way, and I could see how he had earned his reputation as a fine teacher. Next he justified the other half of his reputation.

When the class was halfway over Yeager looked at his watch, then took it off, set it on the podium, dial-side up, and announced an eight-minute break. "But when I say eight minutes, I *mean* eight minutes."

The classroom emptied, most of the students simply stepping into the sunshine to stretch and chat. But since Yeager's course took place in the afternoon, after we had already spent four or five hours in earlier classes, about a half dozen of us felt drowsy enough to head downstairs to the cafeteria for coffee or Coke. There was already a long line at the cash register when we got there, and as the eight-minute deadline approached we grew tense and looked at our watches. One student finally broke out of the line and tossed a dollar at the cashier before pelting back upstairs. Then the rest of us bolted, sloshing coffee and Coke as we ran.

Back in the classroom Yeager waited for students to return to their seats, then put his watch back on and turned to the board to write. Then a door creaked open and a latecomer entered, carrying a Coke behind her back, and one student after another had to swivel in his chair as she made her way back to her own seat, in the middle of the second row. "Excuse me," she whispered. "Really sorry. Excuse me."

Yeager turned. He watched her, glaring wordlessly, a bony hand on his bony waist. Even when she had finally taken her seat, he continued to stare at her for several moments before he spoke.

"I said eight minutes. You chose to ignore me, and I consider that an act of profound rudeness. It will not happen again. *Ever.*"

The woman blushed.

"Do you understand?" Yeager said.

The woman nodded. She blinked back tears.

Yeager turned back to the board. Students glanced at each other as if to confirm what they had just witnessed, and behind me someone muttered, "What a hard-ass." For the rest of the lecture, the mood in the classroom was sullen.

After the first day of classes I studied in the business school library, a library unlike any I had ever seen. The books here did not tell stories, they held data. When I examined two fat books that were on a stand, like unabridged dictionaries, I found that they contained eight decades of data on the prices of grains, pork bellies, and other commodities. The periodicals section, I discovered, contained a few magazines of general interest such as *Time, Newsweek,* and *The Economist,* but was principally given over to trade journals intended for narrow audiences. One journal was devoted entirely to the extrusion metals industry.

In one corner, I found wall maps of the United States. The republic was not shown as a political entity but as a set of markets, by county. On one map, bands of color indicated different levels of wealth. South Dakota was right up there with Greenwich, Connecticut, and Beverly Hills, California. That seemed odd until I remembered what happened to farm land values during the stagflation of the seventies. Half the farmers in South Dakota ended up as millionaires, at least on their bankers' books.

Another map bore the title "The Two Americas." For a moment, I anticipated the familiar political argument that America was a country divided between rich and poor. But the map only divided the country according to purchasing patterns for mayonnaise. The North and West bought Miracle Whip; the South and East went with Hellmann's.

In the classroom at 8:00 the next morning for the first session of Financial Accounting, I was still half asleep—understandably, since I'd stayed up studying until just five and a half hours earlier—so it took a while for my attention to fix itself on the student who was for some reason writing on the board. He wore khakis, a pastel-colored polo shirt, and sneakers. When he finished writing and turned to the class he smiled shyly. He was a big, beefy young man who looked as though he had played tackle or fullback as an undergraduate only a year or two before.

"Hi," he said. "I'm Walt. I'll be your instructor in this course."

After being instructed by the barely postadolescent Omar Kemal the day before, this was hard to take. Walt. Another kid. I pulled the business school catalogue from my book bag. It confirmed that Assistant Professor of Accounting Walter Lindstrom was younger than I and had received his Ph.D. only the year before. That made this the first business course that Walt had ever taught. It was my first week—and his. We were in it together. But while Walt was being paid for being at Stanford, the experience was costing me thousands, an expense I had been willing to incur largely because I believed I would be taught by one of the better business school faculties in the country. Maybe Walt and Omar would develop into outstanding teachers over time. That was possible, but only that, possible. In the meantime Stanford was using my money to place a bet on these guys.

Walt turned to the equations he had put on the board. These, he explained, were the "bookkeeping identities" we would need to memorize. He began his discussion with $SE = CS + APIC + RE$.

"Okay, to put that in words," Walt said, "shareholders' equity, or *SE*, equals common stock, or *CS*, plus additional paid-in capital, or *APIC*, plus retained earnings, or *RE*. Make a note, okay, that shareholders' equity can also be called owners' equity or net worth.

"Now, common stock itself, okay, equals par value times the number of shares issued. And par value is just the nominal dollar value printed on the stock certificate, while additional paid-in capital is the difference between the par value price of the stock and the price the company actually got for the stock, okay?"

Walt droned on to define debits and credits, describe T-accounts, explain the realization of unearned revenues and the expiration of unexpired costs. I wasn't the only one in the classroom who felt ill at ease. Walt looked pained himself. Three or four times Walt simply stopped talking and stood there in the teaching well blinking at the class and swallowing hard, as though he wanted to drop the lecture and start a new subject of greater general interest. "You guys," I could picture Walt saying, "it's embarrassing for me to be down here lecturing you, okay? So why don't we cut this class to play touch football and then have some beers?" But Walt would always regain his composure and drone on.

The first session of Organizational Behavior, or OB, took place on Wednesday afternoon, and by the time I took my seat I was already suspicious. I'd looked over the textbook, *Readings in Managerial Psychology*, and found that it contained chapter headings like "Power: Over and Under the Table," "Communicating: Listening and Being Heard," and "The Whole Person and the Whole Situation: Putting It Together." To my mind these titles suggested a sham discipline, based on pop psychology and sixties jargon. Now the professor, in his late thirties or early forties, appeared before us in the classroom wearing long hair, a beard, a black shirt with a spaghetti-thin red leather tie, and granny glasses. Apparently, no one had told him the sixties were over. "Hi, guys," said Assistant Professor Robert Hammond. "I'm Bob."

Bob devoted his opening lecture to an article in the textbook, by academics named Nadler and Lawler, that described a model of "worker motivation." As best as I had understood the article, the Nadler-Lawler model contained four basic elements. The first was the "performance-outcome expectancy," or the extent to which a worker believed certain behavior would bring certain rewards. A salesman might expect, for example, that bringing in a high level of new business (the behavior) would win him a bonus (the reward). Second came the "effort-performance expectancy," the degree to which a worker believed that by working hard he would be able to achieve his aims. If for instance a salesman's monthly quota was so high that he gave up on it before even starting, the "performance-outcome expectancy was out of whack. Third came the notion of "valance," the value or importance a worker attached to a particular outcome. A company might offer its salesmen a trip to Hawaii as a bonus. But that would do no good if the salesmen attached a low valence to sun and surf, preferring cash instead. Finally, Nadler and Lawler made a distinction between "intrinsic" and "extrinsic" rewards. Extrinsic rewards included money and vacation time. Intrinsic rewards included self-esteem and a feeling of team participation. Nadler and Lawler suggested that workers might care more about how their work made them feel about themselves than about how much it paid.

The Nadler-Lawler model struck me as basically quite simple— define good performance, make sure it can be achieved, then reward it—but during his lecture Bob elaborated the model at length, drawing a giant diagram across two chalkboards. Arrows ran from "needs" on one board to "intrinsic" and "extrinsic" rewards on the other, while "motivation," "performance-outcome expectations," and "effort-performance expectations" each inhabited a chalk circle.

In the last half hour of the class, Bob led a discussion in which he asked us to apply the Nadler-Lawler model to our first case, "Pennsylvania Metals Corporation." Pennsylvania Metals, a producer of metal alloys, faced declining sales in spite of a big sales force. The corporation had discovered that its salesmen were spending too much time on small clients, devoting only about a third of their time to the big clients that accounted for more than four fifths of the company's revenues. According to the case, one salesman explained that "Small accounts depend on us. . . . Big accounts are much harder to crack, you need an appointment and you have to see many people. . . ."

One student raised his hand to say that he used to work for a specialty metals company just like Pennsylvania Metals. "I can relate to the guys in this case," he said. "When the guys at a little company came to you with a product they really needed, their jobs might be on the line. You got that product for them, you felt as though you'd made a difference."

"I spent a couple of years in sales at a steel mill," another said. What salesmen liked to do, he said, was make sales, and by servicing smaller accounts salesmen got to make more sales. "It's like selling pizza by the slice. You get to ring the cash register more often."

"Good," Bob said. "But what about putting it in terms of the model?" He looked frustrated. He went to the board. "What about the performance-outcome expectancy?" He pointed to one of his chalk circles. No one answered. "What about valences?" Still no one answered. "Nobody here thinks these sales guys place a high valence on more money?" Bob said.

"Sure," a woman answered, "but the case says they only get big raises when they leave the sales force for jobs in management." She had come to business school from Ford. "In the car business, there are lots of guys who love sales but would hate being a manager. Maybe the salesmen in the case are like that. Maybe they want more money, but not the management job that goes with it."

The discussion was the most interesting in any of my classes so far. People talked here. Ford? A steel mill? The heaviest industry I'd seen in Washington was lobbying, but now I was able to listen to classmates who had built objects out of steel. Bob, however, looked pained. "This is an okay discussion," he said. "But you should all try real hard to think of these things in terms of the model. That's what we're doing in this course, building models. Anyone? Can anyone apply Nadler and Lawler to the case?"

Bob looked at his watch. Then he shook his head. "Look," he said, "we're running out of time." Even though some of my classmates had worked in steel mills themselves, Bob stopped the discussion to spend the rest of the period putting more diagrams on the board. As I copied down his lines and arrows, I found myself wondering whether the pattern that had established itself during these first two days of classes would hold throughout the term: While other courses had given us material that was over our heads OB had done the reverse, giving us material that was beneath us.

September 28

I have now been to the first session of each of my five core courses. I do not understand Trees. I do not understand Computers. I do not understand Micro. I do not understand Accounting. I do understand Organizational Behavior, since it deals with words rather than numbers. But I don't like it.

So what am I doing at business school?

FOUR

Student Life:
More Snapshots from Hell

October 4

Night. Portola Valley. The house is dark except for a glow from the kitchen, where I'm heating water for a cup of coffee. For the sake of the caffeine, I'll put two heaping teaspoons of Folger's freeze-dried crystals in the mug, not one. The time is midnight. As I pour the hot water from the kettle, I notice two other sources of light in the house, the orange radiance under the doors to Joe's small office and Philippe's room. Is it a source of comfort that my non-poet roommates are still awake, studying as hard as I? No. I conclude that if they must work hard, then I am finished.

If life inside the classroom was intense, life outside the classroom was not a lot of yucks, either. I started fall term with the notion that my classmates and I would do what students do, getting to know each other, going out together for burgers and beers, and throwing parties. I was counting on some relaxation and fun from time to time. But relaxation and fun were not to be had.

It was as though we were all on a bizarre mission to outer space. Every day we would suit up and venture out for a spacewalk, floating to the classrooms, the cafeteria, and the library. We were aware of each other's presence, and we might even wave as we passed. But it was hard to make much of a connection when everyone was concentrating on staying alive.

At night we entered individual black holes. I repaired to the tiny office I'd made out of the pantry, just off the kitchen, Philippe to his room, Joe to the office he'd made out of a closet in the upstairs hallway, other students to the computer lab or to carrels in the library. Seated at the card table I used as a desk, a single light bulb shining on my textbooks and notes, the rest of the house filled with darkness, I felt like an astronaut stranded on the dark side of the moon. Sometimes I found myself concentrating on my heartbeat and respiration, as though I were waiting for my oxygen supply to run out.

My textbooks for the term were *Decision Making Under Uncertainty: Models and Choices, Introduction to Financial Accounting, Intermediate Microeconomics and Its Application, Readings in Managerial Psychology,* and *Fundamental Computer Concepts.* None of these, you will note, had a title that might be referred to as gripping. Nor was any a genuine book, a sustained undertaking in intelligent narrative, intended to be read from beginning to end. Instead they were grab bags. Each presented an array of topics, leaving it to individual instructors to pick and choose from among them. The accounting text, for instance, divided its material into sixteen chapters, then subdivided each chapter into three or more parts. Flipping through the book, I found it so full of charts, diagrams, and tables that it seemed closer to a technical manual than to an argument or exposition.

But what chiefly struck me was the prose. The writing proved turgid, technical, dense. I could open any of my texts at random and find the same. A single sentence, chosen from *Decision Making Under Uncertainty:*

> The ability to generate discrete approximations for continuous distributions allows all the definitions and manipulations for discrete random variables to be used for continuous random variables.

I marked the textbooks and cases in magic markers and highlighters of all colors. I took notes, then formed them into outlines, in effect making notes on my notes. I transferred key formulas from the texts onto three-by-five cards, then taped the cards to the wall over my table. Each week I had hundreds of pages of material to get through, but I lacked any ability to discriminate, to tell what points were of central importance, what merely background, so I felt compelled to learn it all. I was wholly overwhelmed.

Yet the most difficult aspect of the work lay not in its sheer volume but in adjusting from politics to business. Politics was big ideas and talk. Business was implementation, organization, specifics, numbers. Pose a question in politics and a capable Washington hand could fashion two or more answers that would sound plausible, garner some level of public support, and therefore prove correct. For instance: Should the President propose a cut in the capital gains tax?

Answer One: The President *cannot* propose such a tax cut because it would fail to get through Congress.

Answer Two: The President *must* support such a tax cut. Even though the measure would fail in Congress, the President would still have demonstrated his determination to spur investment and create jobs.

Note that from the Washington point of view, Answer Two is just as good, just as correct, if you will, as Answer One.

Now pose a question in accounting. To choose from one of Walt's assignment sheets: "If in 1987 the Stride-Rite corporation had used the Last-In, First-Out, or LIFO, method of accounting for inventory instead of the First-In, First-Out, or FIFO method, how much more, or less, would it have had to pay in taxes?" There was only one answer, exact, precise, and specific to the very penny.

Who cares? I'd think when I read a question like that. *I am here to absorb the grand concepts. I have no interest in mere pettifogging specifics.* Then I'd reflect that my instructors cared—a man like Yeager suggested by his very demeanor that he cared a great deal about pettifogging specifics. So with a miserable inward groan, I'd pull my calculator from its case to begin grappling with the numbers.

And the hours would tick past.

Conor and I were in the same Trees and Micro classes and had lunch together at least a couple of times a week. Even so, it was hard for us to build anything like a normal friendship because we were both operating at our extreme physical limits. After we had devoted our energies to taking notes in class, reading our textbooks, and completing our assignments, all on just a few hours of sleep each night, we barely had enough strength left over to manage respiration, let alone conversation.

"Twenty-seven hours," Conor said one day at lunch, interrupting one of the long, languorous silences that tended to fall on us in our sleep-deprived condition. Conor explained that he had carefully toted up the hours in his day. Each morning began at 7:30, with Conor spending an hour getting his little boy up, dressed, and fed. Conor spent the second hour of the morning driving in rush hour traffic from San Francisco to Palo Alto. He had added ten hours for attending classes, eating lunch, working in the computer lab, finding texts in the library, and attending study group sessions; an hour for driving back to San Francisco; another hour for playing with his son, if the little boy was still up, and talking with his wife; seven hours for studying; and six hours for sleeping.

"No matter how I add the numbers," Conor said, "I keep getting the same answer." He pushed the glasses up the bridge of his nose. "To be a husband, father, and student, I need twenty-seven hours a day. On twenty-four, I can't cope."

Even my roommates and I barely conversed. Occasionally when I was back in the house in Portola Valley I would hear the rumble of clothes in the dryer or hear muffled conversation from Joe's office when he telephoned his girlfriend. Very infrequently I would run into Joe or Philippe in the kitchen. But in the whole first half of the term we engaged in only snippets of discussion.

Joe seemed if anything even more rattled than I was. I was merely hoping to survive, but Joe actually intended to do well. "Gotta run" became his byword. In the morning, "Gotta run. I have to make it to school in time for a good seat in class." In the evening, "Gotta run. I have to be on time for my study group. How else am I gonna nail this stuff?"

Philippe, being Swiss, combined some of the characteristics of both the French and the Germans. Stanford offended the German in him. One night back at the house, Philippe announced that in

Europe, "students do not wear the cutoffs and the flip-flops to class or drink the Coca-Cola during lectures."

Yet Stanford intrigued the Frenchman in him.

"This aggressiveness the American women show in the classroom! They raise their 'ands to the ceiling, trying to attract the professor's eye. They compete. I would say they lack the feminine element. And yet they appeal to me very much."

There were any number of questions I wanted to pursue with Philippe. Why, for one, had he come to business school in California? Why not attend a school on the East Coast, or for that matter in Europe? But there was simply no time during those first weeks to get to know Philippe or Joe, despite our sleeping under the same roof, sharing the same two bathrooms, and keeping our sodas and leftover pizzas in the same refrigerator.

At lunchtimes, the only free time I had, I tried to acquaint myself with the foreigners. In all, there were more than sixty foreign students in our class, including four Frenchmen (each of whom drove a gigantic old American convertible), several Indians, a half dozen Latin Americans, two Israelis, two Filipinos, and a Thai. The two biggest groups, each numbering more than a dozen, were the British and the Japanese.

Judging by their accents, the British ranged from lower middle to upper class, but class didn't matter to them. They represented the Britain of Margaret Thatcher. Opportunity mattered to them. Business and money-making mattered to them. Far from clinging to the restrained, croquet-playing and tea-drinking customs of their island, they embraced California life. "I've driven the Pacific Coast Highway as far north as Mendocino," one Brit told me, "taking it all as fast as I could. I love the tight turns, the sun, the sea, the mountains. Yeah, California is wonderful."

Only one of the Brits lived up to the old-fashioned stereotype of an Englishman. Rupert Dupplin was related to some duke or other. He made a point of drinking tea instead of coffee, and when he spoke his lips barely moved.

Rupert had been head boy at Eton before going on to Oxford.

He'd then commenced his career in an exquisitely upper-class way, taking a position as an assistant to the Chancellor of the Exchequer, Britain's equivalent to our Secretary of the Treasury. Yet by virtue of this very background, so rooted in class and tradition, it was Rupert who evinced most vividly the new, meritocratic, entrepreneurial Britain that Mrs. Thatcher had struggled to call into existence.

"Treasury turned out to be dreadfully stuffy," Rupert told me. "After thinking the matter over I decided that business was becoming the center of interest in Britain, not government."

In the old days, Rupert explained, the honorable careers for someone who, like himself, had gone to a prominent "public school," then to Oxford or Cambridge, were in the church, the army or navy, the Foreign Office, or the Treasury. As recently as his father's generation, the generation that had come of age during the fifties and sixties, that had remained largely true. But the old order was gone. "I don't think anyone in my generation especially misses it," Rupert said. "With so much of our best talent being siphoned off by the state, it's no wonder our standard of living fell lower than Italy's."

Now the careers that attracted the best talent were in business, especially banking and consulting. "Anyway," Rupert said, "I'm rather like you. After serving in government I wanted to get into the private sector whilst I still could."

Rupert didn't qualify as a poet, but he still found Stanford difficult. When I came across him one afternoon in the Arbuckle Lounge he looked especially sallow. There were purple circles under his eyes, and his hair was matted and his clothes rumpled to an extent that was extreme, even for a member of the tweedy English upper classes. Still, Rupert was keeping a stiff upper lip. He nodded to me briskly, then said only, "They do rather put one through one's paces here."

The Japanese formed a subgroup that I found—the word is impossible to avoid—inscrutable. This was for the most basic of reasons. They barely spoke English. The kind of idiomatic conversation that took place between American students at their ease ("Ja eat yet?" "Nope. Joo?" "Nope. Let's grab a bite.") was simply impossible for the Japanese to comprehend. Come to think of it, I suppose they found us inscrutable, too. When Japanese and American students did try to mingle, it was always just that—trying, a big effort. You could see both sides tensing and pasting on especially wide smiles, then watch the Japanese student speak laboriously while the American struggled to make out what was being said. Even much later in the year, when we all had more time on our hands, the Japanese tended to stick together when they wanted to relax. They had to. Being with Americans was hard work.

The Japanese student I got to know best was Zenichiro Takagawa. "Ah am Zen," he said when we met. I forced quite a few smiles while he repeated that simple statement, then figured out that he wasn't talking about a form of Buddhism, just asking me to call him by his nickname. "Ah work with Mitsui. Ah work heah in America. Heah in California. Has been now two years." It was slow going.

Zen and I spent time together just before the beginning of the term, during the couple of free days between the preenrollment courses and the formal beginning of classes. One night we went to a Japanese restaurant in downtown Palo Alto. "I show you how real Japanese eat," Zen said with relish. He ordered sushi and miso soup. Then he had the waiter bring us a heaping plate of vegetable tempura, big chunks of cauliflower and broccoli dipped in a batter that made them taste like Kentucky Fried Chicken. Zen insisted on buying—"Japanese food, so the Japanese man must pay!"—and he ended the evening by ordering bottle after bottle of hot sake. We kicked back quite a number of toasts to the year to come. Soon I started to sound like Zen. "American man and Japanese man, friends!" I heard myself exclaiming. "Bonsai! Bonsai!" (I believed that "bonsai" meant "long life." Zen waited until the next day to tell me very politely that I had been calling him a dwarf ornamental tree.) I had high hopes for my friendship with Zen.

But we lost touch, immediately.

For two weeks after classes began, I called his apartment every second or third evening and got his American roommate. "Zen's out. He's in the library where he always is." When I found Zen one day at lunchtime, he looked pallid, even by the standards of a tired, over-worked group of students.

"Zen," I said, "you need a few hours off. Maybe this weekend we could get together again for Japanese food?"

"Would be very hard," Zen said. He shook his head sadly. "Please understand, English hard for me. Think how much reading our teachers assign. Then please think that for me, everything takes maybe three, maybe four times as long to read."

Of course. The language barrier was so high that Zen had to devote every measure of his strength to scaling it, or tumble to a desperate humiliation. Zen would probably not have been required to commit *seppuku* in the Mitsui boardroom if he flunked out of Stanford, but his harried expression made it clear that his superiors would not have smiled upon failure, and I could see that my trying to keep up a friendship with Zen was only one more claim on his energies. I gave up.

Even though Joe, Philippe, and most of the other non-poets seemed to be working almost as hard as I was, still it must be said that there were a few non-poets who found fall term almost easy. Gunnar Haakonsen, for one.

Gunnar was six-one, lean, muscled, handsome. He had blond hair and blue eyes and looked like a direct descendant of Leif Eriksson. Twenty-five years old, he had graduated from Amherst with a major in economics before working three years in New York as a financial analyst at Bear Stearns. Gunnar had been among the students I had joined for dinner after Orientation, and when over beers and tostadas he had asked why I had come to business school, I had answered only half jokingly, "Because it's a year shorter than law school." Gunnar hadn't smiled. When I'd asked why he had come, he had set down his beer, leaned toward me across the table, and fixed me with an intent, steely gaze. "To position myself for a quantum career leap in financial services." For a moment I knew how villagers must have felt when Viking ships appeared.

Gunnar and I were in Trees and Computers together. In both classes he sat in the skydeck and looked bored. When I joined him one day during lunch, he complained about the pace. I was about to add a word of agreement when I realized that Gunnar considered the pace too *slow*. He was getting tired of spending his nights restaurant hopping in San Francisco and his weekends tanning at the beach. He had come to business school to learn. "When will they teach me something I don't already know?" Even the way he slouched in his chair in class suggested that Gunnar found fall term elementary and inadequate, and it didn't take any wild flight of fancy to imagine how little he thought of poets like me. I started to think of Gunnar as Mr. Cool.

John Lyons was Mr. Perfect. He was six-two, good-looking, a former star football player at Duke University. John had grown up in Darien, Connecticut, one of the wealthiest suburbs of New York City. After graduating from Duke, John had landed a job with a small, upstart securities firm in New York, Leopard Securities. He had done so well that now the firm was paying his way through Stanford, where he continued to work for Leopard on the side, keeping in touch with the Manhattan office by way of a fax machine he kept in his room. John drove a sleek, jet-black BMW and walked with the loose-hipped gait of a completely confident, easy-go-lucky, cheerful jock. But instead of being arrogant he was a remarkably nice guy.

In Accounting and Computers, the classes we shared, John demonstrated his modesty by always sitting in a middle row, eschewing both the teacher's pet front row and the this-is-all-beneath-me skydeck. Walt and Jin soon learned that if students found a question difficult during classroom discussion, they could let poets like me wrestle with the question for a time, offering up one wrong answer after another, then bring the discussion to a tidy close by calling on John, who would get the answer right. John was one of only a couple of first-years who had enough free time to volunteer to help struggling poets in the business school tutoring program. It was during a session with John that I first began to understand some of the essentials of Accounting, and I thanked him as profusely as if he had pulled me from a flaming wreck, which, in a way, he had. "No problem," he answered simply. "Anytime." All fall I kept waiting for John to give a wrong answer or just show up in class looking tired. He never did.

There could not have been many students during those first weeks for whom business school proved something like a breeze, but Mr. Cool and Mr. Perfect proved that some did exist. I tried hard not to resent Gunnar and John. After all, I kept telling myself, they were just young men whose backgrounds and talents were somewhat different from my own. I tried, but I failed. Envy was one of fall term's torments.

When students were neither in the classroom nor, so to speak, in solitary confinement, they were in study groups. In some classes, study groups came together informally. In Trees, Accounting, and OB, for instance, I often found myself working on problems with classmates late into the night, simply because we discovered that working together provided our only hope of getting through the material. In other classes, professors established study groups formally. Yeager told the class in Micro to divide into groups of four. In Computers, Jin permitted groups of no more than three. In both Micro and Computers, study group members were to work on assignments together, then receive a single, group grade.

The time study groups absorbed proved astounding. In Micro, my partners and I met every Saturday and Sunday. Each session lasted at least four hours. No matter how hard we tried to deal with the problems briskly and efficiently, we were . . . human. We got confused. We got frustrated and tired. Consider just one Micro question:

> In an effort to aid the poor, the government introduces a program that subsidizes the first two pounds of butter a family buys and taxes the remaining amounts. If a family that consumes butter is neither better nor worse off as a result of this program, can the total amount of tax on butter that it pays exceed the subsidy that it receives? Explain.*

---

*The solution: The amount of tax on butter the family pays *cannot* exceed the subsidy that the family receives. Yeager's answer sheet presented the following explanation, one that I found myself reading very, very slowly a good four or five times.

In answering this my study group partners and I spent twenty minutes deciding that we needed to draw some kind of graph and another hour or so depicting a budget constraint and a utility function. Then Jim, the holder of a mathematics degree from Harvard, finally proposed an answer. Susan, a tall, friendly redhead from Alabama and, like me, a mathematical illiterate, joined me in assenting. But Doug, a former military man, had a different answer. Doug held out, forcing us to spend time discussing whether we'd operate by majority rule or instead like the old Polish parliament, each of us retaining an absolute veto. Doug finally decided to go along with the rest of us. But by the time he did, the question had taken one hour and forty minutes to complete. It was the first of six.

Steven, the Dartmouth roommate who had himself graduated from Stanford business school, wondered why my study group part-

---

Before the program, the family faces budget constraint AB. Once the program begins, the subsidy in effect reduces the price of the first two pounds of butter the family purchases, then raises the price of quantities in excess of two pounds. This gives the family the new budget constraint ACD.

If the family is neither better nor worse off as a result of the program, a single indifference curve, such as the one shown on the figure as U, must be tangential to both the old and new budget constraints. This is possible only if the family buys less butter, shifting its consumption, in the instance shown on the figure, from E to F.

Since F lies above AB, the expenditure required to buy F quantity of butter is less, by the amount GH, than it was before the program. Overall, therefore, the family receives a net subsidy of GH.

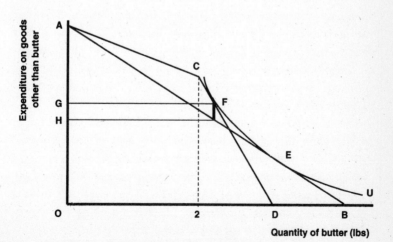

ners and I didn't save each other a lot of time and trouble by just agreeing not to meet. "I remember study groups as the single biggest waste of time at Stanford," Steven said. Within his first two weeks at Stanford, Steven had found that trying to solve problems in study groups took at least four times as long as doing the problems on his own. "So we divvied up the problems and just stapled the answers together before handing them in." Study groups weren't even any good for making friends, Steven said, since everybody felt forced into them.

Maybe. But I wasn't looking for friends. I was trying to survive. And since I wasn't a math whiz like Steven, I had no hope of solving problems on my own. Slow and frustrating as study groups were, I needed them.

In Computers my study group partners were a native of Oklahoma named Alex and, again, Doug the military man. My journal records the following scene. It took place on a Sunday, after I'd already spent six hours in my Micro study group.

October 9

Night—night again. In the computer lab. Although it is nearly midnight the lab is full, with 150 to 180 students clustered in small groups around the fifty or so computer screens. Doug and Alex and I huddle around one computer, working on "Benson Appliance Corporation." The screen is filled with hundreds of numbers arranged in the rows and columns of a spreadsheet.

"Dunno about those knives," Alex says in his Okie drawl. "What if we try raising the unit price from $17.00 to $18.00, then push the advertising budget for knives up to, say, $300,000?"

"Seems like too much to spend on advertising," Doug answers, "but I've got nothing against plugging in the numbers and giving it a try."

Nor have I, really, since we've already been at this for four hours and I long ago gave up the effort to follow what is taking place on the screen. Doug learned engineering in the Navy. Alex served until four months ago as budget director for the entire state of Oklahoma. They represent my sole hope of completing this assignment. I do not wish to distract them.

I prop my elbows on my knees, my head in my hands, and try to catch some sleep.

Since half the business school classes met on Mondays and Fridays and the other half on Tuesdays and Thursdays, this left each Wednesday as a theoretically free day, a reprieve, a fat, twenty-four-hour period when you could do errands and get caught up on your homework and your sleep. My classmates and I needed this time. We had to buy our groceries, do our laundry, open local checking accounts, and register our cars with the State of California. Time. We needed time.

But Wednesdays proved a fraud, as follows.

On Wednesday morning I would stay in bed until 9:00, giving myself an extra two hours of sleep, but would need to be at school by 11:00 to attend a help session. This meant that if I hurried through the shower-and-shaving-and-dressing routine and gulped breakfast, I would have all of an hour to study, pay bills, write a letter, or attempt to balance my checkbook before getting in the car and departing.

I should add that I would have a full hour only because I parked in the A Lot, immediately behind the Littlefield Building. A student would have had still less time if he parked in the B Lot, which lay in the eucalyptus grove, a good two tenths of a mile and a fifteen-minute walk away. But while a B Lot sticker cost $60, a sticker for the A Lot cost $185. This parking lot trade-off between time and money was one that different students handled different ways.

"A fifteen-minute walk," Philippe calculated, "twice a day, six days a week, ten weeks per term, three terms per year—this comes to ninety hours. Are ninety hours of this man's life worth the difference between $60 and $185? They are worth that and more."

Philippe and I both bought A Lot stickers.

Joe, however, found it difficult to relinquish his grip on so much as a penny. "An extra 125 bucks? No way! I'd walk twice that distance to save half the cash." He bought a B Lot sticker.

A classmate of ours named Hugh Oglesby, an embryonic Ivan Boesky, never bought a sticker at all. Instead, he bought a 1971 Dodge Dart for less than the price of an A Lot sticker. "If the car gets towed," he said, "so what? And in the meantime, I'll park it wherever I want." This ruse worked right through to the spring term of our second year, when Gorbachev visited the campus. The Secret Service took one look at Hugh's car and had a police wrecker haul it away.

After parking in the A Lot I would go directly to the help session.

Very quickly, I developed doubts about the usefulness of help sessions, periods of an hour or two each that professors arranged from time to time during the term, invariably on Wednesdays, so that students could ask about the material that had already been presented in class.

It was typical for a graduate student to conduct a help session, especially if the professor teaching the course had senior standing, as did, for example, Yeager, who had been at Stanford for close to three decades. Younger professors—Omar, Walt, Jin—conducted their own help sessions. But in either case, the method seldom varied. The grad student or young professor would stand in the well at the front of the classroom and simply ask, "Who has the first question?" At a stage when you were still taking Sonia Jensen's warning to heart and scheduling your time in ten-minute blocks, you often had to wait thirty or forty minutes while instructors dealt with other students before finally calling on you. It emerged, oddly enough, that students tended to get hung up on different small points, so that listening to all those other questions and answers added up to zero help for yourself.

On the Wednesday of my second week, for instance, I attended the help session for Yeager's Micro class. It was taught by a graduate student, a Ph.D. candidate. (I was surprised to discover that Ph.D.s were granted in business. Is business, I found myself wondering, an academic discipline with enough rigor and depth to warrant five to seven years of study? Isn't it far better, I thought, for a young man or woman simply to go into business and *do* it? I suppose it goes without saying that this was a line of conjecture that promptly twisted around on me. Wouldn't it have been better for *me* simply to go into business and do it?)

The grad student Yeager had selected turned out to be a mild leftist, more eager to exhort and inspire us than to take us through the mechanics of calculus. I myself kept getting confused about what went where in the simplest part of it all, the notation, and I just wanted to have him take us step by step through practice problems.

Instead, we got this:

"I really don't want to waste your time here taking you through the basics. You're all bright. You'll figure it out on your own. But if I do have something to offer, it's a way of looking at the discipline of economics itself."

Eyes rolled. A couple of students got up to leave right there and then.

The grad student persisted.

"You have to keep in mind the history of the eighteenth century."

More students left.

"I know some of you might not find this useful, in a really shallow, mechanical sense. But after all, are you here to pass exams, or to learn?"

I might have been at the business school to learn. But I was in that help session to pass exams.

"What I can try to do is give you some feeling for what's really going on, for the big ideas that underlie all these rather silly word problems you have to do. See, economics was the reaction of the rising capitalist class to arguments against capitalism in the eighteenth century. . . ."

The number of students leaving the classroom had reached the level of an exodus, and I joined it.

During winter and spring terms, attendance at help sessions fell off sharply (except for the sessions that took place just before exams, which were always jammed, even during our second year). But this was fall term. None of us knew any better yet. If the professors went to the trouble of arranging help sessions, we all figured we'd better attend. Even Gunnar, Mr. Cool, went to help sessions at first, though of course he managed to convey the impression that he was doing so only for the sake of form. Among the more than 300 students in our class, help sessions during fall term must have wasted a good 2,000 to 3,000 hours.

After a help session that failed to offer much help, I would go downstairs to the Arbuckle Lounge for lunch. When I saw people I knew I would stop to talk, needing the rest and refreshment of normal human contact. Yet I found that what took place in Arbuckle was far from restful. On the contrary, my classmates and I were so keyed up and running on such nervous energy that every conversation had the feel of a video-cassette tape running just a little bit too fast.

One afternoon barely two weeks into the term a woman I had met only briefly came through the cafeteria line and spotted me.

"I'm starting to panic about this place," she said. "Mind if I sit with you?"

She sat down.

"Yesterday," she said, "I was talking to a second-year. He was a poet in his first year, just like you and me. Know what he said? Oh, this is incredible. He said he studied six nights a week. He only went out for dinner or a beer *once* a week. And he kept it up all the way through the first two terms.

"I don't know. I just can't live my life like that."

Susan, the Alabaman in my Micro study group, joined us.

"The pressure's getting to me," she said. "Sometimes I feel like having a good cry." Whereupon Susan and the other woman began to do just that, dabbing their eyes with paper napkins. I darted a glance around the cafeteria, hoping that no one was staring. No one was even taking notice. Tears during the fall term at Stanford business school were too common.

After lunch, I would meet a study group in one of the library study rooms, each of which was equipped with soundproof tiles and a chalkboard. I would have allocated three hours to this study group session. The session would run closer to six. (It only took a couple of Micro classes before the verb "to allocate" entered the vocabulary of the student population, becoming another instance of business school speak, the new language we were learning together. We "allocated" our "scarce resources," chiefly time. Other scarce resources included energy, attentiveness, and good humor.)

By the time my study group broke, it would be time for dinner and I would face a choice between conviviality and solitude. I could go out with a classmate, perhaps to the sushi bar in downtown Palo Alto, a lavish use of time, likely to burn at least two hours, or I could go straight home and eat quickly and alone.

One way or the other, as I seated myself in my pantry office at

7:00 or 8:00 I would find myself with three classes to prepare for the following day and a good five or six hours of work ahead of me.

So much for Wednesdays as a secular Sabbath, a day of rest.

"It can be done." That had been Professor Cooper's exhortation to us poets during Math Camp. At first I clung to those words, hoping that if I repeated them to myself often enough I would make it up the hill, like the Little Engine That Could. Most of the time, though, the words struck me as empty sounds. I felt stupid. I was convinced I might flunk out. I was exhausted and frightened, characteristics that even most of the non-poets shared. So whenever I came across a classmate who seemed to demonstrate that it really could be done, I regarded him with awe.

Jennifer Taylor grew up in Minneapolis. She was twenty-four, stood five-three or five-four, had bouncy brown hair, bright brown eyes, and a crooked, winning smile. She proved just what Professor Cooper had in mind: that by reasonable effort a student could master the core material and find pleasure and satisfaction in doing so. Although a non-poet, Jennifer lacked an extensive economic or mathematical background. "But I just love the challenge," she said. Jennifer even enjoyed other people's challenges, often helping me with my Trees assignments.

"Sure, it's difficult," Jennifer said during one of these sessions. "But that's why it's so neat when you finally get it right." I knew there was no chance I would start to enjoy fall term myself. But it was a comfort, somehow, to see that Jennifer did.

I drew a more direct form of inspiration from Sam Barrett.

Sam believed he was in danger of failing two fall term courses (a well-founded belief, it would emerge) and had even less idea what to do with a business school education than I did. A twenty-eight-year-old Indianapolis boy with a big grin, Sam loved painting and drawing, and after graduating from the North Carolina School of Design he had formed a design firm with a couple of friends. They had gone broke. "I came to B school," Tom said, "because filling out the application was a lot easier than looking for a job."

Sam came as close as anyone at Stanford to being a cutup. Classroom humor loses a great deal in being committed to writing, but

Sam broke us all up when he remarked in Trees that a certain assignment involved nothing more than "tap-dancing on your calculator." Later, during an Organizational Behavior discussion of stress in the workplace, Professor Hammond asked if anyone could name a single modern job that did *not* involve stress. Sam muttered, "professor."

Sam was in a desperate situation in business school, knew it, yet still cracked jokes. "My motto," he said, quoting an old sham Latin phrase, "is '*Illegitimi non carbarondum est*. Don't let the bastards grind you down.'"

Soon I quit repeating "It can be done." "Don't let the bastards grind you down" seemed more fitting.

October 18

The time is six minutes past ten. I have worked all day, rising at 7:00, attending class from 8:00 until 11:45, eating a quick lunch, returning to class from 1:20 until 3:05, doing some quick shopping at the grocery store, going for a quick run, microwaving a quick dinner, and then entering my pantry office to study. I probably have another five hours of work to go, but I'm not sure I'll be able to complete it because I feel too old.

I don't mean I feel my full thirty-one years. I mean I feel eighty or ninety— old. My joints are stiff, I have trouble remembering what I did the day before yesterday, I doze off intermittently, and I find that I keep checking myself over, the way really old people are always looking for things to tell the doctor.

FIVE

Midterms:
The Horror

It was close to midnight on the fourth Sunday of the term. Joe and I had just gotten back to the house after attending study groups, and since neither of us had eaten we decided to microwave a couple of frozen burritos. As we watched our junk food sizzling, Joe asked how my Accounting was going.

"I've let it slide. Micro seemed more important. This weekend I probably gave Micro 80 percent of my time."

"But the Accounting midterm comes first. Just a week from Friday."

"Oh."

I had taken a deep breath before uttering that monosyllable. Trying to make the gesture look nonchalant, I placed my hand on the countertop. I needed to touch something solid.

Of course I'd known all along that exams would take place beginning in week number five or six. But this knowledge had been purely abstract, lying outside the realm of everyday reality, which, in those first weeks, contained room for nothing more than itself. Never had I come so close to living out the biblical injunction to take no thought for the morrow because "sufficient unto the day is the evil thereof." More than sufficient, actually. Thinking thoughts two or three whole weeks into the future had been out of the question.

Joe finished his burrito. "Gotta run," he said, tearing off a paper towel and wiping his hands. "You want any help on Accounting, let me know."

"Thanks." I gazed at my burrito as it lay oozing grease onto its paper plate. Under happier circumstances I would have looked upon this junk food with delight, splashed it with Tabasco sauce, and chowed down. But now midterms had robbed my appetite.

Midterms fell into two distinct phases. It is hard to say which was worse. One phase was of course the week of exams. That was bad. But the other phase, the week before exams, was so filled with anticipation of the exams to come that it was an event itself. To explain students' anxieties, a word about the Stanford grading system.

Stanford business school had eliminated straightforward grades like A, B, C, D, and F in favor of a Pass/Fail system. The basic grade was P, for "Pass." This was supplemented with P plus, for work somewhat better than passable, and P minus, for work somewhat worse. The bottom grade, U, stood for "Unsatisfactory," and the top grade, H, stood for "High" or "Distinction." The idea was that in each class only the few who performed abysmally or brilliantly would receive a U or an H while everybody else would get a P, P plus, or P minus. And since nearly everyone would get some form of "Pass," we were all supposed to forget about grades and concentrate instead on the quest for knowledge. Right. What actually happened was that as every poet grew clinically depressed at the prospect of a U, every non-poet decided to do whatever it took to get an H.

During phase one, the week before midterms, poets and non-poets alike cut back even further on their sleep. Study groups that had been meeting for five hours a session ran to seven or eight. In class, students pelted their professors with questions about the exams.

"Come on, you guys," Walt burst out in Accounting one morning after we had been pressing him about the midterm. "In the past week I've watched all of you go from being students to being exam takers. The point isn't just to pass the midterm, okay? The point is to learn." Walt insisted he would take only one more question. Thirty or forty hands went up.

Back at the house in Portola Valley, Joe, Philippe, and I saw each other more, starting to eat dinner together in the evening, but talked to each other even less, since each of us brought work to the table. A typical conversation:

PHILIPPE: You enjoy the mushrooms in this omelet? (Philippe had done the cooking.)

JOE: (Tapping at his calculator.) Working out the probabilities on these trees takes so much time, you know? I've gotta train myself to do 'em in my head. Only way I can move fast enough in the midterm to ace it.

ME: A demand curve slopes up to the right, right?

JOE: Now on this oil well case, if hole A is dry but hole B is a gusher, and if holes C and D are both dry, what is the probability that hole E . . . (He falls silent and begins tapping once again on his calculator.)

PHILIPPE: *Supply* slopes up to the right.

ME: Delicious, thanks.

In the middle of the week I shared a dispiriting lunch in the Arbuckle Lounge with Conor. Conor's troubles with the core material had ceased to cheer me. He'd already received a failing grade on a take-home assignment in OB, and we both believed he might flunk the term. As we picked over our Mexican food, Conor looked ashen.

"I was up all night last night studying Trees," he said. "I didn't understand a bloody thing."

"*All* night?" I asked.

"Right," Conor answered. "I haven't slept since Sunday. This taco's my breakfast."

That afternoon I spotted Conor in the library. He was laid out on a sofa in the periodicals room with the accounting text over his face, getting his first sleep in, I suppose, thirty hours.

The next day at lunch I encountered Jennifer. Just a week earlier she had told me that she was still managing to complete all the assigned readings. "Something must be wrong," she had said, laughing at herself, "because I've been told keeping up with the work is impossible." Now Jennifer looked tense. "I just came from two hours in the library working on *one* Micro problem," she said, eating fast. She still had three problems to go to get ready for class, which was just an hour off, and she had yet to start on the reading assignment. "Giving us assignments that nobody can finish," Jennifer said, "seems to be the way that Yeager gets his jollies."

Jennifer resentful, Conor ashen, Joe and Philippe intent on their cramming, myself terrified. Toward the end of the week the midterm anxiety rose to such a hysterical pitch that no one escaped it. There were even reliable reports that Gunnar Haakonsen and John Lyons, Mr. Cool and Mr. Perfect, had been seen studying late at night in the library like ordinary mortals.

Faced with so many students pushing themselves so hard, the deans and administrators did what they could to calm us. Esther Simon and Sonia Jensen circulated in the Arbuckle Lounge at lunchtime, urging us all to get our rest. Simon held a Wednesday help session on exam-taking techniques. Then a group of second-year students joined the effort to dampen the frenzy, putting a letter into every first-year's mailbox. It was a photocopy of a letter that they had received from a second-year the preceding fall, when they had been first-years themselves. The letter was titled "Pain or Pleasure at Stanford Business School."

"Too many tears were shed last year at the business school," the letter began. It argued for a sense of perspective in approaching the workload. "Most of us come [to Stanford] as perfectionists and feel very uncomfortable doing a so-so job on anything. The sooner you give up this habit, the happier you will be." A first-year student could devote an hour to reading one article carefully, the letter contended, but he would be better off using the hour skimming three articles and getting to know a classmate. Then the letter reached its crucial passage:

This is not to deny that you will need to work extremely hard in [your first] year. But if you work hard because you have to, because you are afraid of not passing, because an ugly monster in your nightmares keeps reminding you that the world will come to an end if you don't pass, you can easily resent the experience and find it painful.

But if you constantly remind yourself that passing is not the issue, that you are here because you want to learn and grow, that every minute of hard work is making you a better, tougher, and more capable person, your experiences will be much more enjoyable. . . . What [makes] the difference [is] perspective.

Joe picked this letter out of his mailbox, looked it over, then cackled and asked, "Who wrote this? A nun?" I took the letter seriously, reading it twice when I received it, then again and again during the weekend before midterms. But the letter had no more practical effect on me than on Joe. He went right on pushing himself to get Hs. I went right on pushing myself not to get Us.

Part of my problem was that I kept getting caught up in grand concepts when I needed to master details. In Micro, I found myself fascinated not by the mathematics involved but by the way Micro shed light on the essentially tragic nature of the human condition. I mean this. On the demand side, the discipline of microeconomics explained, consumers had soaring hopes and desires but only so much that they could spend. On the supply side, firms always wanted to make as much money as they could but still had to abide by the decisions of the market, producing only those goods that the market would accept and charging only those prices that the market would bear. Thus all of microeconomics turned upon a central fact of life: Whether as consumers or producers, human beings always want more than they can get.

For me, this placed Micro right back there in the Garden of Eden with concupiscence, pride, jealousy, and all the other effects of original sin. Yet while perhaps useful in a seminary, this turn of mind was of no help in preparing for the midterm. "Either you'll know the material cold or you won't," Joe said. I would not, and I considered it only fitting and right to panic.

At the end of our Micro class on Thursday afternoon, the last class before midterms began on Friday morning, Professor Yeager gave a little speech. Since the students seated before him had the gaunt, hollow look of the hunted, not having slept more than a few hours a night in at least a week, I thought at first that Professor Yeager might simply tell us to relax and do our best. But that would have been out of character. Professor Yeager did not step out of character.

Yeager began by mentioning that there had been some discussion among the deans and faculty about the pressure first-years felt as they prepared for midterms. Most had agreed that the first-years overdid it, working too much and sleeping too little.

"I'm not certain, myself, that I agree with this view," Yeager said. He placed one hand on his waist, still pinching a stick of chalk between his fingers. "I take the classes I teach very seriously, and I expect my students to do the same. But I suppose we do want students to have enough stamina left after midterms to get on with their work for the rest of the term." In any event, he said, the deans had decided that while finals would remain full, four-hour exams, this year midterms would be shortened from four hours each to three.

"I mention this by way of warning," Yeager continued. After writing four-hour midterms for so many years, Yeager was having trouble limiting himself to the new, shorter format. "It seemed fair to warn you that when you take my midterm you will need to work briskly." His thin, rigid lips seemed to change shape for a moment in what might have been a smile. "*Very* briskly," he said. Then Yeager dismissed us.

Thus ended midterms, phase one.

Looking back on it, phase two of midterms, midterm week itself, is a blur. But it was a blur at the time, too.

On Friday morning, Accounting. As I entered the exam room and picked up the blue book, the question I most feared was one on

LIFO and FIFO. Last In, First Out and First In, First Out were the two basic methods of accounting for inventory. When a company prepared its statements, LIFO would usually produce a smaller figure for net income, while FIFO would make net income bigger, and, hence, increase the company's return on equity, a statistic of great interest to shareholders. Crudely put, this gave the company a choice between using LIFO to cut down on its tax bill or FIFO to pump up its stock value. That much I was able to grasp. But whenever one of Walt's assignments had given us an income statement calculated under LIFO or FIFO, then told us to recalculate it according to the other method, I always got lost. Now I joined the flutter as my classmates and I opened the question booklet to begin. Question one: "What amount would Oshkosh B'Gosh have shown as the cost of products sold during 1987 if it had used FIFO rather than LIFO?"

A stuffy silence fell on the room, broken only by the barely perceptible tap-tapping of tens of fingers striking calculator keys. For three hours, I calculated, wrote answers, crossed them out, recalculated and rewrote. None of my answers had the lovely, tight fit that would have indicated they were correct. But I kept working, placing my hopes in partial credit. At noon, Walt told us to put down our pencils and stop. I did not know whether I had passed or failed.

Yeager's Micro midterm took place on Saturday afternoon. In one question, Yeager gave us the demand functions for beer and wine in an imaginary country. Then he asked whether spending on beer would rise or fall if a certain tax were imposed, what that suggested about the price elasticity of beer (that is, how much the sales of beer would fall if the price of beer were raised), and what that in turn suggested about the cross-elasticity between beer and wine (how much the sales of wine would increase if the price of beer were raised). In a second question, Yeager asked what would happen to purchases of Japanese cars if the United States imposed import quotas, if interest rates rose, making car loans more expensive, or if competing, inexpensive cars began to be imported from Korea.

There were six questions in all, requiring a combination of brief essays, graphs showing shifts in demand and supply curves, and some equation-solving. I had to work briskly, as Yeager had warned. When the exam ended, I once again had no idea whether I had passed or failed. I felt only a sense of relief.

Monday, Computers. When I opened the exam I skimmed it quickly, relieved to see that it contained just two word problems. When I went back and read the problems in detail I felt different. The first dealt with NASA space shuttles.

> The Discovery shuttle can carry up to 16 experiments, as many as four communication satellites, and at most only one military satellite on each flight. Challenger II can carry up to eight experiments, as many as six communication satellites, and, like Discovery, at most only one military satellite on each flight.

NASA had contracted to fly a certain number of flights with each craft, carrying into space a specific number of commercial satellites. While the cost of each Challenger flight was $180 million, the cost of each Discovery flight was $120 million.

> Your goal is to develop a linear programming model which will determine how many flights of Challenger II and how many flights of Discovery should be launched next year to accomplish NASA's objective of spending as little as possible, while at the same time meeting its con- tractual obligations.

As I worked on this and the following question, I had something like an out-of-body experience. I especially remember seeming to watch myself from the other side of the room as I worked on the essay. The watching self felt puzzled. It knew the exam-taking self had no idea how to answer the questions, yet there the exam-taking self sat, somehow managing to keep its pen moving across page after page of the little blue exam book.

With the Computers midterm behind me, I had Tuesday and Wednesday to get ready for the Organizational Behavior exam on Thursday. I called Steven for advice. He told me to stoop to the level of the course material itself. What I would need to do, Steven insisted, was spew technobabble.

"The models you've been studying in OB may be a travesty and a sham," Steven said, "but remember that your professor has made them his career. You might also keep in mind that he'll be giving you your grade." Hammond would not want literate little essays. He would want proof that I knew the material. "He'll be looking for a jargon dump."

The exam took place on Thursday morning. It asked us to analyze a case entitled "Why Did the Salesmen Quit?" in which a young entrepreneur had taken over a firm from its aged founder. In short order, the entrepreneur had so alienated his salesmen that they had walked out on him. Why?

I wrote fast, and to make certain Professor Bob noticed all the jargon in my answer, I underlined the important terms.

> Both the literature on <u>culture</u> and the models of <u>leadership</u> suggest that <u>management techniques</u> must be <u>validated</u> over time. The problem for this firm is no longer one of <u>motivating</u> employees through the early, difficult years. The new owner must instead foster a <u>management style</u> more suited to his <u>interdependence</u> with others in the firm.

By the time the exam period ended, I had jargon-dumped my way through two blue books and started on a third. Had I thought about it, the realization that I'd gone in two months from writing speeches for the Great Communicator to spouting technical jargon would have disheartened me. But I lacked the energy to think.

Friday afternoon, the last of my midterm examinations, Trees, and abject humiliation. For although I made my way through the short-answer questions at the beginning of the exam adequately, when I came to Problem 4, entitled "Glittering Trees," I fell apart.

"Glittering Trees" was set in "a remote corner of southwest Indiana," where the Wiley family raised racehorses. The family owned four barns, equally spaced around a circle with a diameter of 100 miles. As the problem opened, word had just reached Jeff Wiley that a tornado was threatening the ranch, and Jeff was jumping into his truck to try to rescue the Wileys' prize racehorse, Glittering Trees. Jeff did not know which barn the beast was in.

A very brief excerpt from the problem, which ran to well over 1,000 words:

> Jeff knows that the tornado is heading towards Barn 3 at this time, but that its course is uncertain. In fact, the tornado has probability 0.5 of arriving at Barn 3 at I pm, probability 0.3 of arriving at Barn 2 at I pm, and probability 0.2 of arriving at Barn 4 at I pm.
>
> Further, if the tornado does hit Barn 3 at I pm, it has probability 0.5 of remaining there, probability 0.3 of moving on to Barn 2, and probability 0.2 of moving on to Barn 4. If it does move on, it arrives at its new barn at 2 pm. If the tornado is at Barn 2 at I pm, it has a probability of 0.5 of remaining there, and a probability of 0.5 of moving back to Barn 3, arriving at 2 pm.
>
> Finally, if the tornado is at Barn 4 at I pm, it has a probability of 0.9 of remaining there, and a probability of 0.1 of moving on to Barn 1, again arriving at 2 pm. Wherever the tornado is at 2 pm, it stays there, and shortly after 2 pm vanishes permanently. The tornado will touch down exactly twice, at I pm, and again at 2 pm.

The problem concluded with the assignment to diagram Jeff Wiley's decision problem, "computing all the probabilities and filling in all the payoffs," and then to "determine Jeff's optimal strategy."

For more than an hour I seized up, unable to think or to write. Not until there were fewer than twenty minutes left did I succeed in forcing myself to begin working. I took the single piece of paper that the answer sheet provided for this question, filled it with a portion of my tree, then ripped a second sheet from my notebook in order to continue drawing decision nodes, event nodes, and branches. I soon filled third and fourth sheets, and I covered a fifth sheet with instructions to Professor Kemal for taping the first four sheets together, as though they were pieces of a puzzle. When the exam ended, my decision tree, still incomplete, contained more than sixty branches. Since I had not even begun to calculate the optimal strategy, I scribbled a guess: "Wiley should go to Barn I, then to Barn 3. If he finds the horse, he should shoot it. If he does not, he should shoot himself."

When the exams came back, I learned that Jennifer had done well, Philippe had done well, Joe had done very well, and even Conor had passed all five of his midterms.

I myself had gotten low but passing grades in Accounting, Computers, and Micro, receiving a P in each. In OB, where Steven had persuaded me to perform a jargon dump, I had achieved a perfect score, getting an H. But in Trees I had achieved a score of 39 points out of 100. Among the 333 students who had taken the exam, I had ranked eighth . . . from the bottom . . . getting a U.

I had flunked.

SIX

The Stockholm Syndrome

November 9

Who do the deans at this place think they are? After charging me fifteen grand a year in tuition, they're trying to pass off as a professor a barely post-adolescent wonder-boy who writes an exam question like "Glittering Trees."

After midterms, everyone knew where he stood. Students had different reactions to this.

As the above excerpt from my journal indicates, I got angry. At first I directed my anger toward the business school, especially Professor Kemal. "Glittering Trees" was the most absurd question I had ever seen on any examination, and as my classmates and I compared our answer sheets we found that almost nobody had answered the question correctly. But in the first class after the exam, Kemal assured us that he had graded "Glittering Trees" leniently, going so far as to give every student an extra five points. Then, as he took us through the rest of the exam, I had to admit to myself that I had not just choked on one problem, "Glittering Trees," but done badly—appallingly, really—on all the problems.

Now I got angry with myself. How could I have messed up so completely? By the end of class I knew I would have to go back and achieve at least a rudimentary understanding of all the material we had covered during the first half of the term while Kemal continued, in the second half, to take up one new topic after another. I would have to study even harder and sleep even less. But I figured I deserved it.

This is worth noting. By the third or fourth week of the term, business school had succeeded in afflicting me with a variation of the Stockholm Syndrome, named after the incident in which a hostage in a Stockholm bank robbery fell in love with one of her captors. I was not in love with business school by any means. But I had stopped holding Stanford responsible for what was happening to me. Even though I was only taking enough time off from my work to sleep five or six hours a night, when I failed to complete assignments or readings I blamed myself. Now that I had failed the Trees midterm I decided it was my fault, and from midterms on it was difficult to say who was punishing me more, the business school or myself.

For Philippe midterms marked just the opposite, the moment when he decided to stop punishing himself and start going easy. When I returned home one afternoon soon after midterms I found him in the hot tub, his head canted back against the side of the tub to expose his face to the sun. "I 'ave been told of a fraternity party tonight where there will be many young women," Philippe said, "so I must work on my tan." Philippe had spent almost no time in the hot tub during the first half of the term, but now he had received three Ps and two P pluses on his midterms instead of the Hs he had expected. "Grades?" Philippe had said, adopting his new attitude the very day we got back our exams, "what do they matter?" I left him in the sun, squinting. He seemed to be forcing himself to lie there and enjoy it.

Joe represented the rare mean. If midterms meant students like Philippe could let up while students like me had to work harder, in Joe's case midterms made no difference. He had gotten two Hs, one P plus, and two Ps, exactly what he had intended to get. "When you come from Jersey," Joe had said early in the term, grinning, "you get used to proving yourself."

Conor got Ps on all five of his exams. This placed him out of danger of flunking, and I expected him to feel elated. He was depressed.

The week after midterms I found Conor seated on a bench in the courtyard. He had his head tilted back against the wall to face the sun, the same position Philippe had assumed in the hot tub. But while Philippe had appeared healthy, Conor looked pale and exhausted. He wore a heavy cable sweater with the sleeves shoved up to his elbows, still dressing like an Irishman instead of a Californian. Droplets of sweat had formed on his forehead. He opened one eye to peer at me through his glasses for a moment, then shut it.

"Five Ps," Conor said, his eyes still closed. "With a P plus on an exam I'd have known one course where I could study less. With a P minus I'd have known where I had to study harder. But five Ps? What does that tell me? Nothing." He wiped his forehead with the back of his arm. "Now it'll be the same thing all over again, me working like a dog for the rest of the term."

Jennifer was as exhilarated as Conor was dazed. I had lunch with her later that week. "Midterms were just so intense," she said, wrinkling her nose and smiling.

The night before each midterm Jennifer had been too nervous to sleep, while the afternoon after each midterm she had felt too euphoric to settle down and study. "It was like putting on *Mary Poppins* in high school," Jennifer said. Jennifer had played Mary. "I remember I was really scared before each performance and really high afterward."

Jennifer had gotten two P pluses and three Ps. Now she was looking forward to the rest of the term. "Being at Stanford business school is probably the hardest thing I've done in my life," she said. She smiled merrily and took a bite of her salad. "But here I am, in with really bright, talented people. And I'm making it."

Thus the aftermath of midterms: Philippe was disappointed in his grades while Joe took his grades for granted; I felt angry, first with the business school, then with myself; and Conor appeared as close to a breakdown as ever. Only Mary Poppins was happy.

Although midterms represented a major dramatic moment, the business school calendar failed to accommodate it. We got no time off. The deans did not call us into Bishop Auditorium to congratulate us on making it halfway through the term. Midterms ended on Saturday and classes resumed on Monday, giving us only a single day, Sunday, to attempt to recover from the ordeal.

In the classrooms our lethargy proved palpable. There were fewer questions. Case discussions dragged. On the skydeck, students buried their heads in their hands and dozed. Meanwhile, down in the teaching wells, the professors were delivering lectures that made the material in the first half of the term look simple.

In Computers, Jin taught us integer programming, a sophisticated method for solving complicated optimization problems. The cases he assigned grew into word problems of bottomless complexity.

One involved a rental car company. The company had seventeen locations and five car models. It knew that 20 percent of the customers who rented cars at location A would return them to location A, 15 percent would drive from A to B, 30 percent from A to C, and on and on. We were to design a computer model that would tell the company how many cars of each of the five models it would need at each of its seventeen locations in order to meet demand during the peak travel period, Thanksgiving weekend. By the time we got to this case, my Computers study group partners, Alex and Doug, had started to like these problems. Madness, madness all of it.

Trees, Micro, and Accounting likewise moved into dense, obscure territory. In Trees, Kemal instructed us in the Bayesian revision of probabilities and in mathematical techniques for dealing with the sharing of risk between entities, subjects I cannot describe because I did not, and do not, understand them.

In Micro, Yeager took us through models of monopoly and oligopoly markets, while in Accounting, Walt dealt with methods of accounting for leases, marketable securities, and intercompany transactions. Since I had never worked in a corporation, the Accounting definitions and word problems proved to my mind as remote and mind-spun and entirely speculative as the debates of the medieval Scholastics. *Calculate how much money Sears should place in its deferred tax provision account. Calculate the number of angels that can dance on the head of a pin.*

The only break in the excruciating routine of class-study-sleep came at Thanksgiving, when we had five whole days off, from Wednesday all the way through to Sunday. I looked forward to those five days. "Thanksgiving break is great," Steven told me. "You'll be able to get rested, then still have a couple of days left over for going to the beach or up to San Francisco." I planned the break in detail. Wednesday I would sleep all morning, then find somebody to go out to lunch. Thursday Edita would fly in, and I would spend the rest of the holiday introducing her to my classmates, showing her the Stanford campus, taking her to Chinatown for dinner, and driving her along the California coast. Thanksgiving break would be great, just as Steven had said.

It wasn't.

Fatigue was nine tenths of the trouble. Since the beginning of the term I'd had something like 100 hours less sleep than I should have. And while I'd expected to feel fairly vigorous on the first day of the Thanksgiving break after just letting myself sleep in for a few hours, when I awoke at noon on Wednesday I felt as though I were lying under the mattress instead of on top.

I did manage to lug myself out to lunch. I had been waiting for a chance to get to know a member of the business school faculty, Professor Jack Healey. A Washington friend had told me to look Healey up, describing him as smart, funny, and probably the only political scientist in the country who voted for Reagan both times.

Professor Healey was a big man in his early fifties. He had small, skeptical, brilliant blue eyes. When I met him at his office he gave my hand a big-knuckled shake. "Call me Healey," he said. "Mexican food okay with you?" Healey drove me to a restaurant just a few miles from campus.

I don't know. I was tired, as I said, and I suppose I was expecting Healey to try to make me feel better by telling me all the hard work would be worth it. But after we had exchanged twenty minutes or so of pleasantries, what Healey said was this:

"I've taught at this business school for seven years, and all I can tell you is you've picked one hell of a group of people to associate with. Fact is, I kind of think MBA students should have their own country.

"The MBA motto? 'I'll tread on you.' The MBA coat of arms? St. George and the dragon, only instead of St. George spearing the dragon, the dragon is eating St. George. The MBA bird is obvious. The California jay. It's loud and obnoxious and it flies around crapping on people."

Healey took a swig of his Dos Equis. "Yup," he said, "one hell of a group of people."

He handed me a second beer.

"Try a jalapeño pepper and wash it down with this," he said. "Put you out of your misery."

When Edita arrived everything went wrong. I slept through my alarm and got to the airport late. From the airport we drove to Route One, the Pacific Coast Highway, ordinarily one of the most scenic roads in America, but the wind sheared rain and salt spray onto the car windows and the sea and sky both looked like greasy lead. Back at the house, after offering to help Philippe cook the Thanksgiving dinner, I scorched the mashed potatoes, knocked over a bottle of wine that Philippe had set out to breathe, and dropped a platter of stuffing on the dining room carpet.

On Saturday night I drove Edita into San Francisco for dinner, but I had to fight back grogginess from appetizers to dessert. Not until Sunday afternoon did I feel rested. By then we had so little time before leaving to take Edita back to the airport that all she and I could do was rent a couple of bikes and ride around the campus.

Edita tried to convince me that a long weekend with nothing much to do was just what she had been hoping for. But I felt guilty. I considered it all my fault. The Stockholm Syndrome.

The lethargy that had begun after midterms ended abruptly at the beginning of week nine. Students who had been sluggish for three weeks suddenly began to act as if they had been nudged with an electric prod. The event responsible for this transformation was Esther Simon's lunchtime help session on finals.

Students ripped open bags of potato chips and popped cans of soda as Simon began. "Year after year," she said in soothing tones, "I've seen first-years surprise themselves at how well they could do on finals. Unfortunately, I've also seen quite a number of nausea and diarrhea attacks that required medical attention, and, on average, one student every second year who suffered a total nervous breakdown."

Students set down their food and sat slowly upright.

"But, please, don't worry yourselves," Simon said.

Simon spoke for almost an hour. She warned us to make absolutely certain that we went into each exam with a thorough understanding of the material, with tabbed and cross-indexed notes, and with plans of attack that involved looking over the questions and calculating how much time to spend on each. She advised us on diet, urging us to eat protein, not carbohydrates, before each exam. She went into sleeping patterns. "In 8:00 classes you can get away with feeling drowsy until 9:00 or 9:30. In an 8:00 exam, you cannot. So now is the time to start conditioning yourselves to wake up at 6:30, perform some mild exercise—a bike ride, aerobics, a short jog—eat breakfast, shower and dress, and achieve full alertness by 7:45."

"Was she dry-humping us, or what?" Sam Barrett said in the courtyard afterward. Sam had been one of only seven students in our entire class to get a grade on the Trees midterm that was lower than mine, and on his OB midterm Sam had gotten a P minus with a note from the professor warning him that the P minus should have been a U.

"I thought I had finals under control," Sam said. "But now I'm trying to figure out when I'm going to get the runs and start puking and which one of us is going to be carried out of here in a full-body restraint. *Screw* this place."

SEVEN

Finals:
The Peasants Are Revolting

December 1

I note that today, the first day of December, the temperature here was in the high sixties and that after the morning fog lifted the whole place was drenched with sunshine. As finals approach, all this unremitting beauty is getting on my nerves. I feel apprehensive, tired, and depressed. I want sleet.

Simon had me so rattled that during the last two weeks of the term I began starting my days at 6:30, just as she had urged. I'd go for a dank, misty jog in the foothills, then scramble two eggs for protein. I was alert at 8:00 all right, but by 8:30 I'd find myself nodding off in class. At night I engaged in still more solitary study. So did Philippe and Joe. When none of us could take it anymore we would gather in the kitchen.

"I want to ski," Philippe would say. He was not pining for Switzerland but for Lake Tahoe.

"All my life I 'ave wanted to ski in the American West," Philippe would say. "In Switzerland, it is common knowledge that the Rockies 'ave powder of a different quality from our own, lighter and deeper. Now the newspapers are reporting the first 'eavy snowfalls at Tahoe. But this Swiss boy must stay in his room and study."

Joe would pace, his fingers wrapped around his mug in a viselike grip. "Gotta ace these exams," he would say. Joe considered getting

Hs an essential career move, even though Stanford banned corporate recruiters from asking students about their grades.

"Oh, they might not be allowed to come right out and ask our grades," Joe would argue, "but I'm telling you, recruiters can smell Hs."

Joe would gulp down his coffee, then spring back upstairs to work. Philippe and I would linger, but only a few moments. Philippe had decided to turn at least one of his three P pluses into an H, and I had a U to overcome.

During the seventh week of the term, my Trees classmates and I arrived one morning for class, took our seats, then watched the big hand on the clock at the front of the room crawl past 8:00 to 8:15 and 8:30. No Professor Kemal. Just as students began getting up to leave—"Kemal's car might've broken down," Sam Barrett said, "and I for one could use the next hour and a half to study"—Dean Slowacki arrived.

"I'll be taking your class today," Slowacki said. He looked flushed, as though he had just trotted downstairs from his office. "Professor Kemal has an illness in the family. Would one of you lend me your textbook?"

For the next four classes we had substitute teachers, either Dean Slowacki or a visiting Wharton professor. In one class the Wharton professor would introduce a new topic such as Adverse Selection. In the next class Slowacki would show up instead and take up the finer points of Normal Distribution. Then it would be the Wharton professor again, this time teaching us about Binomial and Continuous Distributions. "Neither one of those guys ever has any idea where the class is supposed to be," Joe said. "They're killin' me."

Professor Kemal's return in week nine did not help. It was his father who had been ill, and he remained in the hospital. Kemal looked tired and distracted. "Some of you sent Get Well cards," he said, his eyes welling up. "Thank you." Then Kemal began discussion of an entirely new topic, Standard Deviation, and although we had prepared four problems, Kemal permitted the discussion to wander so aimlessly that by the time the period had ended he had failed to finish explaining even the second.

At lunch that day Sam Barrett waved me over to his table. He was sitting with a tall woman I recognized from Trees, Louisa Pelligrino, one of his house mates. "Get this, the latest on Kemal," Sam said. "Tell Peter, Louisa."

"I was really upset after class today," Louisa said. "I mean, I did badly on the midterm, so I've really been trying to understand this material."

"That makes three of us," Sam said.

"So after class," Louisa continued, "I went to see Esther Simon. I thought I was really nice about it. I didn't want to complain at all. I just told her that a lot of us think Professor Kemal hasn't recovered from his father's illness enough to go back into the classroom. I mean, between the two Trees classes he teaches, ours and the 10:00 class, almost 120 first-years have Kemal as their instructor. That means almost 120 students headed for trouble in a core course in their very first term. Am I right? Is this a legitimate concern?"

Sam and I nodded.

"So I told all this to Esther Simon. And instead of being understanding, she got huffy. 'The students need to understand that Professor Kemal is a human being, too,' she said. 'You're not the first to come in here to complain. I don't see why the students can't bear with us and give Professor Kemal some slack.'"

"Can you believe that?" Sam said. "We're *paying* at this place, and they want *us* to cut *them* slack."

I was outraged too.

"Obviously we all hope the best for Kemal's father," I said, "but there's no excuse for letting Kemal's problems get in the way of our education. If Kemal's not up to teaching, the school should clear him out."

I'm not at all proud of this incident. But it shows the state students were in with ten days to go until finals. We felt exhausted, helpless, and overwrought, and it didn't take much to make us hysterical.

The last classes of the term fell during the first week of December. It was the custom to give each professor a round of applause when he finished his last lecture, and in Accounting, Computers, and OB we did. The last Trees and Micro classes merit special comment.

In Trees, Professor Kemal wrapped up his remarks and asked whether there were any questions about the final.

Louisa Pellegrino raised her hand. "I've been checking," she said, "and it's clear that the sections of this course taught by other professors got higher grades on the midterm than we did. So when the final is graded, I hope that basic fairness is observed and the same grading standards are applied to us as to the other sections."

There was a smattering of applause.

Sam Barrett raised his hand to ask whether the final would be administered in rooms in which we could concentrate, since the room in which he had taken the midterm had been noisy.

"When I went in to check, the room was quiet," Kemal said.

"Maybe it was then. But it got noisy outside the window later on—real noisy."

"Did it occur to you to close the window?"

"Oh, come *on*. I'm not a moron. The window *was* closed."

"I find it difficult to believe the ambient noise was such that it actually interfered with your exam. Very difficult to believe."

Sam's face turned red. He started to answer. Louisa interrupted.

"Professor Kemal, here's what I think is going on here. We're all apprehensive about this final for reasons that make sense. I know in my own case, I studied hard for your midterm—harder than I studied for any of the other midterms I took. But I did way worse on yours. I know this term has been rough on you personally, but—"

"Friends," Kemal said, throwing his hands up in exasperation, "I promise you. You do not need to worry. Truly you do not. Study for this final as you would for any other, and I promise you will not need to worry."

"Does that mean this course has gotten so screwed up," Sam said, "that you're just going to pass us all to get it over with?"

"I assure you it will still be possible to fail," Kemal said. "But if you do a reasonable job of preparation, you will not need to experience sleepless nights worrying about the result."

The class period over, various students offered Kemal tepid applause, while Sam and half a dozen others simply stood, shoved their books into their bags, and strode past Kemal out of the room.

That afternoon at the end of Micro, Yeager put his hands on his waist and said simply, "Thank you for your attention. After a slow start you've learned a great deal, as poets tend to do. Good luck on the final. Others might tell you not to worry about finals. I will not. I urge you to take these exams seriously."

As Yeager began to gather his lecture notes, Conor stepped into the teaching well. "Professor Yeager," he said, handing Yeager a package, "we chipped in to get you a gift."

Yeager tore open the wrapping and held up a book. Then he looked at Conor, puzzled: "e. e. cummings?"

"To be sure," Conor answered, "we *are* the poets."

When the laughter died down Conor continued. "Professor, there's one question we've all been wanting to ask: Why *eight*-minute breaks?"

Yeager chuckled. "I learned long ago that MBAs tend to be aggressive. If you tell them ten minutes, they'll take fifteen. But if I tell you eight minutes, I can be fairly confident that I'll have you back in the classroom in just about ten."

The class responded to this final barb by giving Yeager a standing ovation.

The scorn we heaped on Kemal, the ovation we awarded to Yeager—these say a lot about that fall term. Kemal was our age. He wanted to be our friend. But fall term was as traumatic for many of us as a war zone, and we didn't want a pal for a professor, we wanted a field marshal, someone we could rely on to tell us where we were going and then march us there. Yeager was cold and merciless and lived by the clock. But we knew we could rely on him, and by the end of the term we felt toward Yeager the way GIs felt toward Patton. We loved the bastard.

December 11

Midnight Sunday. Finals begin in eight hours.

As usual, when I called him earlier today Steven told me to relax. As usual, I can't.

"Peter, they don't want you to flunk," Steven said. "They want you to become a rich alum who'll give a lot of money to the school. Learn just enough techniques to let you do a decent job on a few of the questions. On the rest, aim for partial credit. Remember, all you need is a P. So chill!"

How do I know which techniques to learn? How do I know when I've learned them? How do I know what counts for partial credit?

On Monday I began five solid days of exams, one every morning, each lasting from 8:00 until noon. During the finals themselves, I felt in the same state of heightened consciousness that I had experienced during midterms. Time did not seem to exist. When the exam period ended each day at noon, my classmates and I would all crowd into the courtyard, laughing and shouting, before breaking into smaller groups for lunch. Halfway through lunch, fatigue would descend upon me. I would go home, sleep for two hours, awake, experience a cold, barbed surge of fear at the thought of another exam the next morning, drink at least two cups of coffee for the sake of the caffeine, then settle myself in my pantry office to study for six or eight more hours.

The Trees exam came first.

There were six questions. In one, a doctor faced a patient whose symptoms suggested that he had contracted either Disease A, B, or C, with a specified probability of each. The doctor could prescribe Treatment 1 or Treatment 2. Each treatment had a certain probability of curing each disease. "Draw a decision tree, work out the probabilities, and decide on a treatment."

In the second question, the head of the IRS was trying to decide how many audit examiners to assign to each of several categories of taxpayers. Yet another discussed rainfall in a certain town, stating the probability that it would rain on any given day, noting that the amount of rain that fell on rainy weekends was a normal random variable with a mean of so-and-so and a standard deviation of such-and-such, and asking, finally, "What is the probability that it will rain on only one day next weekend *and* that the rainfall will total *more* than six centimeters?"

By the standards of the midterm these questions were dull stuff, none beginning to approach the intricacy of "Glittering Trees." True to his word, Professor Kemal had written a straightforward final. As the exam period wore on and I answered one question after another, I found myself growing more and more relieved, so that when it was finally all over at noon I felt as relaxed as if I'd just had a massage.

Tuesday, Yeager's Micro final.

The principal question on the exam dealt, in a flourish of Yeager wit, with Snow White and the Seven Dwarfs. Snow White was the manager. Each of the dwarfs ran a small operation: Grumpy brewed beer, Sneezy produced snuff, and so forth. The problem laid out the wage rates each dwarf charged for his labor, the cost of his materials, the demand for his goods, and the prices he charged for his goods. Then it asked how Snow White should allocate the Seven Dwarfs' labor among the seven enterprises. I made small mistakes here and there in performing calculations, but the problem did not unnerve me.

Yeager had seen to that. Near the end of the term he had announced that he would permit each of us to take into the exam two pages of notes, precisely two sheets of eight-and-a-half-by-eleven-inch paper, and nothing more. This had thrust us all as amateurs into the art of miniaturization. I had spent hours bent over my two sheets of paper, like a scholar examining the Dead Sea Scrolls. But of course I'd found that no matter how tiny a hand I used to transcribe my notes, only so much fit. I'd had to sift through my notebook, the problem sets, and the text, choosing and weighing the concepts and attempting to link ideas in my mind so that a single, minute scrawl would suggest a complete line of thought. By the time I took the exam I had all the concepts and equations so firmly in mind that I only referred to my two sheets of paper two or three times.

The case in the Organizational Behavior final exam on Wednesday centered on a firm that manufactured specialized sheet metal. Five

pages of text described the firm's management, its departments of
sales and marketing, its principal personalities, including the chief
executive and the heads of several departments, its chief competitors,
and its main customer, the Pentagon. An addendum of three pages
provided a description of market conditions and stated that after fifteen years of profitability, last year the firm had sustained a sizable
loss. The final asked, essentially, What's wrong?

I confess that I performed a second jargon dump. The sales and
marketing heads, I noted, suspected each other of faking data in
order to fatten their own annual bonuses—"goal conflict." One of
the personalities, I said, could not decide whether to act like a member of the senior management, as his title suggested, or, since he'd
been hired very recently, like a junior employee—"role conflict." In
this manner I managed to mention "corporate culture," "technical
specialization and innovation," "structure-environment fit," and a
score of other terms.

My behavior on the OB final perhaps sounds cynical, an effort to
get a passing grade without regard for genuine learning. It was. Yet
afterward, as I climbed into bed for my afternoon nap, I found myself acknowledging that the OB material had made it possible for me,
a young man who ten weeks before had known literally nothing
about business, to take a tremendously complicated business situation and make at least rudimentary sense of it.

Thursday, the Computers final, a four-hour ache. I was tired going
in. Then I found that I had to struggle for every answer. It felt like
Hemingway's descriptions of fighting to land marlin. I spent a full
hour on the first question of five, falling well off the pace I needed
to sustain, so that I had to scramble through the last four.

The last problem described the Excel Bicycle Company, an enterprise that made touring bikes and mountain bikes, one model each
for men and women, for a total of four models. Its contracts with
dealers required the company to deliver a certain number of each
model every month for three months. The question detailed the
costs of producing each model, the amount of time each model spent
in assembly and finishing, the costs to the company of carrying inventory, and so on. "Develop a linear programming model that mini-

mizes the Excel Bicycle Company's costs over the three-month period." Here I became not Hemingway but Ahab, taking one lunging,
hopeless stab at it after another.

By the time of the Accounting final on Friday, I found myself capable of only flickering mental effort. I was exhausted. Burned out. I
knew as I took my seat that I could not complete the exam and I
knew that I did not care. Then Walt distributed the blue books and
I experienced the kind of adrenaline surge that evolved to save our
Neanderthal ancestors from woolly mammoths and pterodactyls.

The final asked a long series of questions about the balance sheet
and statement of cash flows of the Petrie Corporation, a merchandis-
ing giant. I worked steadily, encountering trouble only toward the
end of the exam, when, for forty minutes, I got stuck on methods of
accounting for the acquisition of a partially owned subsidiary. I put
down two ways of answering the question, hoping for partial credit
between them.

Then, as the second hand on the big, institutional clock at the
front of the classroom swept up to indicate the stroke of noon, there
was a huge, percussive pop. Sam Barrett had uncorked a bottle of
California champagne.

We all took swigs.

And fall term was over. Over.

Philippe had already left for skiing at Tahoe by the time I got
back to the house. Joe was just leaving for the airport.

"Merry Christmas!" Joe shouted as he hauled his bags to a waiting
cab. "See you next year. Gotta run!"

EIGHT

Home for Christmas

During the Christmas break Edita and I both flew back to Washington, she to stay with her family, I to stay with friends. I quickly discovered that in one sense nothing had changed. Washington was still where I felt at home. Edita and I did our Christmas shopping together, ate at a couple of our favorite restaurants, and went ice skating, just as we had the winter before. One day I went downtown to have lunch with my old colleagues at the White House. Afterward we went out onto a balcony of the Old Executive Office Building to catch a glimpse of President Reagan as he walked back from an event in that building to the White House itself. The President turned and waved, just as he always had, then playfully tossed a snowball up at us.

But of course everything had changed. Reagan would be leaving office in a matter of weeks. My friends in the writing shop were all looking for jobs. And now that I was back in my familiar setting I could see that just one term at business school had begun to make me a different person.

On the drive in from the airport, I noticed for the first time that a number of high-tech firms had offices in the Virginia and Maryland suburbs. When I read the *Washington Post* in the morning I only skimmed the politics on the front page before reading the business section in detail. One afternoon at a department store, I got impatient at the checkout counter. Shoppers all around me were backing up and growing angry. I found myself wondering irritably, Where's the manager? Doesn't he *know* he's incurring ill will? Can't he *see* that hiring just one or two more checkout people for the holiday rush would net him at least a couple of hundred dollars an hour?

For all the agony fall term had inflicted on me I now felt a certain exhilaration at the thought of what I had been through. My learning curve had been virtually vertical. At week one, I had known zero. By the end of week ten I had had to know a great deal. Between the two I had been forced to engage in a long, thrusting climb.

How did a factory manager use computer models to decide how many cars per week to manufacture? How did a major corporation account for its sales? Its costs? Its taxes?

Were these the worthiest questions men could ponder? Clearly not. We were not talking about sin and redemption here. Yet I could see now that business school opened onto its own compelling, if narrower, field of fascination. It might not help you to dispose your soul or reach a conclusion about the meaning of existence, but business school would tell you quite a lot about what was going on in your workplace, your grocery store, or your shopping mall, helping you to understand the economic activities that take up the larger part of most people's waking lives. It seemed to me now that that was no small claim.

I recognized these changes in my thinking and outlook and took a measure of satisfaction in them—I'd earned them.

Edita, for her part, had endured just as much agony during fall term as I had but didn't feel any of the compensating sense of accomplishment. Almost as soon as she had reached Arizona, she had realized that she had gone to business school to try to be like her brothers, all three of whom were bankers. Now she put this experience down as one of life's lessons, thought seriously about what she wanted to do, and decided to pursue her long-standing interest in teaching languages (Edita is fluent in Spanish, French, and Portuguese). She would not return to business school but would remain in Washington.

Paradox though it was, I envied her. For although from the distance of the East Coast I viewed Stanford business school with a sense of pride, I did not by any means look forward to going back. To the work. To the pain. And to feeling stupid again.

WINTER TERM

Inferno, Cont'd

NINE

Winter Term Overture: It's Cold and It's Damp

January 9

I'm back. I'm sick. Those two sentences go together.

During the first weekend of winter term and most of the week that followed, my temperature bounced from just under to just over 100 degrees, a low-grade fever. I had a headache. My throat was raw. I felt groggy from popping so many antihistamine pills.

My solace was that so many of my classmates were also sick. In classes that first week there was an almost junglelike background din of sniffles, coughs, sneezes, trumpetings. At lunch on Monday, Conor pulled a green bottle out of his book bag, opened it, and counted out five big oatmeal-colored tablets. "Vitamin C," Conor said. "Flu." Back at the house in Portola Valley, Joe remained in good health—growing up in New Jersey had given him a constitution no microbe would dare to assault—but one night I found Philippe in the kitchen, brewing herbal tea. "Sore t'roat," he croaked.

You didn't need to have been trained at the Mayo Clinic to read this. Fall term had worn people out. During the Christmas break, they had traveled, skied, stayed up late with old friends, and celebrated their respite from this institution. All this was good for the soul but bad for the immune system. By the beginning of winter term my classmates and I amounted to walking virus museums, featuring strains from all the places we'd gone to over the break, including most of the continental United States and points in Europe, Latin America, and Asia.

Meanwhile, the only activity the California weather was encouraging was bed rest. The weather I'd come to think of as typical during the fall term—sunshine, low humidity, clement temperatures—had vanished. Rain fell steadily for the first ten days of the term, if "fell" is the correct word to use for water that the wind forces into a horizontal rather than vertical route. During fall term, the morning fog had lifted each day by 10:00, 11:00 at the latest. Now the dank morning fog stopped lifting altogether, turning instead into clammy afternoon fog, then wet evening fog, then drizzly, depressing night fog. No longer dressed in shorts and polo shirt, students took to going about with their necks scrunched down into their Patagonia, North Face, and L.L. Bean jackets and their hands jammed into their jeans pockets. For the first time, I understood a phrase from the Frank Sinatra song "The Lady Is a Tramp" that always used to puzzle me. "She hates California, where it's cold and it's damp." The thrill—the constant sense of danger—that business school posed during the first term had given way to a kind of dull, throbbing ache.

Not that the danger had in fact abated.

I'd received passing grades during the fall term, all but ending one aspect of the business school drama, Would I flunk? No, on the evidence of my fall term grades, a P plus in Organizational Behavior and Micro and a P in everything else, including Trees, I most probably would not. Yet during winter term I would face a more profound drama. Who, or what, would business school turn me into? "Careful, Peter," Steven had said with a wink over eggnog during the Christmas break. "If you go back, Stanford might actually make you into somebody who knows how to earn a living. I can see your caption in the yearbook now: 'A Poet No More.'"

Steven was joking, but he was right. My throat raw, my head throbbing, I was struggling with core courses that were continuing the work of replacing my old verbal and intuitive outlook with a set of rigorous, quantitative techniques, systematically building a new me. Later in the term, recruiters would arrive to interview our class for summer jobs in banking, management consulting, manufacturing, and marketing, giving students the opportunity to try on, so to speak, entirely new identities, as if we were trying on rubber chins and noses to find profiles that we liked.

By coming back for this term, I had committed myself to lying down on the table and letting professors stuff my insides with business school cases, mathematical formulas, and long, unreadable books while my classmates handed them scalpels and assisted with the sutures. I hoped that the surgery would transform me into a dynamic, businesslike new man, capable of earning big sums of money—a poet no more. But on all operating tables, mistakes do happen, even during minor procedures. A major procedure, a transformation of mind and soul like this one, was fraught with mortal peril.

Still, it is hard to feel mortal peril when your head feels hot and your feet feel cold. Mostly what I felt during the first couple of weeks was ague.

An incident at lunch one day illustrated the new winter term mood. Marty, a classmate who was fluent in Asian languages, took a seat at my table and started his usual routine of naming all the cities he'd visited in China, mentioning Beijing, Shanghai, and half a dozen others. It struck me as just that, his usual routine. "Marty," I found myself thinking, "give it up. You're not all that cool." A moment later I recognized that a specific dramatic event had taken place, like the first time a new husband comes to the breakfast table without shaving. The romance had gone out of business school.

There was a good side to the winter term mood, I admit. It permitted my classmates and me to become more human.

During fall term, people had put too much energy into trying to impress each other. Marty had talked about China. One of the doctors in our class had shown up several times wearing an orderly's green shirt with string ties, just making good and certain we all knew he had an MD. I myself had encouraged lunchtime questions about the White House. "What is the President like? How does a speech get staffed?" Talking about the White House had put me on my ground, making me feel comfortable and experienced, a man who had gone places and seen sights. All term I had strained not just to keep up with my work but to convince my classmates that I was somebody. By winter term, my classmates and I were seeing each other less as a collection of walking résumés, more as we were. I got fewer questions about the White House and didn't miss them.

In Portola Valley, our house shed the attributes of a bachelor dorm and took on those of a home of sorts. Joe, Philippe, and I put a chart on the refrigerator that showed when each of us was to take his turn putting out the trash or mixing chlorine powder into the hot tub. To buy the groceries all three of us used, we established a pool.

The weekend before the term began, Joe, ever frugal, announced that he intended to buy staples for the house at the Price Club, a huge warehouse operation that offered products ranging from groceries to computer printers at heavy discounts, and I went with him. When we got back, Philippe watched with a kind of horrified awe as Joe and I unloaded industrial-sized cardboard boxes of toilet paper, potato chips, and individually wrapped chicken breasts. Although Swiss, Philippe had enough French in his blood to value good food. He looked at the chicken breasts with particular distaste.

"We're all busy, right?" Joe explained. "So now you can come home, pull one of these breasts out of the freezer, throw it in the microwave, and zap it in just ninety seconds. Then you can give it a squirt of this." Joe produced a two-gallon bottle of hot dog mustard.

"May God forgive you," Philippe said.

It was the first really good laugh the three of us had shared.

TEN

Number Blind

But if winter term made my classmates and me more human to each other outside the classroom, inside the classroom it made us not more human but less so. As the professors lectured and drew their diagrams on the chalkboards, we sat at the horseshoe-shaped tiers of desks like anti-humans, glassy-eyed, slack-jawed, inert.

Our fatigue, our colds and flus, the unending drizzle outside—these certainly bore some responsibility for changing an intelligent, articulate body of students into specimens of the living dead. But so did the Stanford business school core curriculum. I do not mean to belabor the point, but anyone thinking aboout going to business school needs to know that a certain amount of the material is just incredibly dull. Of the five courses I took winter term, three proved completely colorless.

Data Analysis dealt with statistics, an elaborate, complicated set of mathematical techniques for using small samples (for example, the number of defective products that a machine manufactured in one minute) to decide big questions (the number of defective products that said machine would manufacture in one year). The instructor was Stan Slowacki, the associate dean who had taught Computer Camp and substituted for Professor Kemal in Trees. Dean Slowacki reminded me of gym teachers I'd had in junior high and high school.

They were strong men, natural athletes who had always loved sports, and even in their forties and fifties they could keep up with us teenagers on the basketball court or the football field. What they could not do was talk. Having to explain the rules to as simple a game as monkey-in-the-middle left my gym teachers tongue-tied and embarrassed. They would ramble on for five minutes. Then they would look at their feet and say, "Class, you'll understand all the rules once you start to play."

Likewise Dean Slowacki, a big, kind, well-meaning man. Somehow, when young, he had fallen in love with statistics. Now he took this difficult subject and made it impenetrable. He would stand in the teaching well at 8:00 on Tuesday and Thursday mornings looking both angry and sheepish as students strolled in ten or even twenty minutes late (there was no point in getting out of bed early to hurry to a class that was going to put you right back to sleep). When he decided he finally had a quorum, Slowacki would reach into the plastic pocket protector of his short-sleeved shirt, withdraw a telegraphing pointer, and begin to lecture.

One assignment during the first couple of weeks involved football. "When Tony Dorsett was playing for the University of Pittsburgh," the question read, "a sample study of actual games was made to evaluate his overall performance." The question listed the number of yards Dorsett had gained each of the thirty-two times he had carried the ball. "Calculate an appropriate measure of the central tendency of yards gained per carry in order to evaluate Dorsett's overall performance, and justify the measure you have chosen."

I realized later that the question was easy, just a matter of understanding a few basic definitions. But that's not the way Slowacki made it sound.

"We're interested in total or overall performance here," Slowacki said, "not the performance on any one carry. With me? Good. You'll notice that although twenty-nine of the carries fall in the range of three to fifteen yards, the three remaining carries are much bigger, ranging from twenty-five to forty yards. The statistical term for these unusual carries would be 'outliers.' Still with me? Good.

"Now we don't want to ignore these outliers, because it's precisely the outliers that are crucial to victory in a football game setting. But the 'median' and 'mode' do ignore the outliers. This means that the median and mode would be poor overall performance measures. The 'mean,' however, does take the outliers into account. Moreover, the mean serves as a surrogate for the total number of yards per carry. This means that the mean is the most meaningful overall performance measure to adopt. With me?"

All term, I kept waiting to glimpse the wonder and elegance of this material the way I'd seen the beauty of the material from time to time during Math Camp. But back in August, I'd been new at Stanford and the whole experience had been a kind of wild high. This was January.

Everyone was bored in Data Analysis—everyone. My own lassitude even afforded me a certain sense of comfort, making me feel like one of the guys, a genuine MBA rather than a poet imposter. If former investment bankers fought to stay awake in Slowacki's class, if students who used to be crack management consultants before coming to business school found that in Data Analysis their chins slumped onto their chests, well, I was right there, using my fingers to hold my eyelids open with the best of them. But my other two Tuesday-Thursday classes, Cost Accounting and Operations, were different. Although I still found most of the material so flat that during these classes my entire head felt dopey, my classmates evinced precisely the opposite response. They came alive. They really got rolling.

In Cost Accounting, the professor, a funny, likable Australian named Gary Symons, would enter the classroom looking as though he had just come from sleeping one off on his sofa. His hair was matted and his belly sagged over his belt. He always had a flag of shirttail exposed that he would tuck in as he opened the class, often with a comment about beer. "Wheen'll they eenvent a lager that'll take the weight off instead of puttin' it on?"

Symons devoted forty minutes during one of the first class periods to "Preston Machining," a case about a small business that cut and tested metal blocks it then sold to big companies that assembled jet engines. As so often in these strange fictions, there were two products, Series A and Series B, each of which required different amounts of labor, machining time, and raw materials. The case provided dollar amounts for each of these "inputs," then asked students to contrast the "actual *variable* manufacturing overhead cost rate per direct labor dollar" with the "actual *fixed* manufacturing overhead cost rate per direct labor dollar." Finally, the case instructed students to prepare "detailed income statements" using "variable costing," and then, for contrast, using "absorption costing."

As Symons led the discussion he filled the chalkboard with stacks of figures as intricate as a Rockerfeller's tax returns. As I said, many of my classmates really got rolling. Gunnar, the former financial analyst, developed a gleam in his eyes, while students who had been management consultants raised their hands again and again, competing for Symon's attention. Apparently if you had ever been in business, what an operation costs its owners—that was always the central question in cost accounting, *costs*—can prove a question of endless fascination. In government, of course, nobody had cared about costs.

Desperate to stay with the discussion, I kept flipping to the glossary at the back of the textbook. "Absorption costing," the text stated, was "a method of product costing where fixed manufacturing overhead is *included* in the inventoriable costs." Okay. Now, what were inventoriable costs? Under "inventoriable costs" the glossary said, "See product costs." Judging that the discussion was moving too fast for me to look up "product costs," I looked up "variable costing" instead. There I read, "Method of product costing where fixed manufacturing overhead is *excluded* from the inventoriable costs." Inventoriable costs? Again? "See product costs." Lost in the glossary, I struggled to keep from falling dead asleep and toppling over onto my notes.

Steven told me not to worry.

"In my first year," he said over the phone, "I just couldn't figure that course out, and I started skipping classes. Then about a week before the midterm, I said to myself, 'Steven, my boy, you have a problem.'" Steven and a couple of his classmates met at the pub on campus, bought a pitcher of beer, and opened their Cost Accounting texts.

To understand why cost accounting is important, Steven explained, you had to imagine yourself in charge of running a business. "So we pretended we were Lee Iacocca." Steven and his friends figured that Lee knew how much revenue came in every time Chrysler sold a car because the purchaser simply wrote Chrysler a check. That part was simple. But since profit equals revenues minus costs, Lee also needed to know how much every car cost him. That part, they realized, was harder.

"I mean, we just pictured it. Here's Lee Iacocca and he employs thousands upon thousands of workers. He operates umpteen factories at umpteen locations in the United States and Canada and he manufactures sub-assemblies at umpteen more locations in Mexico and Asia. And every year he buys billions of dollars' worth of sheet metal, windshields and windows, rubber bumpers, chrome hubcaps, and who knows what else. That's just a huge amount of *stuff* to keep track of."

Iacocca, Steven explained, could try to keep track of every penny as he actually spent it, but that level of monitoring and accounting would be very expensive in itself. So instead Lee would need to establish "standard costs," assuming that every "input"—every hour of labor, every shipment of sheet metal, every door handle—cost the same. Then Lee could just run a check every so often to make sure his "actual" costs were staying in line with what he had established as his "standard" or "normal" costs.

Lee would also need to monitor his "fixed" and "variable costs." Fixed costs were the outlays that Iacocca would be stuck with whether he manufactured one car or a million. At any of Iacocca's Chrysler plants, for instance, fixed costs might include property taxes, executive salaries, and insurance of, say, $100 million a year, no matter how many cars the plant turned out. Variable costs, by contrast, were the costs that would go up when Iacocca made more cars and down when he made fewer. If Lee paid a supplier $15 for every rear-view mirror that went in a Chrysler Le Baron, for example, then Lee's total outlay for the mirrors would be just that, $15, if Chrysler only made one Le Baron, but $150,000 if Chrysler made 10,000.

"For a guy like Iacocca, keeping your eye on the difference between variable and fixed costs was really important, because your fixed costs could wipe you out." Lee could cut his variable costs just by reducing the number of cars he manufactured. But the fixed costs would remain . . . fixed. Lee could stop manufacturing cars altogether, but he would still have to pay property taxes, upkeep on his factories, insurance, and interest on his debt. Meeting those fixed costs could force Lee to suffer huge losses.

"We realized, by the way, that that's just about what happened to Chrysler during the late 1970s." Back then Chryslers were big, ugly, gas-guzzling monsters, and when the Arab oil embargo raised the price of gas, the public basically stopped buying them. Chrysler scaled back production, but its fixed costs were so gigantic that it went into virtual bankruptcy.

"The whole Cost Accounting syllabus came down to just a couple of really key ideas—standard versus actual costs, and variable versus fixed costs—and about twenty or thirty different little elaborations." Steven explained that the terms in the Preston case, "absorption" and "variable costing," were just different ways of accounting for fixed costs, often called "manufacturing overhead." While variable costing assigned only actual manufacturing costs to items in inventory, absorption costing instead added a slice of overhead costs to each item, as if every car Chrysler produced "absorbed" a part of the company's insurance costs, property taxes, and so forth.

"When we realized that Cost Accounting was nothing more than a few basic ideas, we all looked at each other and said, 'Whoa. Sometimes these courses try to pretend that there's a lot more there than there really is.' So we ordered another pitcher, worked a few practice problems, and had a swell time. And we all got Ps in the course."

Steven could do that. He could look at the Cost Accounting text of almost a thousand pages and see just two or three basic ideas. But I could not. What I saw was one thousand pages, ten thousand diagrams, one hundred thousand formulas, and a million, billion, jillion numbers.

I expected Operations, the core course devoted to manufacturing, to reflect upon one of the chief characteristics that distinguished man from animal, the ability to use tools to create and to build. What I got was word problems.

Professor J. Henry Benchley wore a beard, stylish suits, and neckties with splashy patterns, and I was never able to figure out how such a colorful character had devoted his professional life to this material. Benchley established the pattern for the course during the first two weeks of the term, which he devoted to "process types," various methods of manufacturing. In the first class, for example, we covered "continuous flow," a process type exemplified by paper mills, then turned in the second class to "machine-paced line flows," which were exemplified by auto factories.

The reading for the second class described the General Motors assembly line in Tarrytown, New York. The GM plant, we learned, employed several different lines, one for assembling engines, another for chassis, a third for bodies and interiors. Each line flowed like a tributary into the great river of final assembly, where the engine was dropped into the chassis, then bolted and welded into place. A moment later the body would arrive, descending on huge hooks to be joined with the engine and chassis in a shower of sparks.

To keep the assembly lines moving, the tasks the workers had to perform needed to be divided so that each could be performed in roughly the same amount of time, between thirty and ninety seconds, This was called "balancing." Whenever a new car model was introduced, the lines had to be "rebalanced," that is, the tasks the workers needed to perform had to be redesigned.

"Rebalancing a plant is expensive," Benchley said, stepping from behind the podium. "Very expensive." The entire plant had to be shut down. Equipment had to be moved. The workers had to be retrained. "Then, when you finally restart the line, you discover that you're getting lots of defects, or that the whole flow is getting held up in one place—say where convertible roofs are being added instead of hardtops—and you have to shut the plant back down to fix the problem.

"So what happens? Plant managers start to hate new models. They lose interest in finding out what kinds of cars the customers

want. Instead, they try to hold down their costs by getting the marketing people to go right on selling the cars that the plant is already
set up to manufacture."

But it was different in Japan.

"Japanese car makers don't see manufacturing as a problem they
have to live with," Benchley said, "but as the chance to gain a competitive advantage over American car makers and over each other."
Japanese manufacturers required less time to rebalance plants for new
models, produced fewer defective cars, and operated at a consistently
lower cost per car. "And the Japanese end product is simply better.
The doors fit and the engines hum. Less servicing is required.
Customers tend to like that."

This was fascinating, important material, and I was eager to learn
more. How had the Japanese achieved their superiority in manufacturing? Why were they so much better at making cars than we were?
Were the reasons cultural? Technological? Financial? Yet instead of
elaborating, Benchley stepped back behind the podium. "Assume
that each Tarrytown worker puts in an eight-hour day with two fifteen-minute breaks," I heard Benchley say as he began yet another
word problem, and I thought, *Who cares?*

Yet in Operations, as in Cost Accounting, many of my classmates
really came alive. They were turned on. They achieved higher levels
of consciousness while I was struggling to maintain consciousness of
any kind. Consider, for instance, the Fabritek case.

This was the case that Benchley assigned to illustrate a third
process type, the "job shop," in which a batch of orders was completed in one shop, or at one station, before advancing to the next.
Fabritek, a small company in Indiana, produced machined parts for
more than 100 different manufacturers. Like many business school
cases, the Fabritek case opened with a brief, dramatic vignette:

> One afternoon in March 1969, Frank Deere, milling
> department foreman of the Fabritek Corporation, was ap-
> proached by Stuart Baker, Fabritek's automotive products
> manager.
>
> "Hi, Frank," Stuart said. "I hope you've got good news

for me about this week's order. I don't think my nerves can take a repeat of last week."

Stuart, a young MBA who was new to Fabritek, had landed a big new contract, with a firm in the automotive industry, that required Fabritek to mill and grind castings for use in engine sub-assemblies. The week before, the number of defective castings had suddenly risen, slowing the work of the entire grinding shop.

> "Stu," Deere said, "we've got a real problem. It looks as though I'll have to add more people, replace someone, work overtime, or put on another grinder."
>
> "Wait a minute," Stu replied. "We don't know what's causing those rejects yet. If we sweep this problem under the rug with something like overtime, we'll lose our shirts on this order."

What was going wrong?

I walked into class with the following analysis scratched in my notebook:

> As far as I can see, there are only three possible causes of the high reject rate.
> 1. Moreno, who "rough-mills" each casting before passing it on to Clark, is producing defective work.
> 2. Clark, who "finish-mills" the castings, is producing defective work, possibly because Moreno is working too fast for him.
> 3. Some combination of the two.

In performing such a sketchy, superficial analysis, I wasn't being lazy. I'd read all ten pages of the case twice, made notes, and thought about the problem as deeply as I could. I'll admit that nothing about the case fired my imagination, and while I worked on it, I two or three times found myself dozing off. But I had worked on it, and the answer I've reproduced was the thorough, level best I could do.

It wasn't even on the way to being good enough. When Benchley called on me and I read him my answer, he stroked his beard and eyed me for a moment as if trying to judge whether I was attempting a classroom joke. "That answer is all right as far as it goes," he said, recognizing that I was simply a lost poet. "But you're giving me description. I want analysis. I want numbers. Didn't anyone in this class run the *numbers?*

John Lyons, Mr. Perfect, raised his hand.

"I figure Moreno has 8 hours times 60 minutes, or 480 minutes, available for work every day," John said. "That's assuming the extreme case, in which he takes no breaks."

Benchley wrote these numbers on the board, suddenly smiling. "And?" Benchley prompted.

"The case states that Moreno is earning 167 percent of the standard pay rate," John continued. "That means he's rough-milling 167 castings a day. When you divide 480 minutes by 167, what you get is that Moreno has to rough-mill a casting every 2.87 minutes."

Benchley wrote this on the board, too. "I like this," Benchley said. "Keep going."

John said that according to Exhibit One, a chart of numbers that had been printed as an appendix at the end of the case, the rough-milling "machine time," the amount of time each casting spent on Moreno's machine actually being milled, came to 2.6 minutes. By subtracting 2.6 minutes from 2.87 minutes, John had found that Moreno had only .27 minutes to perform "external tasks," chiefly loading and unloading, on each casting. Yet according to Exhibit Two, the standard time for "external tasks" was .994 minutes. In order to earn his 167 percent of standard pay, Moreno therefore had to be performing his "external tasks" in less than a third of the standard time.

"Moreno's speeding," John said. "He's whipping the castings on and off the machine way too fast to do a decent job of milling them. Maybe he's even reset the machine to go faster than it's supposed to. No wonder they're getting so many defectives."

"Excellent," Benchley said, beaming. He walked to the podium, where he kept a seating chart with our names on it. "John Lyons," he said, pulling a pen from his pocket and making a note on the chart.

"Very good. Very, very good." Then Benchley looked up. "What Mr. Lyons just engaged in is *analysis*. I hope you all get the idea."

The idea I got was that if some people are color-blind, others, like me, must be number-blind. I'd even concluded in all earnestness that Exhibits One and Two—the keys, as John demonstrated, to the solution—had been included only to throw students off.

"Moreno is speeding," Benchley said, continuing, "but what else is wrong at Fabritek?"

Now Gunnar Haakonsen, Mr. Cool, raised his hand. Gunnar reveled in Operations, just as he did in Cost Accounting. "Fabritek's compensation scheme is a problem," he said intently. Fabritek used the piece rate system, rewarding each employee according to the number of castings on which he managed to finish working. Yet this created incentives for each employee to work as fast as he could, producing, in turn, big individual variations, from Moreno, working at 167 percent of the standard rate, to those who were working at the standard rate or just slightly above it. "In a group production process," Gunnar said, "you want the pay structure to provide incentives for working together, not as individuals. So I'd argue that Fabritek should base at least part of its compensation on the output of the entire shop."

"Good," said Benchley, returning to the podium to make another note on the seating chart. Before the class ended, Benchley had made another half dozen marks on his seating chart for especially good work. I suppose a poet like me should have been listening hard. But I felt unable to penetrate the material, as I've said, and it was as difficult for me to follow the discussion as for a blind person to keep up in an art appreciation class.

February 7

Today, halfway through the term, Conor finally did it, managing to doze off in Data Analysis, fall fast asleep in Cost Accounting, and slumber five or ten minutes during Operations. I was proud of him. A hat trick.

ELEVEN

Thermoclines

October 15

> *Fish all look alike and swim with the same desperate energy when they first hatch. But I do not doubt that over time I will grow into a bottom-dweller, a big, ponderous fish, like a grouper, catching only glimpses of my darting, silvery roommates, swimming in a totally different thermocline above me.*

I wrote that journal entry during fall term, when Philippe and Joe were still working nearly as hard as I was. By winter term they no longer were. They had learned how to discriminate among the material, studying essentials but skimming the rest, and now they could start to divert their considerable intelligence and energies to having fun. In a word, they had migrated upward.

A week into the term, Philippe disrupted the schedule of household chores we had posted on the refrigerator by moving out. He loaded his sweaters, socks, underwear, and shaving gear into his gigantic Buick, then drove off to a ski house near Lake Tahoe that he and a group of other non-poets had rented. Philippe and his buddies skied every weekend, drove back to Stanford in time for classes on Monday and Tuesday, returned to the mountains to ski on Wednesday, attended classes again on Thursday and Friday, then headed back off for yet another skiing weekend.

During his brief appearances to do laundry back at our house in

Portola Valley, Philippe would tell us about his ski bunnies. "She is full of life! She is full of laughter! She is seventeen!" Or, "She is mature! She is poised! She is eighteen!"

Joe remained in Portola Valley. His sport was not skiing. It was networking.

"Peter, you've gotta remember that a big part of the value of this place is the people we'll meet here," he said. "Just think of the deal flow I can get from our classmates over the next five, ten, twenty years. They'll be at banks and corporations all over the world. I'm tellin' ya!"

Joe resolved to get to know every member of our class. "I don't mean just know who they are. I mean really *know* them." He went to dinner with study group partners or new acquaintances virtually every evening. He became active in the SBSSA, the Stanford Business School Students' Association, our version of student government. He joined two clubs, the Finance Club and the Entrepreneurship Club. (The school was rich in clubs, including the Finance, Entrepreneurship, Venture Capital, Media, and Health Services clubs.)

Much as Joe enjoyed networking, he soon learned that it had its hazards. One afternoon I ambled out to the hot tub to find Joe already there, soaking intently. As I lowered myself into the tub, he eyed me.

"Met Kevin Sumner last night," Joe said, naming a classmate. "Did you know his father is president of a movie studio?" Earlier that day, Joe said, he had gone to the library and done a computer search for newspaper stories about Mr. Sumner senior. "Last year he sold a bunch of stock options. He made $60 million."

Joe fell into a troubled silence, gazing at the water steaming around his knees.

"Did you know Tim Sterling's grandfather founded a big retail chain?" Joe suddenly asked. Sterling was another classmate he'd met. "I looked the family up in *Forbes*. The Sterlings are worth almost $3 billion."

Another troubled silence. Then:

"I made it to Stanford because all my life I worked hard, stayed off drugs, never stole anything—well, never stole anything really valuable. I figured I'd come to Stanford and do the same thing—work hard, achieve, all that—and then when I left here I'd be able to go out and make a lot of money. But Kevin and Tim, those guys *start* with more money than I even *want*."

At dinner the night before, Joe said, Kevin Sumner was comparing beaches. "But he wasn't talking about beaches in northern California. He was talking about beaches all over Thailand and Indonesia. So I asked him, 'How the hell do you know about all those beaches?' Turns out his father flew the family all around Southeast Asia for three weeks last summer on his own Learjet. And Kevin wasn't boasting or being snotty or anything. For him, living like that is just, like, normal, you know?"

Up until then, I'd envied Joe. He'd been able to master course material that I'd had to struggle to understand in even an elementary way. He'd been out meeting people while I'd still been stuck in my pantry office, studying. But now I saw that Joe had been doing more than shaking hands and noting addresses. He had been measuring what he encountered in our classmates against the possibilities he foresaw for himself. And he was as dazed by business school as I was.

"Those guys," he repeated. Then he just shook his head.

While the non-poets were on the slopes or out networking, the poets stayed behind grappling, often with themselves. The poets, after all, had arrived at the business school as just that, poets. They were dreamers. They loved ideas. They had degrees in English or history instead of engineering or economics. Many came, as I did, specifically to become less dreamy and more practical. But by winter term lots of poets had become uneasy about what business school was doing to them.

One night Susan, the southerner who had been in my Micro study group, Louisa, Sam Barrett's house mate, and I drove into San Francisco for dinner. We sat talking over coffee until late (my one reprieve from study for the entire first half of winter term).

"I came here intending to go back to Alabama and use my architecture background to get involved in designing low-income projects," Susan said. "But with all the student loans I'm taking, by the time I get out I'll be $20,000 in debt. How will I be able to work for the poor?"

"My sister won't even speak to me," Louisa said. "She claims by going to business school, I've sold out. I had plans like Susan's. When I came here I wanted to go back to Boston to work with the underprivileged. But I'll be way too deep in debt.

"But there's something besides the debt," Louisa continued. "I mean, I've seen it now, the way some of our classmates live. I've seen what money can do for you. John Lyons drives a BMW. He doesn't have to worry about what it costs to go to really nice restaurants.

"I don't think John has sold out. I think he's a great guy. He even volunteers his time to coach intramural sports once a week at the junior high in East Palo Alto. [East Palo Alto was a poor township, largely black and Hispanic, just a few minutes from campus.]

"It just sort of makes me wonder. Maybe you don't need to be poor yourself to do good. Maybe you can make money and enjoy yourself and do good all at the same time. What a thought."

I present this conversation as evidence that for some, especially for artistic, intellectual, or left-wing students, business school could represent a spiritual and emotional crisis. Susan, Louisa, and others in our class saw business school as both a seduction and a threat. They struggled in its embrace.

Nowhere was the divide between the poets and non-poets sharper than in my two Monday-Friday classes, Finance and Public Sector Economics.

Finance was *serious*. While in Data Analysis students drifted in late and dozed through the lectures, in Finance they got to the classroom early, ahead of the professor, then arranged their notes on their desktops and assumed an air of sober alertness. It took me a while to figure out why Finance was so different. Then I realized. Finance was about money.

Our professor was Ruth Charen, a tall, dark-haired woman. Charen used an overhead projector, and as she jotted down formulas her hand, magnified many times on the big screen at the front of the room, looked like the hand of God. Poets and non-poets responded to her in opposite ways beginning with the very first class.

"This is my first day back in the classroom in quite some time," Charen began. The year before, she said, a grant had "very nicely relieved me of the burdens of teaching to pursue my research."

The burdens of teaching? Wasn't that an insult? Poets like Conor and me exchanged glances. Here was another instance, our looks said, of the lack of regard for teaching at this school. The non-poets exchanged different kinds of glances. Their eyes sparkled. This is going to be really good, their faces said. Since Charen just came off a year of research she'll be giving us the latest, hottest material in the field.

Charen went on to state that although some students in the class had financial backgrounds many others did not, so for the first three or four lectures she would keep the pace slow. "I can only ask those of you who are bored to bear with me," she said. "As the term progresses we'll begin to move much more quickly."

Now the non-poets looked offended. Gunnar rolled his eyes. Four lectures was a lot of time to lose for a man positioning himself for a quantum leap. But Conor and I leaned back in our chairs and broke into grins. Four whole classes in which we would be able to understand what the professor was talking about. It was enough to make us all but delirious.

Then Charen began her introductory lecture on modern portfolio theory, writing on the overhead projector the formula for compounding interest rates. Conor and I stopped grinning.

$$V_T = V_0(1 + r)^T$$

V, Charen explained, equaled the dollar value of the principal, r the interest rate, t the time during which the instrument would be held, and V_0 the dollar amount at time zero. I glanced at my classmates. The non-poets actually seemed to be following her.

Next Charen moved on to the relationship between zero coupon bonds and interest rates, scrawling on the projector as she derived a formula.

If $d_{12} = .25$, *then* $1 = .25(1 + r_{12})^{12}$

$$or \ \tfrac{1}{25} = (1 + r_{12})^{12}$$

And more generally, $\tfrac{1}{d_T} = (1 + r_T)^T$

$$or \ d_T = \frac{1}{(1 + r_T)^T}$$

$$or \ r_T = (\tfrac{1}{d_T})^{1/T} - 1$$

"The mathematics are so elementary that we won't spend any time on them," Charen said, "but I want to stress that nothing in this course is more important than this formula. Here, in a concise statement, we have the set of interest rates that constitute the discount function, and it is the discount function in turn which gives us the price we must pay today in order to receive one dollar at various dates in the future. . . ."

I place ellipses here because at this point, ten minutes or so into the first of the slow, utterly elementary lectures, I had become irretrievably lost. A look confirmed that Conor had, too. While the eyes of a non-poet like Gunnar shone with interest and comprehension, Conor's eyes had acquired the glassy, unseeing quality that psychologists refer to as flat affect.

Already, it was clear. Finance would belong to the non-poets. As for the poets, we would sink into the frigid, lightless depths.

But there was, as I say, a contrast.

Public Sector Economics was not a core course but an elective, my first. When Conor and I learned that anyone who chose to take Public Sector Economics would not have to take Marketing, a core course, until spring, we signed up. "If Public Sector Economics gives me one more hour of sleep a week," Conor said, "it'll be worth it." We soon learned that Public Sector Economics gave us much more than extra time to sleep. It gave us self-esteem. I note two examples.

The professor, Rajiv Gupta, a slight man with dark glasses who had been raised and educated in Bombay, devoted the first several lectures of the course to the concept of market failure. "Market failure," as he put it, was "the most powerful argument against the unregulated functioning of the free market." (In his musical accent this came out as "dee unregulated vunctioning of dee vree market.")

One form of market failure occurred when an entity conferred benefits on others without getting paid, in effect providing goods and services for free. Since an entity that gave goods and services away would quickly go broke, however, those goods and services would cease to be supplied, and the market for them would have "failed."

"Think of parks," Gupta said. Since the real estate market was more likely to turn unspoiled wilderness into shopping malls than nature preserves, there was a failure in the market for parkland, and the government had to step in. "We enjoy stands of redwood trees within a few miles of this campus only because the government has protected them from commercial development."

Market failure also arose in the reverse case, not when an entity conferred benefits upon others without getting paid, but when it imposed costs upon others without paying them. The obvious example: pollution. "When I drive a car that burns fuel inefficiently," Gupta said, "I pollute the air and impose a cost on all those who breathe. But do I compensate my fellow human beings, in however small a way, for making it harder for them to breathe, in however small a way? I do not." Government had to intervene by enacting automobile emission control standards.

Gupta elaborated upon the notion of market failure at considerable length, but the gravamen of his argument was quite simple. Free markets had intrinsic shortcomings or limitations, and it was up to government to correct them.

At the end of one lecture, I raised my hand.

"Has anybody ever thought about *government* failure?"

My classmates chuckled, but Gupta encouraged me to continue.

The argument for government intervention, I said, presupposed that government was disinterested and omniscient, a body capable of discerning and correcting market failures efficiently and altruistically. In practice, this was hardly the case.

While I was in Washington, for example, acid rain had become an issue. Environmental groups agitated against acid rain, of course, but so did the Canadian government, which intended to pressure our government into imposing costly new regulations on American coal-burning plants. The Canadians knew this would raise the price of the electricity that the American plants produced, in turn forcing American industry, particularly in the Northeast, to buy more of its electricity from the much cleaner Canadian hydroelectric plants.

Both Congress and the executive branch spent millions studying the issue. No direct link between acid rain and specific environmental harm was ever established. Some forests were shown to be unhealthy, but it was also established that the larger trend in the United States was toward more, not less, forested land, as the small farms established in the last century were given up and cultivated tracts reverted to the wild. Certain lakes and streams were dying, but others, notably Lake Erie, were healthier than they had been in decades.

The Environmental Protection Agency proposed a set of regulations to impose on coal-burning plants, just as the Canadians had hoped it would. Then David Stockman, Director of the Office of Management and Budget, had his economists estimate the costs of the regulations to the economy. The figure ran into the billions.

That stopped the regulations. But only for a time. The agitation against acid rain mounted as the interest groups gained advocates in Congress. Eventually, costly acid rain regulations were indeed imposed—on the basis of no clearly established scientific rationale whatsoever.

"The point," I said, "is that when the government took action, it wasn't responding to the facts. It was responding to political pressures." All my experience in Washington had led me to believe that most government intervention was at least as likely to worsen problems as to solve them. "After all, these are the people who brought us the U.S. Postal Service."

There were cheers. "Right on!" one student shouted. "Damn straight!" said another.

Looking around the room I noticed that something more than half the students were sitting in silent disapproval of my anti-government remarks. Those applauding me tended to be big, beefy, robust, and male—the jocks. But that I had only won the support of part of the classroom did not diminish my pleasure. I had spoken up. In a business school classroom, I had at last engaged in an extended act of coherence.

A week later, Conor sallied forth.

Using England as an example, Gupta was discussing the obligation of government to redistribute income and wealth. In the England of 1911, he noted, a tiny number of aristocrats owned pretty much everything. Sixty years later, after socialist Labour governments and paternalistic Conservative governments had enacted death duties, land taxes, and steeply graduated income taxes, the distribution of wealth and income had become far more even.

"This was achieved," Professor Gupta said, "in the interest of greater social justice."

Conor raised his hand.

"With all respect," Conor said, "I don't follow the logic." Surely, Conor argued, the mere pattern of wealth and income was in and of itself morally empty or vacant, neither good nor bad. What mattered instead was the way in which the pattern arose. Did some get rich by robbing others? Or did the pattern emerge as a result of the free and uncoerced actions of all those involved?

"Think about the distribution of income at a professional soccer match," Conor said. One or two star players might make millions of dollars a year while the other players earned far less and most of the spectators less still—a lopsided pattern. "But is that distribution of income wrong? Should it be redistributed? Of course not. The players all play because they want to. The spectators all pay the price of admission of their own free will."

Extending this argument, Conor suggested that the proper role of government was to establish the rules by which the economic game, so to speak, would be played, seeking only to ensure that these rules are observed.

"Take Hewlett-Packard, just down the road here," Conor said. "William Hewlett and David Packard are two of the richest men in the world, worth hundreds of millions each."

"More than a billion each," a jock corrected.

"Right, then," Conor said, "more than a billion each. But they virtually invented the entire electronic measurement devices industry. Today the company they built employs thousands."

"Tens of thousands," the jock corrected.

"Tens of thousands, then," Conor said. "And although their wealth sounds staggering in a world where so many live in poverty, Hewlett and Packard did nothing wrong. On the contrary, they engaged in legal, creative—and, I'd argue, moral—economic activity.

"As an Irishman I believe in the responsibility of the state to secure jobs and a basic level of welfare for all its citizens. But the idea that whenever we see an uneven distribution of wealth and income we should just automatically assume that government has to do something to correct it—well, I'm sorry, but it's ridiculous."

Once again the jocks went wild. "Damn right!" "Way to go!"

Later that day I ran into Conor in the courtyard. "People have been coming up and complimenting me all day," he said, taking a long drag on a cigarette.

"It shows the narrowness of the education at this place," Conor said. "No philosophy. No politics. This institution assumes the world has had free markets since God said, 'Let there be light,' then takes it as its solemn duty to teach us how to outcompete our fellow man."

Conor took another drag on his cigarette. He was working himself into a fine declaiming mode.

"But even the most obtuse engineer or investment banker," Conor went on, "senses that free markets rest on a certain philosophical and political conception of the good. They also sense that this conception of the good comes under attack every day from Marxists and socialists and even liberal Democrats. Knowing this, our classmates grow edgy. They decide they ought to learn some of the arguments for themselves.

"So what do they do? They flock to Public Sector Economics, where half the class rolls over for a naive theory of social justice and the redistribution of wealth. And the half that *doesn't* roll over listens to you and me pipe up with a few obvious remarks and hails us as the class intellectuals."

There was some truth in what Conor said. But there was also a great deal of glee. He and I were the obtuse ones at this business school, not the engineers and investment bankers, and we knew it. If twice a week Public Sector Economics gave us the chance to feel otherwise—to feel as though Conor and I were Mr. Cool and Mr. Perfect—we can perhaps be forgiven for reveling in the sensation.

TWELVE

This Institution Is in Deep Frijoles

It was an established rite at the business school for students to have lunch with members of the faculty. The student government would even reimburse a student up to $10 for the cost of a professor's lunch. Non-poets lost no time in getting to know the faculty, and by the middle of winter term Joe had taken out half the Finance Department. "I want as many friends on the faculty as I can get," he said. "When I start looking for a job, recommendations from Stanford profs can't hurt."

Since I figured there was nothing I could say to a business school professor, even over Cobb salad, that wouldn't sound stupid, I never asked any of them to lunch. Then a couple of them asked me. They told me a great deal, but not about business. About the business school.

Professor Harriman van Cleef was a short man with big, round eyes that looked even bigger behind the lenses of his glasses. A legendary figure at the school for the brilliance of his teaching in a second-year elective on capital markets, he turned out to be a history buff, and he asked me over lunch in a French restaurant what it had been like to work in the Reagan administration. Over coffee, it was my turn to ask the questions. When I inquired how Stanford had turned itself into one of the country's leading business schools, van Cleef, a precise, meticulous man, insisted upon beginning his answer with the historical background behind all business schools.

Until the Civil War, van Cleef explained, the American economy had been agrarian. Businesses tended to be small, local, and run by the families that owned them. Bureaucracies barely existed. "You mentioned that there were over 800 people on the White House staff when you were there," he said. "In Lincoln's time, there were three, Lincoln and two young men who served as his secretaries. That's how little bureaucracy there was."

After the Civil War, truly national enterprises began to take shape: the huge Frick and Carnegie steel combinations; the Rockefeller oil trusts; the railroad lines, built by men such as Leland Stanford, whose fortune founded Stanford University. By the last decades of the nineteenth century, the need for a meritocratic class of trained managers presented itself. Wharton was founded in 1881, followed by Harvard Business School in 1908.

"It was not until 1925," van Cleef said, finally turning to Stanford, "that Herbert Hoover established a business school here at his alma mater."

The Stanford University Graduate School of Business was a direct answer by Hoover and other Western businessmen to the business schools back east. "There was plenty to do in the West that required young talent," van Cleef said. "Mining in the Rocky Mountain states, logging in the Pacific Northwest, agriculture in California, and trade with all of Asia through the port of San Francisco. Western businessmen had gotten tired of seeing young men go to Wharton or Harvard for their training, then stay in the East." (Half a century later, the temptation was reversed; within weeks of arriving at Stanford many of my Eastern classmates were declaring their intention to spend the rest of their lives in California.)

Van Cleef picked up his wine glass, took a sip, then set the glass down, looked at me, and blinked. It was a moment before I realized he had forgotten my question. "Of course," he said when I prompted him. "Stanford's rise to national stature." He cleared his throat.

"For the first thirty or so years of the business school's existence, it remained an institution of only regional importance. Then in 1958 Ernest Arbuckle became dean. He was an impressive man. And he had skills as a fund-raiser that were really quite phenomenal." Under Arbuckle, Stanford began to offer salaries competitive with those at Harvard or Wharton, and the faculty began to improve. Van Cleef joined the faculty himself in 1968.

"Arbuckle also understood that Stanford had to begin supporting research. That was important." When an academic was a good teacher, van Cleef explained, he only succeeded in building a reputation among his students, who then graduated and left. By doing important research, an academic established a reputation among a much more permanent audience, his peers. "To be quite blunt, research is the way an academic advances his career."

Arbuckle gave his faculty the time and money for research. So did his successors. Within a decade and a half, Stanford went from perhaps thirtieth place in business school rankings to first or second.

"But in recent years," van Cleef said, "I'm afraid we've hit something of a plateau." I encouraged him to elaborate, eager to learn more about the business school's inner workings. But van Cleef was reticent to disclose the institution's problems to a student. He glanced at his watch, and when the waitress brought the check he paid at once. "Sorry," he said, "but I must hurry back."

"Plateau, hell," Professor Jack Healey said. "It's a lot worse than that."

This was two weeks later, and Healey had invited me to lunch in the big dining room of the University Faculty Club. "Figured I owed you after taking you to that cheap restaurant during Thanksgiving break," he had said. The room had a high redwood ceiling, and it looked out through tall windows onto azaleas and bougainvillea. As we made our way to our table, Healey said, "Not bad, huh?"

"Not bad," I agreed.

"Not the *place*," Healey said. "The people. *There.*" He jerked his head toward a table where three pleasant-looking older men were drinking coffee and picking at their desserts.

"Ken Arrow, Paul Berg, and Burton Richter. Get it?"

"Get what?"

"Three Nobel Prize winners at one table. This campus may be liberal as hell, but the brains here are world class."

We took our seats. Healey flagged a waitress and ordered two Mexican plates.

"Okay," he said, "the problems with the business school." In contrast to van Cleef, Healey spoke as openly as if he were talking about a football team he followed.

"Start by taking a look at what's happening in this country from about the middle of 1982 onward," he said.

During the 1980s, practically every component of the American economy was being bought, sold, or reorganized, largely by MBAs under the age of thirty. New businesses were being formed at a historic rate. Employment by the huge corporations of the *Fortune* 500 may have been shrinking somewhat, but small businesses, often started and run by young MBAs, were creating hundreds of thousands of new jobs every month. In Silicon Valley alone, dozens of new high-tech firms sprang up, including the giant Sun Microsystems, founded by a Stanford business school grad. Business acquired a kind of glamour, and business schools, in turn, were hot, their enrollments rising.

"Under JFK and LBJ," Healey said, "the best and brightest went into government. Under your man Reagan, the best and brightest started hauling themselves to B school."

Yet had this been good for Stanford? Not exactly. "Two problems with the eighties as far as the business school is concerned," Healey said. "Problem one: They happened. Problem two: They're ending."

Problem one had made it hard to keep the faculty at Stanford first-rate. There was too much money around, and the best members of each department were constantly being tempted to leave Stanford for higher pay.

The money the Stanford business school faculty were making to begin with sounded pretty good to me. Even assistant professors, the most junior members of the faculty, earned $70,000 to $80,000, and in certain fields, such as Finance and Accounting, that figure was as high as $90,000. Then there were add-ons. Much of the faculty got subsidized housing. Many moonlighted, giving paid lectures and seminars and teaching at summer programs for corporate executives. Virtually every member of the faculty could earn an extra $20,000 a year by moonlighting, while the stars on the faculty were able to double their salaries.

"Trouble is," Healey said, "a lot of the faculty here could do even better at Wharton or Harvard."

High as Stanford business school salaries seemed to me, they were low by the standards of other major business schools, in part because Stanford authorities had imposed an informal but well-understood ceiling on business school pay. "The thinking is that you'd have a hard time holding the university together if a full professor of history, with a Ph.D. and ten books to his credit, got paid less than a twenty-nine-year-old assistant professor of accounting."

Wharton and Harvard also presented richer opportunities for moonlighting. Here in northern California there was only so much industry, L.A. was a long way away, and in between there was nothing but farm and ranch land. On the East Coast, however, an aggressive young business school professor found himself at the seat of corporate America, only a half-day's plane ride from New York, Boston, or Chicago to either of the other two.

"So far none of our really big names has defected," Healey said. "But it's getting a lot harder to recruit junior faculty.

"What happens is, you find yourself bidding on incredibly young guys who have good research records but no teaching experience at all—if they had research records *and* teaching experience, no way you could afford them. So you buy these young guys off the market. Then you hope like hell you can train them."

I allowed that this must explain Kemal and Walt, the child professors in Trees and Accounting.

"For frig sake," Healey said, "don't get me naming names."

Since the business school was unable to pay its faculty top dollar, it had to grant them other concessions. Just the year before, for example, the deans and senior faculty had simply surrendered when the younger members of the Finance Department staged a revolt.

Healey explained that in the original core Finance course, students had learned the basics: the differences between stocks and bonds, the way corporations calculated their cost of capital, and the factors companies took into account in deciding whether to raise money by issuing bonds, selling stock, or borrowing from commercial banks.

"Then the young guys in the Finance Department said, 'This bores us.'" Since they were the ones who had to teach the introductory, core course, they argued, they should be permitted to drop the old curriculum and instead teach material that interested them. This new material, as I had already learned in Charen's Finance class, was technical and theoretical. Now the only place a poet like me could learn the basics was in a second-year elective.

"With any luck, Peter," Healey laughed, "the finance elective next year will explain some of the stuff they're teaching you now."

Problem two, the end of the eighties boom, was even more serious. The job market for MBAs was starting to tighten. Already, the companies that recruited at Stanford were beginning to press for more practical, applied material in the curriculum, and this was creating divisions among the faculty.

On one side were the professional academics. They wanted to go right on teaching abstruse material based on their research. "We've got guys in the Finance Department," Healey said, "who want to devote their entire working lives to garbage like game theory, which hasn't got a rat's ass of relevance to anything."

On the other side were the lecturers, a dozen or more businessmen, mostly retired, who held untenured positions teaching second-year electives in such subjects as real estate and venture capital. The lecturers were all in favor of adding more practical material. They were practical men. They had gotten rich by being practical men. There was not a Ph.D. among them.

Like the lecturers, the students themselves wanted more practical material. "MBAs are after jobs," Healey said. "So as far as they're concerned the academics might as well just get out of the way and let Procter & Gamble and Morgan Stanley come in here and write the curriculum for us.

"Compare business students with law students," Healey continued. Law students esteemed their professors. They yearned to be like them. They saw teaching the law as perhaps the highest calling in the entire legal profession, and they dreamed of reaching that summit themselves. "Being looked up to day-in and day-out is real easy to take," Healey said. "Hell, for a law professor it's half the reason for teaching."

But MBAs?

"You think you guys look up to us? No *way*." MBAs did not want to wear tweed jackets and drive Fords; they wanted to wear Italian-made suits and drive Porsches. They wanted big, glamorous jobs that paid huge amounts of money, and they felt absolutely certain that they deserved them. So when business school students looked upon their professors, they looked down upon them. No one, Healey contended, believed more fervently than MBAs that those who can, do, while those who cannot, teach.

"Instructing a classroom of loud, aggressive MBAs is like feeding sharks in a tank. Only instead of tossing in fish from a bucket, you climb right in and let the sharks gnaw your limbs. As the job market gets worse, the sharks'll be biting deeper and deeper." Healey shook his head. "Then somebody like you comes along and asks why the faculty would rather do research."

The lecturers versus the tenured faculty versus the students. The teaching of applied, practical material versus the conducting of pure research. In Healey's view there was no solution here, only a point of equilibrium for the school to reach, a balance to strike among the competing interests. And right now the balance was off.

"It's a great school," Healey said. "But there's too much theoretical garbage and not enough decent teaching." Nor was the balance about to be improved. The Dean, although a capable man, had been at his post almost a decade. Neither he nor his associate deans appeared to be responding to the changes that were already taking place in the market for MBAs.

"Ask me," Healey said, taking a bite of chicken fajita and refried beans, "this institution is in deep frijoles."

Part of this analysis bothered me. Healey was talking about the school as if it were in business to manufacture and market a product. But was that the way to think about an academic institution?

Both Healey and van Cleef had as much as stated, for instance, that in their own way the business school faculty were as concerned about building their careers and making money as the business school students themselves. But academics were *supposed* to earn low salaries. In return, they gained a remove from the world of getting and making, permitting them to dedicate themselves wholly to the life of the mind. That was the deal. At least that was the deal that the best of my professors at Dartmouth and Oxford understood themselves to have accepted.

At the business school, the faculty seemed to want it both ways. They were eager to engage in commerce, but only as lecturers and consultants—on terms, in other words, that permitted them to keep their minds impeccable and their fingernails clean.

"So what *is* business school," I asked Healey, "business, or school?"

"That's the problem," Healey said. "It's both."

Any business school, Healey argued, was always trying to combine two highly reactive chemicals, business and academia. "Think of it as an inherently unstable compound like—oh, what the hell, I don't know a damn thing about chemistry." Healey glanced at the guacamole dip in the center of the table. "Let's call it Guacamolium," he said. "One part avocado and one part salsa."

Get the proportions exactly right and you'd have a miracle compound. People would love it. It would make them better equipped to live in the modern world. But get the mixture even a little bit wrong, and one of two things would happen. "Either it'll be insipid, like plain avocado—that would be nothing but applied stuff, lecturers coming in and telling stories about how they built their companies, without any theoretical basis at all. Or it'll be too sharp, like really strong salsa—and that would be nothing but the theoretical stuff that makes the kids' heads spin, stuff like game theory."

Healey stuck a tostada chip into the dip, then popped it into his mouth. "That's a hell of a metaphor," he said. "But that's what a business school is. A big, unstable vat of Guacamolium."

I would like to be able to say that after my lunches with Healey and van Cleef I pondered what they said, but all that really made an impression on me was Healey's remark that the eighties boom was about to end. That mattered, big time. A shrinking job market for MBAs would have no effect on truly talented students like Mr. Perfect and Mr. Cool. But in the job interviews that were now just a week off, somebody like me could discover that he was unemployable.

THIRTEEN

Summer Job Interviews: Buddy, Can You Spare Ten Grand?

February 13

In Finance class today, I was surprised to see Philippe show up dressed not in the usual sweater and corduroys but in a beautifully tailored, dove-gray suit and a red Hermès tie. Interview season has begun.

Perhaps I should state, for the record as it were, that winter term midterms proved the same grim affair as midterms during fall term. In Data Analysis, Finance, Operations, and Cost Accounting (there was no midterm in Public Sector Economics), I crammed into the small hours of the morning all over again. Then during the exams themselves I shuffled through my notes, clicked away on my calculator, scribbled answers, erased them, scribbled new answers, and then erased *them*. Yet the truth is that winter term midterms just didn't matter very much. What mattered was getting a summer job.

A few words of background.

The job search drama opened during fall term with BBLs ("BBL" stands for "brown bag lunch"). These were noontime presentations conducted in the big classrooms just off the courtyard by firms that intended to interview at Stanford. By the middle of winter term I'd attended half a dozen BBLs. They were all remarkably alike.

"Thank you for joining me this afternoon," a good-looking, expensively dressed young man or woman would say. "I'm John [or

JoAnne] Smith, Stanford Graduate School of Business, Class of [insert a year within the last five]." Then the presenter would hand out booklets about his company. Printed on heavy, glossy paper, these booklets would be filled with photos of young employees, men and women who looked just like the presenter himself, shown engaging in earnest conversations at conference tables, barking buy and sell orders into phones on trading floors, or striding through airports on their way to world capitals. Each photo would carry a caption along these lines:

> Jane Jones, Wharton grad. "I find working here at [insert company name] endlessly stimulating. It gives me an outlet for my desire to operate at high levels, to make a real difference, and to deal with bright, determined people. And by the way, it's also fun."

Next the presenter would deliver a carefully rehearsed presentation accompanied by slides or charts. He would describe the history of the company, indicate how privileged he felt to be working there, and state that it would be a fine place for members of our class to work, too. He would sternly add, however, that no individual should set his hopes too high. His company, after all, would hire only the select few.

None of us paid much attention to the part about not getting our hopes up. If anybody shouldn't be getting his hopes up, these BBLs seemed to suggest, it was the companies themselves. They were the supplicants. They were the ones who were so eager to hire MBAs that they submitted their representatives to the indignity of listening to potato chips being munched and soda cans being popped open while they talked. Some of the most important enterprises in the world put on BBLs for us. IBM and Apple. Bain and McKinsey and the Boston Consulting Group. General Foods and Procter & Gamble. They wanted us. They *needed* us. Or so the BBLs made it appear.

The second act of the job drama was the winter term résumé crunch. By the third week of the term, each of us was required to submit a copy of his résumé to the business school's Career Management Center.

Ten days before the résumés were due, the Career Management Center began running lunchtime seminars on résumé writing. I refused to attend, scoffing at the notion. "How complicated can writing a résumé be?" I thought. "You list where you worked and where you went to school. If there's space left over at the bottom of the page, you put down your favorite sports." I neglected the whole matter until four days before the deadline.

When I finally went downstairs to the computer lab, I found the lab jammed. The atmosphere was frantic. Students were working at terminals while others stood in tense groups, waiting their turns to use the laser printers, or paced back and forth, circulating drafts of their résumés to each other to proofread and comment upon. The lab looked like the floor of the New York Stock Exchange.

"If I were you, I'd put my name in fourteen-point bold typeface, not twelve-point italic. You want your name to look big and confident, not small and fussy."

"Should I center my address and phone number under my name? Or put my address flush with the left margin and my phone number flush with the right? Hey, it *matters.*"

"Don't just say you 'worked on several refinancings' while you were at Goldman. Say something with more energy. Something like 'participated in a number of major financial restructurings.'"

"Are you *still* using the printer? *Please.* There are 333 of us who need to meet this deadline."

I ended up spending three hours a day in the computer lab for all four days, getting every item on my résumé just so, printing the résumé out, passing it around for comments, then going back to the computer again and again to make this or that tiny adjustment.

"How are we supposed to get any studying done?" I complained to Sam Barrett.

Sam continued to tap at his terminal. "You thought you were here to study? Wrong-o. You're here to get a job."

The Career Management Center bound our résumés into book form, then distributed the résumé books to scores of companies. Just before midterms the companies began to woo us. I got letters from all the consulting firms. General Foods sent me a box of one of its new products, chewy candy dinosaurs, and Clorox gave me a little bottle of bleach.

Finally, just after midterms, students began to turn up in class dressed not in jeans and sweatshirts but suits and ties (the women wore dresses that looked like men's suits, with scarves that appeared intended, chiefly, to suggest men's ties). It was time for the third and last act, the interviews themselves.

For the three weeks of job interviews, Philippe moved from the slopes at Tahoe back to our house. He and Joe threw themselves into the job search, closeting themselves in the library to read up on the eight or ten banks with which each had signed up.

When talking only to me, Philippe and Joe each discussed his job-interviewing strategies quite freely. Joe wanted to go back to the bank he had worked for before business school, Salomon Brothers, but was intent on spending the coming summer with one of Salomon Brothers's competitors. "Puts me in a stronger position when I'm talking signing bonus with Salomon next year," Joe explained. "My old boss will say, 'Hey, we can't take Joe for granted. We don't treat him right, he'll go straight back to the bank he worked for during the summer.' "

Philippe, too, seemed to know just what he was doing, down to the Hermès tie. Back in Switzerland, Philippe said, Hermès ties were considered vulgar. "Only an imbecile would spend so much on a length of silk." But Philippe had read in a magazine that Hermès ties were popular with American investment bankers—the article had referred to them as "power ties"—so he had bought several in the airport duty-free shop on his way back to the States after Christmas break.

Philippe's plan was to talk to all the banks. Since he had a legal rather than financial background, however, he felt certain that only the less important, second-tier firms would make him offers. That would be good enough. He would take one of these offers, spend the summer learning everything he could, then return to Stanford next fall poised for an assault on the first-rate banks. "Next year?"

Philippe said. *"Then* I will get offers from Goldman Sachs and First Boston."

As I said, Joe and Philippe discussed their plans with me quite openly. Yet when they spoke to each other, they lied.

> JOE: Who you thinkin' of talking to?
>
> PHILIPPE: I 'ave not decided. Maybe the packaged goods companies. Procter & Gamble perhaps. I 'ave always been fascinated by soap.
>
> JOE: Same here. Been thinkin' about spending the summer with Clorox.

Philippe and Joe would both chuckle, each knowing, of course, that he was being had.

After the interviews actually began there was a lot less chuckling. Indeed, the interviews effected a basic change in the temper of the school. Stanford ordinarily prided itself on the spirit of cooperation among its students. At Harvard, with its harsh grading system, students fought each other incessantly for grades and the attention of their professors—or so we at Stanford believed. "But here at Stanford," Esther Simon told us during Orientation, "we're not like that. We believe that students receive a richer education if they work together."

This ideal of cooperation was more than just Stanford's official view of itself. It actually affected the way students conducted themselves, as I learned in Organizational Behavior during fall term. Many students had let their work in OB slide during the second half of the term, devoting their time instead to the harder, more quantitative subjects such as Computers and Trees. A couple of weeks before finals, Everett Adams, a tall athlete from Georgetown, had recruited me and two dozen other students to make an outline of the course. Then as the final had drawn nearer, each of us had been approached by classmates who wanted to photocopy our outline. Everett had called a meeting of the group at lunchtime.

"So what does everybody say?" Everett had asked, looking from

face to face as we huddled in the courtyard. "Do we keep the outline
to ourselves? It's our work, after all. Or do we share it?"

"I really dislike the perception that we're trying to be aggressive or
hostile," one woman had said. "Let's just share it."

Everett had waited for someone to take up the other side of the
argument. No one did. In class that afternoon, Everett had asked
Professor Hammond if he could make an announcement.

"If there's anybody who still doesn't know," Everett had said, "a
group of us have made an outline of the course. Our names and
phone numbers are listed on the piece of paper that's going around
the room now. Anybody who'd like to copy our outline, just get in
touch with one of the people on the list."

This had elicited wild cheers.

"Hey," Everett had said, "if we'd wanted to go for each other's
throats, we'd all have gone to Harvard, right?"

Now, just one term later, Joe and Philippe were telling each other
lies. Even stable personalities like Jennifer Taylor began to exhibit
wild mood swings, up after a good interview, snarling at classmates
after a bad one. One afternoon back at the house I picked up a newspaper that Joe had left on the dining room table. He was seated in
the living room, doing nothing but drinking beer. "You can read my
paper," he snapped, "but don't lose my place." Lose his place? In a
newspaper?

Joe pursued his plan, interviewing with every bank except
Salomon Brothers.

"But, Joe," I asked, "aren't the recruiters able to tell that you're not
being sincere? Don't they even ask why you're interviewing with them
after spending four years with Salomon Brothers?"

"Yeah, they ask," Joe said. "But I just look real honest and say I
want to go to work for Bear Stearns or Morgan Stanley or whoever
because they're the best investment bankers in the world. You can always count on an I-banker's vanity, Peter."

It worked. Joe got an offer from every bank he talked to, finally
settling on Shearson Lehman Brothers, chiefly because Shearson was
located in downtown Manhattan, not far from Salomon Brothers.

That way Joe would be able to get together with his old Salomon friends at lunchtime.

Philippe, too, talked to bank after bank. In his dove-gray, double-breasted suit and Hermès ties, Philippe looked just what he was, an urbane, sophisticated European, and I thought the investment bankers would jump at him. They didn't.

"Morgan Stanley," Philippe announced one afternoon, holding up a small sheaf of rejection letters, known at Stanford as ding letters. "Goldman Sachs. First Boston." But instead of looking dejected, Philippe appeared quite cheerful. Everything was going according to plan.

"It would have been foolish for these banks to hire me," he said. "But when I interview with the second-tier banks, they will see me as a bargain."

It happened as Philippe had said that it would. Kidder Peabody, one of the smaller Wall Street banks, made him an offer. Philippe accepted. Then he strapped his skis to the rear bumper of his Buick, climbed in, and, with a roar and a plume of purple exhaust, headed back to the slopes.

Non-poet after non-poet landed job offers with ease. John Lyons interviewed with half a dozen investment banks, got offers from all of them, and turned them all down to go back to Leopard Securities. Gunnar Haakonsen interviewed with a single firm, Wasserstein Perella. While the typical salary for a summer job lay in the range of $1,000 a week, or $10,000 for the entire summer, Wasserstein Perella was rumored to pay substantially more. "Isn't he taking a big risk by interviewing with just one firm?" I asked Joe. "Nope," Joe answered, "Gunnar will say, 'I want this job so bad, I'm not even *talking* to anybody else.' Wasserstein Perella will eat it up." Mr. Cool got the job.

Jennifer Taylor landed an offer from General Mills. "I wasn't aggressive enough for the bankers," she said. In her first banking interview the recruiter had begun with, "So, you think you're good enough for us?" Jennifer had blushed, struggled to regain her composure, then said politely, "I suppose that's really for you to decide." The recruiter had just shaken his head.

"But the marketing people all really liked me," Jennifer continued.

Marketing recruiters were looking for team players, not cutthroats. They wanted candidates who could establish a sense of rapport. Jennifer fit. "Once I figured that out," she said, "I was golden."

Management consulting firms not surprisingly saw the well-educated, articulate Englishman Rupert Dupplin as someone they could deploy to good effect in Britain, and Dupplin got offer after offer. His only problem was that California had shaken his loyalty to the sceptered isle. Dupplin negotiated at some length with one of the big consulting firms.

"They agreed to let me spend half the summer in L.A.," Dupplin told me, smiling.

"And the other half?" I asked.

His face fell. "London."

Although handicapped by his halting way with English, even my Japanese friend Zen got job offers.

"Many invitations," Zen said when I ran into him in the courtyard. He showed me a loose-leaf binder in which he had collected all his offers, neatly placing holes in each with a paper punch. There were letters from all the big investment banks.

"But I thought you wanted to stay with Mitsui," I said.

Zen explained that Mitsui would only keep him in the United States another two or three years before sending him back to Osaka. "You know Osaka?" Zen said. "Osaka is not like Stanford. Osaka is not pretty.

"But if I leave Mitsui and join an American company?" he continued. "Maybe they send me to Japan for four, five years. But always I can come back to America. I like America very much. More friendlier." Zen took an offer from Paine Webber.

Poets had a harder time. It wasn't so much that we didn't get offers as that we underwent agonies to achieve them. Conor was so anxious about finding a job that he had started looking while he was back in Dublin during the Christmas break, speaking to a number of Irish banks and insurance companies. These encounters had not been encouraging.

"Irish people are always ready to knock down anybody who looks to be putting on airs," Conor explained, pushing his glasses up the bridge of his nose. "All the executives I saw had the attitude, 'An MBA? We don't have any of that fancy American education here. Why did you go and leave a good job in the civil service in the first place?'"

Now Conor found himself roundly dinged by every investment bank and management consulting firm with which he interviewed. He finally took matters into his own hands, making half a dozen trips to Apple headquarters in Cupertino, half an hour south of Stanford. Somehow, he convinced the company that since Apple owned a factory in Ireland, it needed to give Conor a summer job in California.

I myself responded to the job search pressures badly. Instead of throwing myself into the search, signing up for a dozen or more interviews and preparing thoroughly for each, as Conor had done, I tried to pretend that the interviews weren't even taking place. I stuck to my business school work. When Philippe and Joe started talking about jobs I often slipped into my pantry, shut the door, and put on some music. I never even entered the dates of the interview season in my calendar (the reason I was startled when Philippe showed up in Finance class wearing a suit).

But the trouble with denial is that it only works for a time. Sooner or later, reality makes itself known. In my instance, reality called me on the phone. "You're giving up two years of your life to get an MBA—and skipping the interviews?" Steven asked. He claimed I was failing to grasp the very nature and meaning of business school. Maybe people got master's degrees in English just so they could appreciate literature, Steven said, but the reason for getting a master's in business was to prepare yourself for the working world. Talking to the banks and consulting firms was part of the education.

The next day I went reluctantly to sign up for interviews with two firms, one consulting company and one investment bank. I figured that was the minimum that would permit me to retain a semblance of self-respect. I chose McKinsey & Company, one of the three or four biggest consulting firms, and Dillon Read, a small investment bank, chiefly because they seemed to have the most open spots. I am not pleased to report how those two sets of interviews went.

Not that they didn't both begin well enough. "This is one of the most impressive résumés I've seen," the McKinsey recruiter said. Like all first-round interviews, this one was being conducted in a small room in the Career Management Center. The room contained only a Formica-topped table, a couple of chairs, and a potted plant. I supposed that when an interview was going badly the room could feel as sterile and depressing as the examination room in a doctor's office. But this interview was going well. So far as I was concerned the setting and ambiance were nothing short of charming.

The young man conducting the interview explained that he was in McKinsey's L.A. office and did a lot of work for oil companies and aerospace firms throughout Southern California. He was at least four years younger than I, and in asking about the White House he seemed almost obsequious, which I liked very much. Since he concluded the interview by saying, "McKinsey would be lucky to hire you," it was no surprise when I got a phone call inviting me back for the second-round interview two days later.

"I see you have no quantitative background to speak of." Now I was being interviewed by a McKinsey partner, a man in middle age. We were not in a stark cell in the Career Management Center but in a plush hotel suite—second-round interviews were conducted off campus—yet it was only now that I began to experience that sinking, examination room feeling. He glanced once again at my résumé. My political background was impressive, he said, and McKinsey did value what he termed people skills, especially at the higher levels of the firm. "But before you reach those levels, you've got to spend a few years doing the hard, nuts-and-bolts analytical work that's the basis of the service we provide. Shall we go through a case?"

In second-round interviews, consulting firms would often spring a case on a candidate, asking him to solve it out loud. But knowing that this was typical did not help. I felt as though I'd reached the part of the physical where the doctor tells you to drop your trousers and bend over.

"I'll just give you a case out of my own experience, if that's all right," the partner said. He wore a starched white shirt and trousers with creases that could have sliced cake. He assured me dryly that he had worked on this case when he was my age and just starting at McKinsey.

"The case involved a freight forwarding company. Any idea what a freight forwarder does?"

This sounded ominous. I certainly had no idea. But instead of giving the partner a simple no, I reacted as I often did when I felt uncomfortable. I tried to be funny. "Nope," I answered, "Ab-soh-LUTE-ly none." I attempted a winsome, aw-shucks smile.

No reaction. The partner merely proceeded in a cool, even, completely businesslike way.

"A freight forwarder," he said, "picks up freight, packages it—usually they'll build a standard-sized wooden frame or crate around each shipment—takes it to a ship or airplane for transport, picks it up at the dock or airport at the other end, stores it, then uncrates it and delivers it to its final destination on the appropriate date. So the business is basically trucking, storage, and handling."

The partner explained that his client had been in the freight forwarding business for several decades, always profitably. Then over a period of just a few months, the client suddenly found itself losing money. As often happened in a business that hadn't changed much in many years, the managers had grown lax in their bookkeeping.

"Cost accounting?" the partner said. "Non-existent. So they couldn't figure out what had happened, and they turned to us."

For McKinsey, the partner said, straightening out the cost accounting proved elementary—"not that it didn't take a lot of time and brains." McKinsey concluded that the freight forwarder had begun to lose money because of a single expense, air charges.

"The airlines," he said, concluding his presentation, "were suddenly charging our client more—a lot more—to carry its freight. My question to you is, Why would that happen?"

I froze.

After a tense moment of silence, the partner repeated the question. He looked at me grimly.

"You understand the question, right? Why would the airlines start charging more?" He wasn't trying to make this easy.

"Fuel costs?" I finally said. "Was this by any chance taking place during the Arab oil embargoes of the early seventies?"

"No," he said flatly. "It was after that. The higher price of oil had already been absorbed into the airlines' price structures."

Another tense silence.

The partner said, "Let's look at it another way." During the same period, he stated, airfares for passengers were holding steady or actually dropping. Yet here the airlines were, imposing sharp increases on freight forwarders. "To recommend what our client should do about it, we had to figure out what was going on. So what would you guess?"

"There was no other airline that would have charged less?" I asked. Even I recognized this as a stupid question—before spending tens of thousands of dollars to hire McKinsey, the client would obviously have spent a few quarters to telephone other airlines. And yet I was desperate. "All the airlines were raising their fares?"

The partner confirmed that all the airlines were raising their fares. "But you're getting someplace," he said. That surprised me. "If all the airlines were raising their fares at the same time, what could be the reason?" I had no idea, which did not surprise me.

Once again, I froze. If I'd been in that physical, it would have been now that the doctor put on a rubber glove and dipped his index finger in ointment. As it was, the McKinsey partner simply gazed at me. Then he gave up.

"What about supply and demand?" he said.

If all the airlines were charging higher fares, the partner said, the demand for cargo space must have risen to a new level. Yet despite this increase in demand, the supply of cargo space was more or less fixed; it took many months for airlines to order new planes, get them delivered, and finally put them into service. "So the airlines were charging our client higher rates because they didn't really need his business. Other freight forwarders were out there, bidding up the price of a relatively fixed supply of cargo space. Makes sense, right?"

Of *course* it made sense. The explanation was *so* obvious that I felt the partner had tricked me. Supply and demand? The words "supply and demand" would in one way or another have represented the answer to virtually any question about any market. I'd assumed—quite naturally, I still think—that he'd wanted a more sophisticated response. Wasn't the real question why there was suddenly so much more freight being forwarded? Granted that it would take a long time for airlines to add to capacity. But you wouldn't expect business in shipping crates around the world to double overnight either, would you?

"Let me put it this way," the partner said. The McKinsey summer program was short, just ten weeks. Over long experience, McKinsey had learned that the business school students who benefited most from the program were those already capable of handling a consulting workload.

"I don't doubt that you'd be able to learn the basic consulting skills—eventually. But I have to be frank. In my judgment, we'd have to spend too much of the summer training you to be able to give you a really good experience."

I'd blown it. Totally. I was furious with the partner and furious with myself. It wasn't that I'd been too stupid to answer the question. It was rather that I hadn't understood the rules. I had been trying to figure out how a specific problem could have arisen in an industry I knew nothing about when the partner had only wanted me to demonstrate the most basic awareness of market forces. Uttering the words "supply and demand" would have sufficed. But now there was nothing to do.

I stood, shook the partner's hand, and left.

A week later I walked into one of the tiny interview rooms in the Career Management Center to find the recruiter from Dillon Read, the investment bank, seated at the Formica table making notes on a pile of résumés. Although the room was not a great deal bigger than a refrigerator box, the recruiter managed not to acknowledge my presence; I quietly sat down across from him, and, with nothing much else to do, looked him over. He wore a pink shirt with big gold cufflinks and a pair of red suspenders. His hair was slicked back. He was making notes with a fat Mont Blanc fountain pen. Here in

California, his attire screamed Manhattan and money. He could not have been older than twenty-six.

He sat for a few moments in silence, continuing to make notes on the résumés, presumably to make it clear that I was but one of the many students he would be seeing. Then he glanced up suddenly, as though he had just become aware of my presence. Reaching to shake my hand he said, "I'm H. H. Hennessey the third."

Mr. Hennessey the third spent twenty minutes of a half-hour interview giving me a socioeconomic background check. He wanted to hear whom I'd known at Dartmouth and Oxford. When conversation turned to the White House, he gave me the feeling that he thought less of the Californian, Reagan, than of the Eastern establishment figure, Bush. He asked whether I knew a certain Cabinet secretary who had been a prominent figure at the bank before leaving for Washington. It happened that I'd known the secretary's daughter. "Oh?" Hennessey said. "Good. Very good."

At last Hennessey shifted the interview to business school. "What subjects are you enjoying most here at Stanford?"

I couldn't very well respond that at least half the time I hated them all. So instead I told him that I liked Accounting and Finance. This was truthful but incomplete. After so much time in politics, I liked the *idea* of Accounting and Finance, disciplines that involved considerable intellectual rigor. In practice, which is to say, every time I ever actually had anything to do with either subject, I found Accounting and Finance especially tiresome and difficult. Still, I doubted that Hennessey wanted me to go into it at that level of detail.

"Good to meet you," Hennessey said, concluding our half hour with a second handshake. "I'll tell you now that I intend to recommend you for the second round."

This second interview took place in another hotel near the campus. The two bankers who questioned me were senior to Hennessey, though not by a lot; they looked to be at the most in their early thirties. It was a freakishly warm midwinter day, and throughout the interview I had to fight to keep my gaze from wandering past the bankers, in their striped shirts and monogrammed cufflinks, out the window to the people lying around the hotel pool on chaise lounges and salving themselves with coconut oil. The Dillon Read men submitted me to an hour of intent questioning. Then they asked me to step into the hall for a moment so they could confer. Finally they called me back into the room.

"We'd be taking a risk on you," one said. Since investment banking wasn't as exciting as working at the White House, I might spend the summer at their bank, then decide that what I really wanted to do was go back to politics. "But if you truly want to be an investment banker, we think you'd make a good one."

They would have to speak to New York before making a definite offer, the other explained. But that would only be a formality, since they had both agreed on me. "We'll be in touch," he said. "And congratulations."

As I drove back to the campus, my first reaction was simply to enjoy my good luck. Me? A banker? The very night before I'd spent two hours working on a problem set for Finance class that I never did finish. Now two investment bankers had all but assured me of a summer job on Wall Street. Life was funny, I thought, but as long as it worked in your favor, who could complain?

That night I had second thoughts, making this entry in my journal:

February 22

Something very odd was going on during my interview with Dillon Read today. The bankers asked me repeatedly if I was certain I wanted to go into investment banking after working in the White House. But why? In Bonfire of the Vanities Tom Wolfe described investment bankers as "masters of the universe." How could they possibly wonder why I would want to become one of them?

I now suspect that what took place in that hotel room had less to do with any firm understanding of reality than with a collision of illusions. They thought the White House the seat of all earthly glory. I knew better. Working at the White House involved a lot of long hours and merely routine toil.

And I? I thought investment bankers somehow existed on a higher plane of being. While I was spending six years in one office tapping out speeches, for instance, my old roommate Charles, a real estate banker, was flying around the world buying and selling entire office buildings.

But maybe the two bankers who interviewed me knew something about investment banking that I didn't—maybe Charles knows too, but just isn't telling. Maybe investment banking involves a lot of long hours and merely routine toil. Maybe even flying around the world can get old.

When I got back to the house after classes the next afternoon, there was a message on my answering machine. It was Hennessey the third. Dillon Read had decided to make me a formal offer.

Once again, I considered my reservations. Investment banking didn't seem to fit me. It had nothing to do with words or ideas, at least as far as I could tell from Finance class. Investment banking was about math.

Even the Dillon Read men themselves viewed me as a risk. They had made it clear that any skills at dealing with people I had acquired in politics would be of no use to me in banking until I started dealing directly with clients in four or five years. Until then I would have to serve an apprenticeship, struggling to achieve proficiency in research and the building of financial models. To the Dillon Read men I was a bold gamble, an investment that wouldn't pay off for years, if then, and I knew I was even more of a long shot than they thought. Should I be playing roulette with their bank and my career?

There were two answers to this. One was, Of course not. The other was that I could use a summer job and this was the only offer I had. I called Hennessey back to accept.

FOURTEEN

Upswing

It first occurred to me back during the early weeks of fall term that the characteristic emotional pattern of business school was one of wild, erratic mood swings. I felt stupid during the first couple of days of Math Camp, as I've said. Then when I began to gain some purchase on algebra I felt elated, only to feel stupid, once again, when we moved on to calculus.

So the pattern went. Down after being unable to complete an assignment in Trees or Accounting. Up after getting a good grade on the OB midterm or making one or two coherent comments during a class in Public Sector Economics. Down after being rejected in one interview. Up, way up, after being accorded warm treatment in another. Yet even the ups often involved less a sense of contentment or accomplishment than of giddiness, and I got sick of the ride.

But after interview season the mood swings abated. My classmates and I settled down. Back at the house in Portola Valley, we settled into an easy pattern. In the mornings Joe and I had our coffee and cereal together and shared the Wall Street Journal. On the nights when Philippe was home from the slopes, the three of us would have a few beers at 10:00 or 11:00, when Joe got back from networking. The business school itself ceased to feel like an institution for manic depressives and began once again to resemble a collection of reasonably well-adjusted young students. Some of us had to scramble to catch up in coursework we had let drop while we interviewed, but we felt no mortal peril. At lunchtime downstairs in the Arbuckle Lounge, the business school cafeteria, there was a sound I had all but forgotten: laughter.

What had changed? Simple. We had jobs.

"I spent weeks worried that no one would make me an offer," Conor said over lunch. "But now I've got a job. Employment. Do you know what that means to an Irishman?" Conor took a big bite of his submarine sandwich, notable in itself since while he was job-hunting he had had no appetite. "The day Apple made its offer I took my wife out to dinner in the city. Then I did something I've been wanting to do since I started at this place. I spent the weekend in bed, asleep. By Monday I felt rested. Really, truly rested. It was glorious."

When I told her about my own job, Edita was impressed. "That's *great!*" I still harbored the doubts I have already described. Me? In an investment bank? Yet hearing Edita sound so happy made me see matters in a different light. The men from Dillon Read were professionals. They had looked me over and decided to pay me the compliment of hiring me. It would have been churlish of me not to feel gratified. Even if Dillon Read was mistaken about me, as I suspected, ten weeks with an investment bank would still teach me a lot about the world of making and getting. It would also leave me $10,000 better off.

All of us had come to this school to achieve some specific improvement in our careers. We had risked a lot, including two years of our lives and a great deal of our money. Now the risk was beginning to pay off. It felt good. We were Stanford MBAs. We were hotshots, after all.

Not that things changed much inside the classrooms. In Finance I continued to suffer a peculiar sensation of tedium laced with doom, as though I were the defendant in a protracted Pakistani trial at the end of which I was certain to be hanged. In Slowacki's Data Analysis class, it soon came time for the special project, a regression analysis of each study group's own, original design. Clark, a friendly, wiry former consultant for Booz Allen, perhaps the most quantitative of all the prominent consulting firms, and Bill, a big, lethargic jock and computer nerd, accepted me into their study group as an act of charity. They designed a project about a muffler repair shop. They found a shop, interviewed the mechanics in each of four repair bays, and gathered data on more than thirty cars. Then they designed a regression analysis that attempted to explain the breakdown of mufflers in terms of the number of miles each car had driven, the make of each car, whether the muffler in question was original or a replacement, and the sex of each car's owner, an item added to test the model for absurdity. My role? After Clark and Bill had performed all these labors, the three of us got together one evening at Bill's apartment. I sat at the keyboard of Bill's computer and typed as Bill and Clark paced the room, telling jokes, playing catch by bouncing a tennis ball to each other off the ceiling, and dictating our report. I understood nothing. Truly nothing.

In Public Sector Economics each study group had to submit four long case analyses over the course of the term. Since my study group had four members, myself, Conor, Susan, the Alabaman who had been in my Micro study group, and Greta, a medical doctor from Austria, we decided that each of us would write one analysis. I had done the first, intending to get the bulk of my work in the course over with early in the term. The writing of the last of the four had fallen to Greta.

The case, set during the presidency of Gerald Ford, involved an effort by the federal government to provide the public with a flu vaccination. Table after table of data detailed the expenses of producing and distributing the vaccine and the probabilities that in a certain fraction of instances the vaccine would produce virulent or even fatal side effects. To whom should the Ford administration administer the vaccine? Everyone in the country? Only those at gravest risk, such as the very old and the very young? Greta had to calculate costs and benefits under different scenarios, quite intricate work. Then she had to write a lengthy report based on her findings.

Six days before the paper was due, Greta had done nothing but make notes. Five days before, nothing. On the afternoon of the fourth day we held a group meeting.

"Of course I vill finish this report," Greta insisted. "I know these issues. I am a trained physician."

Then she showed us her notes. Greta had amassed a good twenty pages of jottings, far more than necessary, and Susan, Conor, and I concluded that Greta would probably never get around to running the numbers. We were also alarmed by her grammar. In one place Greta had written, "Not vaccinated, many children sick will fall," reminding Conor of Mark Twain's quip that he detested German opera because he always had to wait until the last act to hear the verb. Susan, Conor, and I broke the report into pieces and distributed the work. The section I got stuck with landed me in the computer lab for a good six hours, ruining a Saturday afternoon.

Yet none of this bothered me much. Now I saw the business school curriculum as instrumental, not an end in itself but a means to an end. The end was getting a job. Sitting in Professor Charen's Finance classroom or helping to save Greta's report was just something you had to go through.

I reported my sudden change of view to Professor Healey.

"I'll never complain about this school again," I said. "In just a term and a half it took a dope like me and gave me enough of a business education to get a really good job."

Healey rolled his eyes. "Bull," he said. "Education had nothing to do with it."

Someday, Healey said, he would conduct an experiment, having the business school admit two identical classes at once. The students in one class would follow the Stanford curriculum, earning their MBAs in the usual manner. The students in the other class "wouldn't do a damn thing, just play golf and throw hot tub parties." At the end of two years, these idlers would be awarded MBAs just as if they too had earned the degrees. Then the business school would track the students in both classes, noting their income levels, the rates at which they got promotions, and so on.

"It's my contention," Healey said, "that five years after they graduated you wouldn't see a diddlysquat's worth of difference between the two groups." Business school was a signaling device. It told the marketplace that a student was good enough to get in. Whether the student also got a decent business education was, Healey claimed, beside the point. "MBA degrees are union cards for yuppies."

Healey had a point. There was no denying that the Dillon Read men had made me an offer because I was a Stanford MBA student. If, like the McKinsey partner, they had given me a case to solve, they would have found that my knowledge of finance was nil. But they hadn't given me a case to solve. I would soon be a holder of the yuppie union card, and that, to them at least, was credential enough.

Yet just as during Christmas break I had recognized that business school had made me different, now, six weeks into winter term, I was once again aware of changes taking place within me.

Take Data Analysis. Was I able to follow Slowacki's lectures? No. I did manage to scrape through the midterm, but only because I was able to manipulate a few formulas. Yet Data Analysis had enlarged my understanding. If nothing else, now I knew that statistics *existed.* In politics I had often wondered how pollsters could claim to present the views of the entire nation after questioning only a few hundred individuals. Now I knew. Statistics. I remained unable to design a poll myself, needless to say. But now I knew about a sophisticated, rigorous mathematical discipline that could set out reliable views of big realities based upon extrapolations from very small samples.

I was in something of the position of a janitor on the Starship Enterprise. Each day my rounds would take me to the control room, where I would look up from my sweeping and dusting every now and again to gaze at the screen. I would see a planet, glittering with gold, where the streets were paved with coins and the inhabitants spoke in numbers, not words: the Planet Corporate Finance. Or I would see an immense craft, studded with tickers and counters that whirred madly like colossal digital clocks or odometers: the Space Station Cost Accounting. Captain Kirk and Spock, played by non-poets such as Joe and Philippe, were the ones who beamed down, met the natives, and had adventures; I remained on shipboard, mopping the floors and cleaning the lavatories. Yet if only from a distance, I was seeing what they saw. I too was boldly going where nobody but business students had gone before. And even though I had only been on the starship for a few months, I already sounded different when I spoke with a fellow janitor back on Earth.

"What does a management consultant like Steven actually do?" Josh asked over the phone one day during winter term. Josh, a close friend, was a speechwriter at the White House, just as I had been.

"Lots," I answered, testy that he should display such ignorance.

Management consultants, I explained, might survey the markets a company wanted to enter. They might advise a corporation on how to raise capital. Or they might analyze a company's expenses and revenues on every last one of its products.

"To take an elementary example," I heard myself saying, as though I had been lecturing at business schools for years, "imagine you run a mom-and-pop grocery. Do you stock more breakfast cereal or more produce? More men's toiletries or more baby products like diapers and baby bottles?"

Even in a little grocery decisions of those kinds could become complicated. So Josh ought to be able to see why Exxon or GM or Hewlett-Packard might be inclined to hire specialists—energetic kids who were whizzes at business analysis—to help them out. "I mean, it would be worth it to pay Steven's firm $1 million if Steven and his fellow consultants helped you figure out how to enter a new market and earn ten times that amount. You can see that, right?"

"Okay," Josh answered, "I'll take your word for it. Consultants do stuff I'll never understand."

When I got to business school, that had been my view too—consultants like Steven did stuff that I'd never understand. These few months later, I was still unfit to act as a consultant myself. But now at least I understood what consultants did. What was more, Josh recognized this and deferred to me. After weeks of making me feel stupid, business school had finally made it possible for me to make other people feel stupid. This was progress.

I went on with Josh at some length, boasting, as it were, about my fellow crew members on the Starship Stanford. One of my classmates had been a management consultant. On his last case before coming to business school he had worked at a hospital, reviewing its paper-work procedures "It sounded boring to me, too," I said to Josh "But just listen."

My classmate, a short, stocky guy with a lot of animation in his face as he spoke, had pointed out that even a simple procedure like a tonsillectomy required pages of reports and records. When the patient entered the hospital, the admitting clerk filled out forms. Every time a nurse entered the patient's room, she completed a status report. Doctors did the same. At the hospital where my classmate had worked, eight people, on average, handled each piece of paper several times apiece before the paper went to the billing department. Since so much paper got lost or became illegible, the billing department made mistakes on 10 percent of its bills.

"There were millions of dollars involved in those mistakes," I told Josh, "and every billing mistake involved a high risk of litigation from patients, insurance companies, and government regulators. My classmate and his team designed a paperwork system that cut the billing mistakes in half. Pretty neat, huh?"

Another classmate had worked at a venture capital firm. Her job had been to read the dozens of business plans the firm received each week, searching for proposals sound enough to interest her bosses, the firm's partners. "She was like a reader in a Hollywood studio who plows through five or six scripts a day, hoping to find two or three really good ones in a month," I explained to Josh. "And her bosses were like movie producers. They'd put up some money of their own, raise more, and go from having an idea to having products in the marketplace."

She was a tall, quiet woman who loved computers. One of the proposals she spotted was for manufacturing computer monitors much bigger than any then available. My classmate and her bosses met the electrical engineer who had written the proposal, did enough research to satisfy themselves that a market for oversized monitors existed among architects and graphic designers, then raised millions of dollars, found a high-tech factory capable of manufacturing the product, and hired a team to market it. "They got the monitors into the marketplace at a profit in just eighteen months," I told Josh.

"Not bad, considering that's about how long it can take to get a simple piece of legislation through Congress."

I didn't put it quite this way, but my tone of voice stated quite clearly that while writers like Josh and the person I used to be sat in front of word processors all day, MBAs made things *happen*. Now that I had a job, I was one of them. Lowly janitor I might remain, but I was on board. I was making the MBA journey.

During the last few days of February, even the weather brightened.

February 26

The sun has finally returned, and up in the foothills, the effect of the sunlight is dramatic, all but splashy. Parched and brown all autumn, the hills now have a cover of fresh, tender shoots of grass, and in the afternoons the hills shine with a greenness that almost seems to carry its own luminescence, a glow like the glow of the sunlight itself, brilliant, glorious, alive. The big blue and purple clouds stay to the west of the mountains as if forced against their will to the chilly ocean side of the high ridge. A single, fat cloud might sometimes break free to scud across the sky, sheeting down drizzle; but the green of the grasses only turns greener still in the wetness, and after a quarter of an hour the cloud rains itself out and the sun returns. The sun—the sun is back. I could sing. I could dance. I feel like Noah when the torrent ended and the dove flew back to the ark with an olive sprig.

All right, I was overreacting. It was only sunshine. But until then winter term had been so cold and damp and so fraught with job interview terror that a few rays of sunshine were all it took.

The upswing continued when during the first week in March students and faculty jammed Cubberly Auditorium, a theater on campus, for the Saturday night performances of the Second-Year Show, an annual event. I didn't expect much. Business school students, I thought, could not be very entertaining. I was mistaken.

In one skit, second-year students, dressed as business school cases, hung out in a bar. One wore a pointy-headed costume covered with aluminum foil—a knife from Benson Appliance. Another waddled into the bar dressed as a chicken, a play on the Marketing case about a company that sold contact lenses for poultry. (Hens, apparently, often pecked each other to death. Someone, somehow, discovered that if chickens wore rose-colored contacts, they could live together in harmony. A company thus came into being to produce and market chicken lenses. I am not making this up.) The chicken on stage wore huge, Elton John–style glasses. "Honey," it said to the knife, "those contacts did nothing for me, but ain't you just wild about these funky frames?" At the end two students struggled on stage in a horse outfit. Most of the audience figured out the character a moment before I did and hissed. Then it came to me. Of course. The horse costume represented Glittering Trees. I booed.

A second skit depicted a production line. A dozen second-year students took positions, moving in short, jerky motions, like robots, to turn themselves into a Rube Goldberg device for processing tennis balls. One student lifted balls out of a box, handing them, one at a time, to a second student, who spray-painted each ball pink. A third examined the paint jobs, passing the balls along when they met his standards and dropping them into a discard box when they did not. Still another second-year tested each ball by using a tennis racquet to bounce it, just once, on the floor. A final set of students inserted each ball in a box, tying each box with a string.

Then the human machine began to go awry. The spray painter sprayed his fellow workers instead of the tennis balls. The first tester tossed discarded balls at the boxers and wrappers instead of into the discard box, while the second tester lobbed balls into the balcony. Soon a lovely, total chaos reigned on stage. The effect was all but professional, as good as a sketch on "Saturday Night Live," and the audience hooted and cheered.

The final skit was based on the premise that Elvis was alive—and enrolled at Stanford. In the climax, Dave Chen, the president of the second-year class, descended to the stage on a rope, dressed as Elvis in a sequined, baby-blue stretch suit. To the accompaniment of brass, guitars, an electric piano, and a three-woman backup chorus, Chen gyrated and sang, "You ain't nothin' but a hound dog." The audience stood and stamped its feet. Chen sang an encore, "Don't step on my blue suede shoes."

The Second-Year Show demonstrated that Stanford business school students could dance, sing, perform reasonably good jazz, write funny skits, and act. For me, this was an important lesson. Business school, and by extension business itself, did not just attract drones and nerds but gifted, creative people. This was a happy thought, and at the huge party after the show I enjoyed myself for two solid hours by joining half a dozen classmates in singing around a piano.

The show, the sunshine, our summer jobs—all contributed to a lightening of the winter term mood. At noontime, students began to carry their lunches upstairs from the Arbuckle Lounge to sit outdoors, lingering in the sunshine to talk after they had finished eating. Study groups started holding shorter sessions. Students began to gather at night in local beer and hamburger places, and you could walk into the Dutch Goose or the Oasis and find four or five booths in a row jammed with MBAs, talking and laughing.

Then, suddenly, the entire institution went into shock. *Business-Week* magazine published its annual survey of business schools. It ranked Stanford ninth.

FIFTEEN

The Frijoles
Hit the Fan

You might suppose that for Stanford to be ranked ninth out of the more than 500 business schools in the country was good, not bad. But Stanford had gotten used to being ranked first or second, nip and tuck with Harvard, and in the eyes of the students, being downgraded almost amounted to a breach of contract. Thirty thousand bucks to go to what is widely recognized as the first- or second-best business school in the country was one thing. It was another altogether to devote that kind of money to attending number nine.

The day the magazine came out, gloom hung over the school. Students looked as shaken as if a war had been declared or an assassination had taken place. In the Arbuckle Lounge at lunchtime, Joe sat staring at his cheeseburger, picking it up every so often, then setting it down without taking a bite. He complained that at Salomon Brothers, the bankers ranked each other partly according to how good a business school each had attended. "Now all the Harvard guys will laugh their asses off at me," Joe said. He shoved a French fry from one side of his plate to the other. "Even the Tuck and Darden guys will be laughing their asses off."

Gunnar had no more appetite than Joe. He mentioned that while he was at Bear Stearns he had heard a couple of the older traders talk about the New York City debt crisis in the late 1970s. One day a trader was golden. Then the next day a rating agency would down-grade city debt and the trader would be out millions. "That's what this reminds me of," Gunnar said. "We have a huge investment in this business school and the market just swung against us." Gunnar looked pale.

Philippe had responded to the survey in a lawyerly way, examining the documents. He had taken himself off to the business school library and spent several hours comparing the *Business Week* survey with those in other publications, notably *U.S. News*. Over lunch, he presented his findings.

Stanford, Philippe explained, did well in surveys that based their rankings on the views of academics. This made sense. Academics thought highly of research, and Stanford business school's reputation for research was excellent.

Stanford also did well in surveys that based their rankings on the views employers expressed about business school graduates they had hired. This too made sense. Stanford admitted small classes—fewer than 350 a year, compared to yearly classes at many business schools, including Harvard, of more than twice that size—and the admissions process was correspondingly very selective. The students who got into Stanford tended to be impressive, and it stood to reason that they would perform well when they left.

But the *Business Week* survey was different. Granted, it, too, took into account both the views of academics and the opinions of employers about MBAs they had hired. But *Business Week* also took into account the views companies expressed about *interviewing* at business schools.

"But of *course* Stanford will rank low in a survey of this nature," Philippe said. When companies put on BBLs, Stanford students sat gobbling sandwiches and slurping Cokes. Then, during the interviews themselves, companies were forbidden by Stanford policy to ask students about their grades. And when companies finally managed to hire Stanford MBAs, "They 'ave to pay us," as Philippe said, "like bandits." Stanford MBAs commanded an average starting salary in their first jobs of over $65,000, more than MBAs from almost any other institution. The companies that interviewed at Stanford could be expected to gripe.

"So," Philippe concluded, "the survey tells us nothing we do not already know, no?" He seemed quite merry.

"There's just one little problem," Sam Barrett said. Sam looked angry. He sat hunched at the table with one leg jittering up and down. "Philippe isn't about to get his views published in a national magazine."

After lunch I ran into Conor.

"Ever since I got here," Conor said, "I've been telling myself that I'm not like the I-bankers and consultants. I didn't come just to get a credential. I came for an education."

"Same here," I said. "At least that's what I've been telling myself."

"So this survey shouldn't bother us, should it?" Conor said. "We're getting the same education now as we were before the survey was published. No big deal. Water off a duck's back." He shrugged. Then he adjusted his glasses and looked at me.

"But don't you see it?" Conor continued. "The irony? I came here for an education, but one of the things I've learned is that brand names matter. When I was interviewing with Apple, it mattered a *lot* that I was from a school they considered one of the two or three best in the States. Now I'm as furious as any I-banker or consultant that Stanford could let this happen to its reputation."

All that day and the next students hung around in the Arbuckle Lounge and the courtyard with hangdog, beaten expressions. The cheerfulness of the week before had only been a remission. Now we had relapsed into a major downer. At 5:00 P.M. on Wednesday, the Dean held an open meeting in Bishop Auditorium.

The room was packed, every seat taken, students standing in the aisles and crowding the doorways, murmuring. As the Dean, associate deans, and administrators entered through a side door and took their seats on stage, the students fell silent. The deans and administrators fidgeted. Sonia Jensen rose and introduced the Dean. There was no applause. The Dean stepped to the microphone. His shoulders were stooped.

"I guess I'd better admit right away that this is a low day for me,"

the Dean said. "But this school is a great institution. I really believe
that. And ever since a certain issue of a certain magazine came out,
I've told myself over and over that what the press says about this institution doesn't matter, not as long as all of us know how great
Stanford business school really is.

"But that article still hurt. It hurt me. It hurt everyone here on the
stage with me. Nobody enjoys going to work in the morning and
finding out that your reputation is a lot lower than it used to be.

"And I have to say that what really hurts the most"—he paused,
his voice choking—"is that the article contains quotations from
some of our students, from some of you right here in this room, who
said things about this institution that were . . . well, that hurt.

"So the associate deans and I thought that we'd get together and
ask your views. We're here to listen. If you see something that we
could be doing better, I want to give you my assurance, right here,
right now, that we want to hear from you."

The Dean returned to his seat. Associate Dean Slowacki stood to
take over the meeting.

"Uh, if anybody wants to say anything or ask a question,"
Slowacki said, "just raise your hand."

For a moment, there was an embarrassed silence. Then one hand
went up after another.

One student rose to attack the core curriculum. "So much of the
core seems really badly designed. Why should we have to learn the
Black-Scholes Option Pricing Model before we even know what options are used for?"

Slowacki answered that just last year the Finance faculty had held
long discussions about what to include in the introductory Finance
course. "I think we have to rely on their judgment," he said.

Hisses.

Another stood to ask why exemption exams were only offered
once a year, before fall term even started. He hadn't been able to take
the exams. "To tell the truth," he said, "I needed to work until the
very last day possible before leaving for California because I needed
the money." So even though he was a Certified Public Accountant
and had spent four years working for Price Waterhouse, a major ac-

counting firm, he had had to take both of the core accounting courses. "I'm sorry, but that's ridiculous."

"You've got to understand the registration process," Slowacki answered. "We need to know how many students are in each course. We can't have people constantly taking exemption exams and dropping out of core courses."

More hisses.

The teaching came under attack again and again. One student complained that too many instructors were young and inexperienced. Another objected to being taught Micro by an assistant professor from Latin America. "I know it's not his fault, but the guy doesn't even speak English." (I'd sat in on a few minutes of one of this professor's classes, and it was true. The professor's accent was so heavy no one could understand him.) Yet another rose to remind the deans that during Orientation one of them had claimed that every member of the Stanford faculty was one of the best in his field at either teaching or research and outstanding at the other. "A third of the teachers here really are outstanding," he said. "But a third are only okay, and a third stink."

"Uh, thank you for those comments," Slowacki said at one point. "We deans have been having talks among ourselves about how some of the teaching can be improved." They had already arranged to have certain instructors videotaped in the classroom, he explained, so a professional consultant could work with the instructors on their teaching techniques.

Boos and laughter.

So it went, students attacking the school, Slowacki offering lame answers and getting hissed or laughed at. The entire event struck me as a minor tragedy. It was so needless. The deans must have been hoping we would tell them what swell work they were doing in running their great institution, and just a couple of days earlier we would probably have done just that. The sun had come out, we'd lined up jobs, and our complaints were starting to look small compared to what being at business school was doing for us. The *Business-Week* survey had cast us back into a fretful, resentful mood appropriate to the beginning of winter term, not the end. I still think we would have come out of it in a few more days if the deans had only left us alone.

After almost two hours Slowacki brought the meeting to an awkward close, and students stomped out of Bishop to find that after a week of good weather it had started to rain.

March 19

Finals start tomorrow and the mood is still morose. Conor says his wife keeps asking whether Stanford will give some of his money back.

It was hard for me to force myself back into exam-taking mode until halfway through the last week of classes. Then I got scared. After treating midterms as a distraction, then ceasing to study altogether for the better part of two weeks while I interviewed for summer jobs, I was behind, and it suddenly occurred to me that flunking even one of my finals would tarnish my standing as a hotshot Stanford MBA, the only credential, so far as I could see, that Dillon Read cared about. With my summer job at stake, I began to closet myself once again in my pantry office to study.

On the Data Analysis final on Monday of exam week, the hardest problem dealt with a credit card company. The company had mailed promotional coupons to 500 of its customers. Now it wanted to know whether its customers had used the coupons to charge more to their cards.

The customers held two classes of cards, "ruby" and "diamond" cards, an obvious, heavy-handed play on the American Express gold and platinum cards (all humor on business school exams was obvious and heavy-handed). The problem provided data in heaps, detailing the number of cardholders for each kind of card, the number of cardholders sampled, and on and on. Then the problem ended with a series of commands:

"Test the hypothesis that the mean amount charged if the coupon plan were adopted would be different from the mean amount presently charged." "Specify the null and alternative hypotheses." "Indicate whether this is a one- or a two-tailed test."

I knew when it was over that I'd probably passed, but I felt no elation, just a measure of relief that I had managed to sit through a whole term of Data Analysis classes without forgetting to breathe.

On the Cost Accounting final on Tuesday, it was more of the usual word problems. These proved less a matter of dealing with an alien and difficult body of knowledge, like the questions on the Data Analysis final, than of racing against the clock to work tens upon tens of calculations, each small and easy enough in itself. One problem addressed itself to the Kuddly Kangas Corporation (that humor again, in this case playing on Professor Symons's origins as an Aussie).

Kuddly Kangas, the problem stated, made toys, including its premium product, Joey, a stuffed kangaroo that stood 100 centimeters tall and wholesaled for $150, a markup of 50 percent on the standard cost of manufacture. The text went on like this for a page, providing information about the various stages in the manufacture of Joey, about inventory levels, about standard direct materials, about direct labor costs, and so forth. Then the problem issued its instructions: "Calculate the factory overhead variances, in as much detail as the material allows." "Calculate the materials price and materials usage variances." Calculate this, calculate that.

By the time Symons entered the classroom and told us to close our exam books, my fingers were so stiff from working the buttons on my calculator that my knuckles were inoperative. Yet except for two small parts of one question, I'd completed the whole exam. I was sure I had passed.

On Wednesday I had a day off, so I crammed for the Operations final on Thursday.

All term Operations had struck me as a particularly frustrating course. It was always posing big, important questions, only to reduce them to bitsy word problems. Look at this one question from the essay part of the final: "It is generally felt that piece rate compensation for factory workers [that is, paying workers according to the number of pieces of work they managed to complete] is inconsistent with the Toyota production system. Why?"

After cramming the night before I knew the answer. Toyota used a quality control system known as TQC, or Total Quality Control, devised by the American W. Edwards Deming, but put into effect first and most widely in Japan (few Americans had ever heard of Deming—I certainly had not—but in Japan he was revered, right up there with MacArthur). TQC gave Toyota workers the freedom to halt the entire production line whenever they discovered a defect. But if the Toyota workers were paid by the piece they would be reluctant to halt the line since doing so would cut into their pay.

But *why* did the Deming quality control ideas take deeper root in Japan than in the United States? Why were the Japanese so much better at *making things* than we were? Operations never even attempted to answer these questions.

The Operations final went on, word problem after word problem.

How much flour should the Bulldog Baking Company order, and how often should it order it, given that Bulldog needed so-and-so much flour per year, that its inventory carrying cost was such-and-such per pound of flour per month, and so on?

How many counters should be set up at a fast-food restaurant when the customers arrived in a random pattern at the average rate of v per hour, each counter cost w per hour to operate, the average customer order was for x dollars, and y percent of the customers would leave without ordering if they found themselves forced to wait longer than z minutes?

After half an hour of this I had reached the level of frustration at which white mice in mazes lie down and die, yet I managed to keep putting answers in blue books for all four hours.

Since there was no final in Public Sector Economics, that left Finance.

Throughout the term Finance had devoted itself to increasingly sophisticated models and terms. Since the midterm we'd covered the Capital Asset Pricing Model, a mathematical description of the relationship between a security's risk and its return; the Black-Scholes Option Pricing Model, a formula that used seven different variables to value options; and the first several letters of the Greek alphabet—the alpha, A, a measure of a stock's volatility; the beta, ß, a measure of market risk; and the delta, Δ, a measure of the relationship between an option price and the underlying futures or contract price. I could copy those definitions from the glossary in the back of the textbook, as I just did. But understand them?

On the final I stumbled through questions about option puts, calls, and exercise prices, about market volatility, annualized yields on bonds, arbitrage strategy, and synthetic instruments. It was all math. I understood nothing. But by now I knew I could pass business school exams even when I'd failed to grasp the material. Part of the technique was putting formulas on index cards, the other part, adrenaline. I'd taken care of both, compiling a stack of index cards as thick as a pinochle deck and placing the following sentence on the top card: "You have a summer job with an investment bank. If you flunk this final you'll look like an idiot." A full five minutes before Professor Charen entered the room and told us to stop writing, I had managed to get down an answer to every question.

Winter term was over.

I joined my classmates in the courtyard, where they stood stomping their feet and scrunching their necks into their windbreakers to keep warm since it had turned drizzly and cold yet again. The weather felt depressing, which, given everyone's mood, was fitting. There were only a few minutes of milling and talk before students began to disperse, going off to have lunch or straight home to pack for the break.

"It's funny," Conor said as he and I headed downstairs to the cafeteria for lunch. "Out of the four billion people on earth, everyone in our class must be in at least the most fortunate two-tenths of one percent. But we figure if this school were ranked first or second instead of ninth, we'd be in the top *one*-tenth of one percent, so we're all pissed off."

He adjusted his glasses. "That's MBAs," he said. "Always wanting more."

SPRING TERM

Purgatorio

SIXTEEN

Spring Term Overture: Sing Like a Cuckoo

It had been cold and rainy when I left Stanford during the third week in March, after winter term finals, but when my plane from Washington landed back at San Francisco International the afternoon of Saturday, April 1, I found myself peeling off my sweater and fumbling in my carryon bag for my sunglasses. The temperature was in the mid-seventies. The sky was cloudless. The weather would stay that way all term.

Back at the house, Joe was in the driveway engaged in a rite of spring, washing his car. Joe, the clean freak. He waved to me with a hand in a Playtex rubber glove, then gave me a cheerful squirt of the hose. Philippe was lying on the back porch taking the sun. As I lugged my bags past him he tilted his Ray-Bans back on his head. He sighed theatrically, then uttered a single word. "Bliss."

I threw my bags in my room, changed into a swimsuit, slipped out to the back porch, slathered a squirt of Philippe's suntan oil onto my shoulders and face, and climbed into the hot tub. When classes began the next morning I would have to start work on one elective, the History of U.S. Business, and four core courses, Macroeconomics, Strategic Management, Business in the Changing Environment, and Marketing. But that could wait. The sun was out. I had a job. And if I could get a passing grade in Finance, which I had, then business school held no more fears. After a few minutes Philippe went into the kitchen and came out with a bottle of California Chardonnay for the three of us to split. That night I wrote:

April 1

This term will be different. I feel it. I know it. Stanford will be a warmer and sunnier place, of course, but it will also be a different and a better place, a place that reflects the deepest understandings of the mystics and poets about spring as time of rebirth and re-creation. Grim worries about grades—Begone! Ceaseless, gnawing fears about finding a job—Off with you! It is spring, the world is young and new, and with the ancient Anglo-Saxon poet I sing,

> *Sumer is icumen in,*
> *Lhude sing, cuckoo!*

Looking back, I see that I was being an April fool, as completely carried away as I had been when the sun came out for a couple of weeks during the winter. But I still think that singing was a fitting response to spring term. Now my classmates and I were indeed in a different and a better place. We had moved, in effect, out of hell. We had come through. We were saved.

What I failed to appreciate was that we had not proceeded directly to heaven.

SEVENTEEN

Managing Strategic Management: Starve Problems, Feed Opportunities

We were, of course, in purgatory, a last purification, where core courses remained core courses. Consider Macroeconomics and Strategic Management.

Macroeconomics, or Macro, met on Tuesdays and Thursdays at 8:00 in the morning and was taught by Professor Joseph Rogerson, a short young man with a beard and the bland, quiet manner of a greeter at a funeral home. While Micro had dealt with the economics of individual firms, Macro concerned itself with the economics of entire nations, and Rogerson spent the full ten weeks of the term building one gigantic, mathemetical model of the economy of the United States. The only person who could conceivably have put this model to any use was the Chairman of the Federal Reserve. Replacing Alan Greenspan was not a job any of us was likely to get.

In a typical class Rogerson spent the period droning out accounting identities. The gross national product equals consumption plus investment plus government expenditures plus the surplus of exports minus imports. Net investment equals savings plus the surplus of tax receipts over government expenditures plus the surplus of exports over imports.

Remaining even minimally alert through an hour and fifty minutes of this would have been difficult at any time of day. First thing in the morning, it was out of the question. Uninspired though he was, however, Rogerson of Macro proved a sprightly and engaging instructor compared to Harold Morris of Strategic Management. Morris was so boring and ineffectual that you loathed him. Yet at the same time he was so pathetic, so clearly a well-intentioned, fundamentally decent person who had somehow or other ended up in a job that he just could not do, that you loathed yourself for loathing him. This, of course, made you loathe him more.

"Students in the past have complained that they couldn't hear me in the back row," Professor Morris began on the first day. In his early forties, he was short and heavy. He had shaggy, mousy hair. "But this is as loudly as I can speak without straining." Morris looked sheepish. "I know. I've tried to speak louder. But I always end up going hoarse." In the third row, Joe and I exchanged glances. We could barely make him out.

The course materials Morris had assembled proved so vague that I found myself struggling simply to understand what Strategic Management *was*. The purpose of the course, Morris's syllabus stated, was to "gain insight into the ways that firms respond to changing competitive conditions and the things that managers can do to guide the firms through those changes." "Changing competitive conditions" and "things that managers can do" were in one way or another the subject of every course the business school offered.

The assigned readings contributed to this sense of a subject that didn't know what it was. One article, entitled "Crafting Strategy," argued that executives should develop their business strategy the way potters crafted clay, abandoning conscious, analytical thought in favor of feel and intuition. The very next reading, an essay called "Economic Analysis and Strategic Management," suggested instead that business strategy required such supremely sophisticated analysis that it could only be discussed in technical jargon. "This . . . endeavor," the article began, "will involve mining the emerging economic theory of internal organization for normative propositions of practical import to those concerned with organizational design and 'efficient boundary' issues." I read that sentence two or three times, scratching my head.

After devoting the first several classes to meandering lectures, in the fourth class Morris surprised us, holding up a fishbowl that contained a slip of paper for each of the study groups we had formed. Morris drew one of the slips, then blandly asked the study group it named to present the day's case, the first of the term. The three students in the group, clearly stunned, fumbled as they pulled together their notes, then made their way down the steps to the teaching well. Morris took a seat at the side of the room.

Melanie, one of the study group members, asked, "Um, how long would you like us to present?"

Morris smiled. "Take as long as you'd like."

As long as you'd like turned into nearly three quarters of an hour.

The three students merely recapitulated the case, even though everyone in the room had already read it in detail. Two of the students, Melanie, an articulate but shy woman, and Lee, a jock, shuffled and stomped, embarrassed. The third was a brash former computer salesman named Drew Fisher ("Call me Fish") who kept talking, unable to resist the opportunity to take over as the star of this little scene. For one long stretch he slipped into a parody of an anchorman.

"Good point there, Lee," Fish would say. "And now, Melanie, back to you."

Twenty minutes into it we could all see that nothing was taking place but a waste of time. "Am I paying tuition to be taught by that jackass Fisher?" Joe said under his breath. Morris simply sat at the side of the room smiling.

Not that the students in the study group were stupid. The case was difficult. It concerned a metal tools company called Cleveland Twist Drill, "a firm in a declining industry that is attempting to restore its competitive capabilities." Jim Bartlett, the company's new president, had replaced virtually all the company's department heads and cut back drastically on the product line. But he was convinced that in order to operate Cleveland Twist Drill profitably, he still needed to reduce his labor costs. The central question: Should

Bartlett try to persuade his Cleveland workers to make pay concessions, or should he move production out of the Midwest to regions of the country where labor costs were lower?

The case went into great detail about working conditions, the various personalities in management, the unions involved, and the company history. It ended with exhibits, including a couple of pages of financial data, an internal memo, and several organization charts. You could read both the case and the assigned readings ten times and still have no idea what Bartlett and Cleveland Twist Drill should do. Apparently Melanie, Lee, and Fish had made the same decision about the case that my own study group had made: Sit back and wait for the professor to give you the hang of it. Who could have guessed that it was the professor who would be sitting back?

Lee and Melanie soon began glancing nervously over at Morris. "Take your time," Morris said mildly. This only encouraged Fish, who had actually begun to copy Cleveland Twist Drill organization charts from the back of the case to the chalkboard. After some forty minutes Morris at last stood, walked over to Fish and his group, and stood rubbing his hands, evidently intending to suggest by standing there that Fish should turn the class back over to him. It was a couple of minutes before Fish even noticed him.

"Well, Fish," Morris said, "what conclusions did your group reach?"

"Conclusion?" Fish said in mock surprise. "I was amazed we got through the financials and org charts."

Morris maintained an even smile. "Did anyone in the group reach a conclusion?" he asked. "Lee? Melanie?"

"I did, sort of," Melanie answered. "I think the company has an obligation to its workers," she said. The case stated that many of the workers had been with the company for more than twenty-five years. "That means they're older," Melanie said. "It'll be hard for them to find new jobs. Staying in Cleveland just seems the right thing to do."

"That's an understandable point of view," Morris said. "But unless I'm mistaken, Melanie, you're basing your recommendation on ethical considerations rather than business strategy. Can you relate your view to Cleveland Twist Drill's strategic needs?"

Melanie thought for a moment. "Not really," she said.

"Well, it's still early in the term," Morris said.

At this point, there were fewer than twenty minutes left in the class period. So far, no one in the room had learned anything.

"Class, have you read Michael Porter yet?" Morris asked, naming the author of several articles in the syllabus. We hadn't. No Michael Porter readings were assigned until after the midterm. "Really? I must have made a mistake. Well, to anticipate one of the readings, Porter suggests three basic strategies for companies in declining industries."

Morris recounted these strategies. A firm in a declining industry could try to expand its share of the market as its competitors pulled out; redirect its efforts toward segments of the market that were healthy and growing rather than dying; or simply exit, getting out of the industry altogether.

This seemed interesting enough. But although the class period now had not much more than five minutes remaining, Morris still hadn't applied any strategic concepts to the case. Should Cleveland Twist Drill stay in Cleveland?

"The case gives the impression of Jim Bartlett as a meticulous planner," Morris said, "and this would relate to the Vancil reading." The Vancil article had noted that during stable periods businesses tended to build up elaborate systems of control. "But while you need control systems during stable periods, these can become the very things that suppress change in a period of discontinuity or crisis, like the one Cleveland Twist Drill was facing. Here's where Mintzberg comes in."

Mintzberg was the author who had compared running big companies to making clay pots. We had two minutes to go. "To some extent, this is the way Bartlett is operating in the case," Morris said. "He's intuitive. He's making up his strategy as he goes along.

"This will be a big issue for you as managers when you leave this school," Morris said. By now Morris had been speaking for several minutes on end and his voice had grown raspy. But even as it became harder to hear him, we were all hoping he would get to the point. The whole classroom was leaning forward. In the back row, people were cupping their hands to their ears. It was like the family of a dying man straining to hear his last words.

"The balance," Morris continued, "between Vancil's strategy of stability and Mintzberg's emergent, organic strategy—this is really the central issue of the case, and it's one you'll be dealing with all your working lives. Tight versus loose. Analytical versus intuitive. Neither one alone is enough. So what I'm saying here, class, is that you'll need to learn how to use both sides of your brain. That's all for today."

By now the class period had been over for three minutes. Students began to collect their papers and stuff their notebooks into their backpacks, exchanging looks and rolling their eyes. "What happened?" Melanie suddenly asked. Then she nearly shouted, "What happened to Cleveland Twist Drill?"

Morris looked startled. "The Cleveland workers voted against giving Bartlett pay concessions," he said. "So Bartlett went ahead with the plan to shift production to sites in Rhode Island, Kentucky, and North Carolina."

"And?" Melanie asked. Students were on their feet and leaving now.

"And what?" Morris asked, perplexed.

"Did it work? Did the company pull through?"

"No," Morris answered. Even after shifting production out of Cleveland, Cleveland Twist Drill was losing $10 million a year. Bartlett was only able to save the company by entering a joint venture with a German firm to produce specialized carbide products. "As a producer of tools made out of steel," Morris said, "Cleveland Twist Drill never really made it."

As we walked out together, Joe looked disgusted. "What was that all about? 'Tight versus loose?' Where did they *find* this guy?"

All Morris's classes were dismal. One afternoon it got so bad that a market developed in the couple of copies of the *Wall Street Journal,* *The New Republic,* and *National Review* that students happened to have brought to class in their book bags. I mean a market, literally. I myself paid 75¢ to read *National Review* while Morris lectured, then sold the magazine for a nickel profit.

No one loathed Morris more than Joe. There were a couple of reasons for this. One was that Joe wanted to learn something about strategic management. "This is the first time at this school I've felt we had the chance to think about more than this or that accounting issue, you know?" Joe said. "If the course were well taught, we could be learning how a company should position itself against its competitors, how it should decide what new products to invest in, stuff like that. Big stuff. But this guy Morris is wrecking it for us."

The other reason was money. Joe divided the number of classes we would have during our two years at Stanford into the cost of attending the school (he followed the Yeager formula, adding the price of tuition to the amount he would have made if he had stayed at his job as a banker). Joe concluded that every class cost him a couple of hundred bucks. Over the course of the term, Joe figured, Morris was throwing away more than $3,000 of Joe's money. The evening Joe figured this out, he had to go lie down.

Joe and others lodged protests. It did no good. "Incredible," Joe said after one appointment. "Slowacki told me Morris was working with a teaching coach. He said we should be patient." Yet a term only lasted ten weeks, and this term, already four weeks old, would be our sole exposure to the whole subject of strategic management during our two years at business school. "A few more weeks and we'll all be gone for the summer," Joe said. "The deans are just waiting us out."

By the middle of the term Morris's classroom pattern became invariable. Twenty minutes for Morris to apologize for the last class, half an hour or more for a study group to flounder in presenting a case, then the remainder of the period for Morris's own inaudible, useless summing-up. On any day a third or more of the students would crowd outside the classroom door at the beginning of the period, listening in intent silence. When Morris pulled a slip of paper from the fishbowl, those in the unlucky study group would enter the room groaning while the rest of us would offer a muffled cheer before stampeding off.

Joe grew frantic. Then he hit on a plan. It came to him in looking over the syllabus for a Strategic Management class taught by another professor. This syllabus was in lucid English, and on one page it reprinted a maxim of the famous management expert, Peter Drucker. "Starve problems, feed opportunities."

"When I read that," Joe said, "I asked myself, 'Why waste time on talking to deans who aren't going to do anything, or on going to classes where you aren't going to learn anything?'" Joe took the syllabus to a photocopying shop in downtown Palo Alto and made two complete, crisp copies, one for him and one for me. Then he arranged for friends in the other section to keep us supplied with class notes. From then on, whenever Joe and I did attend Morris's class, it was only to sit in the back row and catch up on our reading for the other class.

"Starve problems, feed opportunities." Joe and I both copied this out and thumbtacked it to the wall over our desks. Morris had taught us one strategy.

EIGHTEEN

Cold-Called

I had never set eyes on Reed Dawson, the instructor who taught Marketing, until I attended the first class. But I had heard about him all year long. All of us had.

"Dawson is one of the two or three best teachers at the school," one second-year had told me. "Dawson is nothing but a showman," another had said.

Dawson was listed in the faculty guide as a lecturer, indicating that he was not on the track to a tenured position. Most lecturers at the school were retired businessmen, as I've noted. Marvin Lieberman, who taught a second-year elective on entrepreneurship, had made huge sums in a cable TV venture. Gordon Damer, who taught the second-year real estate course, had made millions developing Irvine, south of Los Angeles. But Dawson had had no previous career in business. He was an academic still in his middle thirties. Teaching *was* his career.

"He came up for tenure a couple of years ago, but the faculty turned him down," Joe had said during one of our late-night coffee breaks during the winter term. The reason, as Joe had gotten it from second-years, was that Dawson had produced too little research. Even now Dawson still had only a couple of articles listed under his name in the faculty guide. "But word is that it was his style, too.

Dawson is too flashy to fit in with the faculty members who like to think of themselves as real scholars."

At first, the rumor went, everyone had assumed that Dawson would only remain at the school until he found a new job at another, less prominent institution, the usual pattern for a professor turned down for tenure. But then Dawson and the school had come to an arrangement. Dawson had gotten to stay, and the school had gotten a teacher who could teach. "In the classroom," Joe said, "there's supposed to be nobody like him." It only added to his legend that Dawson had grown up in Texas and looked like a young Clint Eastwood. He was Stanford business school's handsome, driven man from nowhere, the cowboy who rode into town.

Dawson's mystique made me skeptical, and I inclined toward the view that Dawson was probably a skilled performer and not much more, a huckster who got away with his act only because his Stanford audience was starved for anything that could pass as sprightly or animated teaching.

My attitude toward Dawson in turn reflected my attitude toward his subject. Marketing? The notion summoned to mind images of carnival barkers and Fuller brush salesmen. Marketing was seamy. Marketing meant looking slick, talking fast, selling people items they didn't need or want. I assumed that Dawson would devote the course to this underside of capitalism, teaching us, essentially, how to manipulate people.

By the end of the first class, I knew that I had been wrong about Dawson and Marketing both.

Dawson dedicated the first class to the history of Pringles potato chips, one of scores of products made by the giant consumer goods company, Procter & Gamble. "Class," Dawson said, speaking in a rapid twang and wearing a look of intense concentration, "first you need to understand that there just never was a company that was bigger or smarter than P&G."

In the 1960s P&G assigned some of its best talent to a study of the potato chip business. The P&G team found that since potato chips were difficult to ship and spoiled quickly, even the biggest potato chip companies, such as Wise and Lay's, were actually made up of loose networks of small factories with their own fleets of delivery trucks. No firm had achieved a genuinely national scale.

Because P&G's established markets, largely in soaps, were already saturated, the company was eager to expand into snack foods. So in 1968, P&G introduced Pringles.

"Pringles were perfect, rayht?" Dawson said. "To make Pringles you cooked potatoes in a vat, just the way you made soap. Then you packaged the Pringles in crush-proof cylinders and treated them with preservatives so they never went stale. Pringles could be shipped from one factory anywhere in the country. Class, it was brilliant."

Except for one problem. Pringles didn't sell.

"Now, class," Dawson said, "in order to figure out what one of the biggest, most successful companies in the world was getting wrong here, let's do some thinking about potato chips ourselves."

Dawson began to dart up and down the aisles, peppering students with questions. "Why do people buy potato chips? Why do *you* buy potato chips?"

One student answered, "For the crunch."

There was laughter. Dawson cut it off. "Class, we're talking about potato chips, not nuclear physics. Crunch is a good answer." He went on to other students, dashing from them to the board, listing potato chip characteristics as students named them. "The crinkle sound of opening the bag." "The surprise of pulling a different size and shape of chip out of the bag every time." "The salty, greasy flavor." "Goes great with soda."

As Dawson continued his questioning, I suddenly realized he was calling on each student by name even though he hadn't asked us to use name cards. By the end of the period, Dawson had called on at least half the class, making it clear that he had used the student handbook to memorize every face and name. I could understand how some students might see this as a gimmick or showman's trick. But it made a point—if Dawson took the class that seriously, so should we—and I was impressed.

"Flavor, crunch, crinkle," Dawson said, reading from the board.

"Now, would I be wrong to suggest that a big part of what people enjoy about eating potato chips is that they're *fun?*"

P&G had missed this very point, Dawson argued. Why? Because P&G was concentrating on its own problem, the need for a new product that would exploit the company's manufacturing and marketing strengths, rather than on customers' desires. In later research, P&G learned that Pringles were popular with just one group, old people. Senior citizens were the only citizens interested in potato chips that would keep for months, perhaps because they wanted chips that would remain fresh, if that is the word, between visits from the grandkids. Every other kind of consumer had in effect told P&G's focus group that Pringles took the fun out of chips. (With their perfect sameness, one respondent supposedly said, "Pringles look like potato chips designed by Nazis.") P&G finally resorted to a second, much more modest marketing plan that positioned Pringles as a specialty product.

"Write this down, class," Dawson said, ending the first session. "Good marketing is driven by value delivery. First you learn exactly what customers value. Then you work to deliver just that."

So the man I'd thought would be a huckster took pains to stress that Marketing was not huckstering. Talking about potato chips might not involve the intricacies of Accounting or the sophisticated mathematics of Finance, but I liked it all the more for that. It gave me the feeling that business school was finally getting down to *business*, leaving behind dry theory to move closer to the working world where people made products and sold them.

My humiliation took place in the very next class, a session devoted to a case entitled "Southwest Airlines."

Southwest, the case explained, had been founded in 1967 by Rollin King, a graduate of Harvard Business School. Living in Texas as a financial advisor, King had become convinced of the need for better air service on the triangle of routes between Houston, San Antonio, and Dallas–Fort Worth. The region was growing. Houston already had a population of nearly two million, Dallas of one and a half million, Fort Worth of half a million, and San Antonio of

800,000. Two carriers, Braniff and Texas International, served the triangle, both, in King's view, poorly.

Braniff and TI had huge route structures—Braniff covered most of the Western Hemisphere, while TI had routes in nine Southwestern states and Mexico—and were accordingly geared to long flights, not hops like those between Texas destinations. The Texas leg of a Braniff flight, for instance, could be delayed by a thunderstorm in New York. Getting reservations on Braniff or TI was often difficult. Both were known to cancel flights on short notice, Braniff so often that Texas customers called it the world's biggest unscheduled airline.

King got financial backing and took the big airlines on. He bought airplanes at a discount from Boeing. He devised a campaign touting Southwest as a fun, local airline, dressing his stewardesses in pink miniskirts and running ads that used love as their theme (remember, this was still the 1960s). "Love Can Change Your Ways," one ad proclaimed. "The 48-Minute Love Affair," read another. And King priced his tickets at just $20, undercutting Braniff and TI, which both charged $27 on the Dallas to Houston run and $28 to fly from Dallas to San Antonio.

Passengers flocked to Southwest. But the airline still lost money. As the case closed, Braniff had just announced a two-month, half-price sale on tickets from Dallas to Houston, Southwest's only profitable route, a move clearly intended to cripple Southwest. What should Rollin King do?

My study group included two poets, myself and Conor, and two non-poets, Jennifer Taylor and a serious, articulate woman named Sarah. Conor and I decided to let Jennifer and Sarah do most of the work on cases until he and I got the hang of it ourselves (not, I admit, that we mentioned this to Jennifer and Sarah). Marketing cases were just too important to risk letting poets like Conor and me mess them up. Case discussions, Dawson's syllabus stated, would account for a full 40 percent of our grade. And if a study group was badly prepared for even one case, *"the group will fail class participation for the entire course."* The italics were Dawson's own.

We met in the library just after dinner. Jennifer and Sarah analyzed the financial numbers in the case in considerable detail, tapping away on their calculators while Conor and I took notes. When the library closed four hours later, Sarah and Jennifer had decided merely that Southwest should cut its own fare to meet the Braniff sale price. After that, Southwest could only await Braniff's next move. Jennifer and Sarah did have one other thought. They considered Southwest's advertising sexist. The airline should drop love as its theme, they believed, and stress its local, Texas flavor, dressing the stewardesses as sober cowgirls rather than indecent go-go dancers.

Dawson began the class the next morning by setting up a laptop computer on a desk in the teaching well. Then he attached the computer to a device that projected the computer monitor onto a big screen at the front of the room.

He flicked a switch. A list of names appeared on the screen. Among them, I was alarmed to see, was "Robinson, P." Dawson had instructed each study group to give him a list of its members at the end of the last class, and Jennifer had apparently put me down as group leader.

"Class," Dawson said, "this is a high-tech cold call." The program on the computer, he explained, was a randomness generator, in effect an electronic wheel of fortune. "Here goes," he said.

An arrow appeared on the screen and began running quickly down the column of names, accompanied by loud blips. As the arrow began to slow the blips changed to ticks, ticking, ever more slowly, name by name by name. The room erupted. "No, not me!" "Keep ticking, baby!" "Next name, go on to the next name!" With a final tick, the arrow came to a halt. It pointed at "Robinson, P." My classmates burst into an ovation, overwhelmed with relief at seeing someone other than themselves get what was perhaps the most dramatic cold call of the entire year. I felt too stunned to speak.

"Congratulations, Peter," Dawson said when the applause died down. "You win. But before you take us through the case, there's someone I want you to meet. Rollin?"

At this a big, well-dressed man in his late fifties descended the stairs from the back of the room. He joined Dawson in the teaching well. He was wearing cowboy boots.

"Class," Dawson said, "meet Rollin King, the founder of Southwest Airlines. Rollin will be helping us discuss the case."

My classmates burst into a second ovation, laced, this time, with laughter. The first had expressed their pleasure at escaping a cold call. Now it was clear that they had escaped something much worse, an event as grisly as an *auto-da-fé* or public beheading. I, who knew nothing, would have to undergo an examination by Rollin King, the central character in the case, who knew everything. My classmates could scarcely contain themselves. I was the victim. They were not.

Quite why, I do not know—nerves perhaps. But I opened with a joke.

"Mr. King, my study group decided that this case was simple. You should have sold your planes and gotten out of business as fast as you could."

Then I added, "Just kidding."

This elicited yet another round of laughter and applause, and I realized that the scene had taken on the dynamics of an eighteenth-century British hanging. The rabble was indeed eager for me to die, but in the meantime they would cheer me for any show of defiance. Dawson and King for their part made fine executioners. Neither so much as smiled. I reddened. Then, recovering, I played shamelessly to the crowd.

"But to be serious, we concluded that Mr. King had made his biggest mistake a long time before he even launched the airline."

"Now what was that?" King asked. He had a husky, no-nonsense voice. "I analyzed the market wrong?"

"No, Mr. King," I answered. "You went to Harvard Business School instead of Stanford."

The rabble rewarded me with a sustained round of hoots and applause. But now Dawson and King looked annoyed.

"Peter," Dawson said, "we're attempting to discuss a case. Do you have anything to say?"

Thus began the most excruciating hour of my life at Stanford.

I tried to explain the simple conclusions that our group had drawn, but Dawson and King kept interrupting, drawing me out, demanding analysis, presenting entirely new questions of their own.

"Southwest figured it would break even on each flight at $20 per ticket and thirty-nine passengers per flight," Dawson said at one point. "Did you check that assumption?"

I had no memory, either of the assumption itself or of whether we had checked it. But before I could panic, Jennifer slipped me a note. "Yes we did," I read, attempting to make my answer look spontaneous. "The numbers worked. Thirty-nine passengers at $20 each would have been break-even."

"But you're only telling me that you checked my math," King added, growling. "I already know I can add. Reed asked about our *assumption*. Was it reasonable for us to think that we could *get* thirty-nine passengers on every one of our flights? What kind of market share would that have implied?"

I stalled, waiting for another slip of paper from Jennifer or Sarah. None appeared. I furrowed my brow, pretending to think. Still no paper. Blushing like a grade-schooler, I admitted that these were numbers we hadn't run.

"What?" Dawson said, affecting incredulity. "You didn't run the numbers? But, Peter, this is *business* school. This institution is *about* running numbers. You and your group had better run the numbers right now. The rest of us will wait."

I reddened yet again, then turned to my group. Jennifer already had her calculator out. There was a tense silence in the room while Jennifer and Sarah wrote down a set of numbers and explained them to me in a whisper. I turned back to Dawson and King.

I said that on the Dallas to Houston route, to name one of the three, the average number of passengers each day came to 1,334. Southwest intended to operate 24 flights a day, one every hour on the hour. Twenty-four flights times 39 passengers per flight meant that to break even on that route, Southwest needed to attract 936 passengers a day, or 70 percent of the entire market.

"Now that you've finally given us the numbers," Dawson said, "can you tell us what they mean to Rollin and his airline?"

"I guess I'd say that we're not just talking about running a third airline," I answered haltingly. "Southwest either has to expand the market pretty dramatically or put at least one of its competitors out of business."

"Expand the market or wipe out a competitor," Dawson repeated. "Thank you, Peter. We're starting to get somewhere."

Dawson pressed on, forcing me to deal with one topic after another. When Dawson had me address advertising, King bristled at my suggestion that his ads were sexist.

"Stop right there," King said. "We're talking about Texas businessmen in the 1960s, not Stanford feminists two decades later."

Most of the women and quite a few of the men in the classroom hissed.

"You don't have to like it," King said. "But those businessmen enjoyed a little fun in the air. And our girls were just one hell of a whole lot younger and prettier than those old gals on Braniff and TI."

More hisses, many groans. Dawson moved the discussion on, asking me what our group had concluded about market segmentation.

I fumbled around. We'd talked some in the study group about the two basic kinds of airline customers, business travelers and passengers who traveled for pleasure, mostly retired couples and families with children. But even Sarah hadn't been able to work out any way for Southwest to be able to take advantage of the difference between these two kinds of travelers. Dawson acted astonished.

"But, Peter, it's so simple. What does the business traveler want?"

I'd been reduced by now to putting my answers in the form of meek questions. "To get where he's going on time, maybe with some chance for relaxation?"

"And those traveling for pleasure?" Dawson asked. "The tourists? What do they want?"

"They want to get where they're going on time, too, don't they?"

"But I'm asking how tourists and business travelers are *different*. Let me put it this way. What is a family with three children on its way to visit the grandparents in Houston concerned about that an executive flying to Houston to close a deal isn't?"

I froze, as paralyzed as I'd been during my second interview with

McKinsey. Dawson simply observed me for a moment. Then he threw me a prompt.

"Remember, Peter. The executive put the fare on an expense account. The husband and father of three pays for it himself."

I hung my head. "Money," I said. "It's so obvious. Tourists want to save money."

Dawson led me on through the rest of the case in a manner that would take too long and prove entirely too painful for me to recount here. Every time he steered me to an important insight or a correct answer, the answer seemed so obvious that only an idiot could have failed to see it in the first place. So there it was: I felt like an idiot. Yet I felt something else, too, a sense of excitement, even exhilaration. Dawson's teaching technique may have been painful, yet he was not applying this technique to an absurd word problem, like ordering flour for the Bulldog Baking Company, but to an actual instance of the drama of business life. And the man it had all happened to was standing in the teaching well beside him, a big, brash, rich Texan who had founded an entire airline.

After an hour of grilling me, Dawson had forced me to admit that Southwest Airlines was facing a crisis our study group could not present any plan to forestall. The airline had already attracted all the passengers it could reasonably hope to get but was still losing money. Braniff was about to turn the plucky little upstart into a squashed little memory.

"Maybe Southwest really should have sold its planes and gone out of business," I said weakly.

Dawson turned to King. "Rollin, help Peter out. Tell him what you actually did." King picked up the control of a slide projector and asked a student at the back of the room to dim the lights.

"We did give a few hours' thought to closing the operation and selling off the planes," King said. "But my managers and I decided that we were just better than the other guys." He paused for a husky chuckle. "So we fought 'em."

Southwest quickly moved to segment the business and pleasure markets, offering cut-rate tickets after 8:00 P.M. and on Saturdays.

The airline filled these flights to capacity. Then Southwest launched an all-out war on Braniff.

Southwest met Braniff's reduced fare and opened a massive advertising campaign, taking out full pages in all the San Antonio, Houston, Dallas, and Fort Worth newspapers. King flashed a slide of the newspaper ad on the screen. "Nobody's Going to Shoot Southwest Airlines out of the Sky for a Lousy $13," the headline read. The copy explained that Braniff was engaging in predatory pricing, baldly trying to force Southwest out of business, and that Southwest was responding by giving passengers two choices. They could pay Southwest $13 on the Dallas to Houston flight, the same fare they would pay if they bought a cut-rate Braniff ticket. Or they could pay Southwest's full fare of $26 and receive a gift as a token of Southwest's appreciation. The ad concluded, "Remember What It Was Like Before Southwest Airlines?"

The ads led to media attention that amounted in turn to hundreds of thousands of dollars' worth of free advertising. "We had pro-Southwest editorials in all the local papers," King said. "There were cartoons like this."

King clicked his control and a newspaper cartoon appeared on the screen showing ducks, crows, and eagles, climbing the ramp to enter a Southwest jet. One startled stewardess was saying to another. "I think they've decided it's cheaper to ride."

For the sixty days that its cut-rate offer lasted, Braniff lost money hand-over-fist. "We lost money, too," King said, "but not as much, because most of our customers went ahead and paid the $26 fare." The gift Southwest gave each of its full-fare passengers was a small bottle of Chivas Regal. "The Chivas people told us that during those two months, Southwest Airlines was the biggest whiskey distributor in the world."

When Braniff raised its fare back to $26 at the end of two months, Southwest was even stronger than it had been beforehand. "We'd generated goodwill," King said. "We'd expanded our market the way we'd needed to. And the crisis with Braniff had made us *think*."

King explained that he and his managers had reviewed every aspect of Southwest's operations, then organized the airline as a "value de-livery system" based on four principles.

First, simplicity. Southwest owned only one kind of aircraft and used only one maintenance facility. It offered no food service. Southwest didn't even transfer bags to other airlines. And it refused to purchase a computerized reservation system. "We just had our gals set up cash registers at the departure gates."

Second, high productivity. Every one of Southwest's planes was in the air an average of eleven hours in every twenty-four. Between most flights, the airline had a turnaround time of ten minutes.

Third, concentrating only on passenger business. Southwest re-jected all overtures from freight forwarders and never even considered trying to win a contract with the U.S. Postal Service. "Get a real vivid picture in your mind of what it was like the last time you waited in line at a post office to buy stamps," King said. "Now try to imagine what it would be like to do *business* with that group."

Fourth and last, sticking with one kind of market, the short-haul, mass-transit market, with flight segments of two hours or less. "We knew how to operate so well in that kind of market, we could even keep competitive with bus and auto travel."

King turned off the slide projector and asked for the lights. "Y'all might be interested to hear what's happened to our little airline since this case," he said. Southwest Airlines had expanded into short-haul markets across the western United States. It now owned eighty-five aircraft and serviced thirty cities. Its stock was listed on the New York Stock Exchange. In the next year or two, Southwest's annual revenues would top a billion dollars.

King concluded on a note of pure triumph.

"One more thing," he said. "Braniff is out of business." The class gave King a standing ovation.

A rich man being applauded by business school students isn't a surprising spectacle, of course. But I don't think it was just that King had built a company and gotten rich that mattered to the class. It was *how.* Here was a man who had quit a staid career as an investment advisor, taken on established, gigantic airlines, and then broken them. King hadn't relied on some brilliant financial analysis or shaped his enterprise according to academic business theory. It wasn't even clear that he could have if he'd tried. (When Dawson finished examining me, he asked other groups to offer their own solutions to the case. Not one was able to present a plan that consorted well with the numbers.) King's real solution?

"Guts," Dawson said, ending the session. "Sometimes, class, that's what it takes."

NINETEEN

The Intellectual Life of the Baby Wolverine

Far as I'm concerned," Professor Healey said, "the name of the course shouldn't be Business in the Changing Environment. It should be Business *Schools* in the Changing Environment."

Business in the Changing Environment, a core course, was divided into two segments. The first six weeks were devoted to the interplay between business and government, the last four weeks to ethics. I could see how the government part made sense. In recent decades doing business in America had come to include doing business with regulators and legislators, so MBAs needed to know how government worked. But just how a month of ethics had worked its way into the curriculum puzzled me. So I had stopped by his office to ask Healey, who would be teaching my section of the course.

"Remember that the faculty at this business school goes to cocktail parties with the faculty from the rest of the university," Healey said, reaching for a match to light his pipe. "In the early eighties, the faculty here started getting snotty comments about how they were contributing to greed on Wall Street and training modern-day pirates and buccaneers. After a while it got hard to laugh off. So the faculty said, 'Hey, let's just put an ethics unit in the curriculum. That'll shut everybody up.' " Ethics was added to the core curriculum in 1985.

Healey added tobacco to his pipe and tamped it with his thumb, then struck another match. "Not that you can teach much ethics in just four weeks," he said. He puffed. "Come to think of it, not that you can teach much political science in six."

Healey devoted the first class to public opinion about business. "You may think of the press as high-minded, altruistic servants of the public's right to know," Healey began. "I'm here to tell you that newspapers and TV stations are for-profit organizations, every bit as much as any oil company or defense contractor."

Conor and I had both dealt with the press, and we saw Healey's comments as elementary, all but obvious. "But I'm telling you," Conor said the next day, "there's talk that Healey's cynical." Conor had heard Everett Adams, the classmate who had recruited students to write an outline of Organizational Behavior, say that he was shocked. In the next class, Everett confronted Healey directly.

Healey began the next class by passing out a note on interest groups. "An interest group," the note read in part,

> would be expected to form among individuals and organizations with aligned interests when the benefits from collective action exceed the anticipated costs of organizing and implementing that action.

"In other words," Healey said "when people get involved in the kinds of hard-fought, expensive political battles that are required to get legislation through Congress, they're not usually motivated by altruism. They've done some figuring. They've decided the benefits of the fight will outweigh the costs."

Healey then turned to a case, "Detroit versus Washington," about a push by environmentalists to get Congress to enact tough automobile emission standards. The Big Three auto manufacturers, Chrysler, Ford, and GM, opposed the legislation, claiming it would make their cars less powerful and more expensive. The environmentalists and the press called the validity of these claims into serious question. But it didn't matter Congressman John Dingell was chairman of the relevant committee in the House of Representatives, and in Dingell's Michigan district, car manufacturers were important employers. The quip on Capitol Hill had it that Dingell was "the congressman from General Motors." Dingell blocked the legislation.

"The environmentalists," Healey said, "were taking a stand on behalf of the diffuse, general interest in clean air. But that's just not much of an organizing principle compared to the millions of dollars at stake for the Big Three or the votes at stake for Congressman Dingell."

Everett Adams raised his hand. "Professor, I just have to say that I find your attitude very disturbing." He spoke with emotion, visibly upset. "You're teaching a cynical view of government. I mean, what about ideals?"

"Two answers to that," Healey said. He began calmly. "The first is that you can define costs and benefits to include high ideals."

Some people might find that the mere existence of a social ill, such as pollution or corruption, made them so angry that it imposed a tangible cost upon them. If they succeeded in getting the government to correct the ill, cleaning up the pollution or corruption, they might feel a sense of satisfaction so powerful that it amounted to a genuine benefit. "So, sure," Healey said, "Ideals can have a big place in this model, if you take psychological costs and benefits into account.

"And you're entitled to do that if you want. But what I'm trying to do in this class is teach you the way the system really works, without much comment on whether it's good or bad. And I've got to tell you, Everett, that there's a lot less idealism in government than you might think. That's the second answer."

Healey began to speak with emotion himself, his voice rising. None of us MBAs, he said, would be surprised to see people in business act according to the bottom line. That was the way business worked.

"Well, I want you to consider that possibility that politics has a bottom line. Votes. If you're a politician, when you win enough votes you get to keep your job. When you don't, you're out.

"So how do you win votes?"

Healey paused for a moment, peering from face to face. "I suppose one way is to perform your duties according to high ideals, working for some refined notion of the public interest, then hoping on election day that your constituents will march into the voting booths burning with a sense of truth, justice, and the American way. But the more common technique is to appeal to interest groups that will donate money to your campaign and work to get the voters out on your behalf."

Virtually every union in the country contributed to political campaigns and spent money on lobbyists in Washington and the state capitals. So did virtually every big business.

"So do the American Association of Retired Persons, the American Automobile Association, the American Trucking Associations, and the American Association of name any damn thing you want. Hell, the last figure I saw was that there are more than 2,000 associations with paid reps in Washington. Two *thousand*. That's just part of the game, Everett. Even the Audubon Society and the Sierra Club spend money on politics. That's just the way it is."

"Maybe it is," Everett said. He looked exasperated. He spent a moment searching for words. Then he blurted, "But government ought to be about a whole lot more than just—*politics*."

Healey took a step back, as though he had been kicked. "Just politics?" he repeated. Then Healey exploded. *"Just politics?"*

"It happens that I've devoted my professional life to studying 'just politics,' Everett. I admit I'm just a two-bit academic. I'm stuck here in a university. I'm not bound for glory in the world of deals and big money that awaits Stanford MBAs. But one thing my academic work has given me is a liking for politics. No, let's make that stronger. What I have, Everett, is a *reverence* for politics.

"Imagine a President who ignored politics. Of course, nobody minds that idea as long as he pictures himself as President. But no matter who you are, the chances are very good that the President will always be somebody else.

"Do you want that man—or that woman—just to do whatever he thinks is right? Do you really want the President to ignore interest groups and voters and polls? Suppose the President wants to outlaw the Sierra Club? Or triple taxes? Or take us to war? Do you really want the President and Congress and all those in power in this country to ignore the interests—even the straightforward economic interests—of everybody else?

"The system is messy. Is it corrupt? Yeah, in many ways. But I invite you to show me a system that works better.

"And I'll tell you something else. If the Founding Fathers came back today and saw the mess this government is in, you know what they'd say? They'd say, '*Great!* There are so many checks and balances that debate on every stinking issue goes on forever and the government can barely get a damn thing done. This is *exactly* what we had in mind. Gentlemen, the liberties of the people have been preserved.' "

Healey stopped. He and Everett eyed each other. Then Healey went back to talking about the case.

I glanced around the room. There were students present who could price complicated financial instruments to the penny. Others knew how to construct enormous spreadsheets to determine the net present value of vast, complicated real estate developments with mortgages that would take years to pay down. But give my classmates political analysis one bit more sophisticated than senior high civics, and a lot of them had no idea how to respond. Many simply sat there, staring at Healey.

"I hate this part," Healey told me one morning when he had completed the segment on government and was about to begin the segment on ethics. I'd found him sitting on the steps near the courtyard, taking the sun for a moment before heading off to play tennis. He wore a dirty sweatshirt that sagged at the elbows and a pair of canvas basketball sneakers. He held a cup of coffee in one big-knuckled hand and a pipe in the other.

"This ethics stuff. Either the students at this school have learned right from wrong by this stage in their lives, which I tend to doubt, or they haven't learned right from wrong, and what the frig can I do to fix *that?*" He puffed on his pipe.

"You MBAs. I'm telling you. Did you see Everett Adams in that class on auto emissions? Talk about nigh-frigging-eve. Do MBAs want to learn about politics, or just hold little feel-good seminars on how we should all write to our senators and make the world a better place?"

He sipped his coffee, then took another puff.

"So anyway, in this ethics unit, I take a few philosophers, and in—what is it?—eight classes, I go over three basic ways of making value judgments. That's it. After that, you all go off to Wall Street. It's like trying to give an intellectual life to baby wolverines."

Healey's treatment of ethics proved every bit as cursory as he said it would. He dealt with the utilitarianism of Jeremy Bentham, the rights-based morality of Immanuel Kant, and the modern ethical system devised by the Harvard philosopher John Rawls.

Since what Healey was trying to cram into just eight classes was actually quite a large chunk of Western thought, it's no surprise that it didn't all fit. The way Conor put it was that in the segment on ethics we were like waterbugs, skittering over profound issues "without even breaking the intellectual surface tension." What did surprise me was that to many of my classmates the material was entirely new. This was visible in their faces. There were positive looks of wonderment when Healey held up a copy of John Rawls's massive book, *A Theory of Justice.*

"Don't worry," Healey said, "I'm not going to assign you to read this, although it wouldn't kill you if I did. I just wanted you to see that somebody thought all this stuff on ethics and justice was important enough to write about it for 600 pages. And we're not talking ancient philosophers. John Rawls is still teaching."

John Lyons just looked at the book and shook his head. "Wow," John said. "Some people live in a whole other world."

Which is my point. Stanford did offer MBAs a smattering of philosophy, political science, and history. But these were disciplines that sought to understand for the sake of understanding, not in order to produce. They were a whole other world.

Yet it was the History of U.S. Business that held intellectual life at the business school up to the strongest light. The course was taught by David Font, a middle-aged, bespectacled scholar and a Fellow at the Hoover Institution, the think tank across the street from the business school. In vivid, skillful lectures, Font dealt with the whole sweep of American economic development, from the establishment of the first, tiny, Puritan enterprises of the seventeenth century through the rise of the railroads after the Civil War to the emergence of globe-spanning corporations during the Cold War. Two lectures stood out.

In the first, Font examined the notion of the Puritan or Protestant work ethic, first put forward by the German sociologist Max Weber. Weber held that their belief in predestination led Protestants to practice hard work and frugality in an effort to acquire the worldly goods that would demonstrate they were among the saved or elect. In this way, Weber argued, Protestantism played a central role in the emergence of capitalism. This thesis had held wide currency ever since the publication of Weber's 1904 book, *The Protestant Ethic and the Spirit of Capitalism*. But according to Font, there was a problem.

"On the historical evidence," he said, "the thesis is impossible to sustain."

Where had capitalism first appeared? In the medieval city-states of Catholic Italy. And in Switzerland, a country of both Catholic and Protestant cantons, there was no systematic correlation between the level of prosperity a canton achieved and the religion it practiced.

Weber, Professor Font argued, was mistaken in identifying a specifically Protestant work ethic. "All religions place a high value on work, including Catholicism, Buddhism, and Islam. The important aspect of Protestantism per se is that it was the doctrine of dissenting minorities."

Protestants in seventeenth- and eighteenth-century Europe, Font said, often found themselves discriminated against, being excluded from political life, the professions, and the universities. They turned to trade by default, and with their energies so narrowly focused, they prospered.

The experience of Jews in many ways paralleled that of Protestants. Barred from owning land, confronted with pogroms in Eastern Europe, Jews learned to accumulate wealth in the form of portable materials, including jewels and gold. This in turn put them in a position to act as lenders. In many instances, Jews became the most prominent bankers in a village or town—in the case of the Rothschilds, the most prominent bankers in Europe.

"This tradition remained strong among Jews even in my own youth," Font said. His grandparents, Jews from Eastern Europe, had urged the boy Font to become a doctor or professor, and all his friends on Manhattan's Lower East Side got the same promptings from their parents and grandparents. "Not until many years later did I see that this attitude came straight from the old country. If you had your wealth in your head, no one could take it from you."

Much the same pattern was visible among the overseas Chinese, Font continued. In Vietnam, Singapore, Malaysia, and the United States, the Chinese had found themselves largely excluded from politics and the professions. So they had devoted their energies to business and trade. "Today the overseas Chinese are a potent economic force from Saigon to San Francisco."

Weber was almost as much a part of the ambient American culture as Freud (you're as likely to hear some poor wretch on the "Donahue" show ascribe his woes to the "Protestant work ethic" as to "low self-esteem" or to "neuroses"). But Font gave Weber a drubbing. It was a powerful intellectual performance.

In a later class Font turned to the economist Joseph Schumpeter, whose 1911 book, *The Theory of Economic Development*, made Schumpeter one of the principal figures in capitalist theory. Font himself based his views of economics on those of Schumpeter, and he wanted us to know why.

"As you know from your courses here at the business school," Font said, "most economic models are static." The typical model saw human activity as mechanical and repetitive, always settling at an equilibrium between expenditures and receipts. "The problem," Font said, "is that this bears almost no resemblance to reality."

By contrast, in Schumpeter's view the important events in any economy were sudden and discontinuous, innovations that overturned the settled patterns rather than reconfirming them.

"Here in Silicon Valley," Font said, "you can't drive to the grocery store without seeing two or three high-tech start-ups that weren't there the week before. Is that static equilibrium? Not a chance. It's Schumpeter's process of dynamic change."

Behind the sudden, disruptive innovations stood the entrepreneurs who introduced them. According to the usual models, entrepreneurs only wanted to maximize their profits. "But according to Schumpeter," Font said, "the puny motive of profit maximization barely explains anything at all. Just listen to Schumpeter in this passage." Font picked up a dog-eared book, adjusted his glasses, and read aloud.

"There is the will to conquer, the impulse to fight, to prove oneself superior to others, to succeed for the sake, not of the fruits of success, but of success itself. Finally there is the joy of creating, of getting things done, or simply exercising one's energy and ingenuity.' "

Font set the book down and looked at us. "Capitalism," he said, bringing the class to a close, "is not in my view a matter of counting coins. Capitalism is a romance and an adventure."

Font was a professor whose understanding of business rose above the technical disciplines to acknowledge the existence of the human soul. He was a professor with a view to profess. How did MBA students respond to him? His classroom was often a third or even half empty.

"That's the way it seems to go," Professor Font told me. Year after year, most of the students who took the course were second-years, many of them interested only in cutting classes to enjoy the sunshine during their final term at Stanford. MBAs were in any event a lot more interested in acquiring specific techniques, like cost accounting, than in learning underlying principles or ideas. "Accounting is part and parcel of business practice," Font said. "The works of Max Weber or Joseph Schumpeter belong to a different realm."

A very different realm. A whole other world.

TWENTY

Race and Gender

I'm lonely," Jennifer Taylor said. It was her birthday. I'd taken her out to a business school hangout, the beer and hamburger place called the Oasis, or in the lingo, the O. We sat in a booth with a pitcher of beer and a pizza as a jukebox in the corner played sixties music. At the bar, a group of business school men watched a baseball game on TV. Jennifer had turned twenty-seven. It was the first time I had seen her feeling low.

Jennifer told me that she had broken up with her boyfriend back home in Minnesota almost a year and a half ago. "Don wanted to get married, buy a nice split level in the Minneapolis suburbs, and start a family." But Jennifer was intent on staying in northern California, where she was working for Hewlett-Packard, for another year or two. The weekend after she heard that she had been accepted at Stanford, they had split. Jennifer had started hoping that she would meet someone at business school.

"But you know what? The guys here just aren't into it." Business school men preferred to go out with undergraduates. Even when they did date business school women it was only that, dating. "What MBA men are in love with is their careers."

"But, Jennifer," I said, trying to make her feel better, "there are plenty of men in the world who aren't MBAs."

She shook her head. "I didn't really think about it before I came here," Jennifer said. "But now I think about it a lot. All the women in the business school do. It's like there's this rule. A woman is allowed to marry a man who has more education than she has. But no man wants to marry a woman who has more education than he has, *especially* not a woman who might make more money."

Even prominent feminists took pains to date and marry men who had more money than they did. "Look at Gloria Steinem, the biggest feminist in the world. I read in *People* magazine just the other day that she dates rich guys like big real estate developers. Look at Jane Fonda. She dumped that dweeb political activist, Tom Hayden, to hook up with Ted Turner.

"You could even do a Reed Dawson–style Marketing analysis on it," Jennifer said. She took a sip of beer and imitated Dawson's Texas accent. "I thank we can agree, class, that every time a woman adds a hundred thousand dollars to her likely lifetime earnin's, she decreases the number of men who would be interested in marryin' her by a factor of x. The number of men who would be interested in marryin' Jennifer Taylor, class, is directly and *inversely* related to the fact that Jennifer is gettin' her MBA."

Jennifer had another sip of beer. "Sometimes I think that when I graduate, the only guys who won't feel threatened by my Stanford MBA will be Harvard MBAs."

Women were by no means the only distinct subgroup or minority in our little business school society. There were, as I've already mentioned, the foreigners, the French, the British, the Japanese, and others. There were also thirteen black students.

Everything I say about my black classmates will run the risk of political incorrectness. (Some might argue that I've already made a PC mistake by calling my classmates "black" instead of "African-American." One of the students came from Ghana, however, and was just plain African.) Yet for present purposes, politics—or rather, as we shall see, the absence of politics—is just the point.

The black students were as impressive as anyone in our class. They had gone to superb undergraduate institutions, including Princeton,

Harvard, Yale, Berkeley, and Stanford. Two of the men were medical doctors. Another had been a bank vice president. One of the women had designed computer hardware for Hewlett-Packard. The black students would have succeeded anywhere. They did not need anybody's help.

Yet during the winter term interview season, as students compared their offer and rejection letters it became clear that our black classmates were in more demand than almost anybody else. Judging from the number of offers the black students got, recruiters seemed almost desperate to hire them.

"Tom Sowell's explained the whole phenomenon," Professor Healey said over dumplings at a Chinese restaurant one winter night. Sowell, an economist at the Hoover Institution who was himself black, maintained that while affirmative action did indeed confer advantages on blacks in the work force, it conferred those advantages only on certain blacks. According to the argument, employers knew that if they ever had to fire a black worker they might very well find themselves hauled into court and accused of racism. This placed a premium on hiring only safe blacks, blacks with strong educational backgrounds and good working records that employers could be reasonably certain they would never have to dismiss. The three black women and ten black men at Stanford business school were safe blacks.

I always thought my black classmates had grounds for indignation. They had to contend with a system that patronized them, giving them special treatment they hadn't asked for and didn't need. Yet they dealt with the politics of race by ignoring it. None tried to foster any sense of a separate or aggrieved black community (there was a Black Business Students Association, but it was almost entirely social, not political). The black students were simply thirteen members of a business school class of 333 bright young men and women. They believed with the rest of us that after graduating they'd get interesting jobs, make good money, and eventually rise to positions of influence and prestige. "I'm here to learn as much as I can," one black classmate told me, "enjoy myself whenever I can, and get the best job I can." In other words, to take the same approach to business school as anybody else. When during spring term we elected our class officers, a black man won as president, but his color had nothing to do with it. Students just thought he would do a better job of handling the finances and making sure the student government threw good parties.

Sowell and other economists have argued that where there are opportunities for economic advancement, racial differences tend to become irrelevant. I am not an economist. But I do know that at Stanford business school race just didn't matter very much.

Gender did matter.

"This place is *completely* sexist," Louisa Pellegrino told me during a Saturday night barbecue at the house she shared with Sam Barrett. Even though Louisa was one of the class feminists and I had worked for Reagan, Louisa saw me less as an enemy than as a backward child. While I munched my ribs and she nibbled her tofu, she gave me the feminist critique of Stanford business school.

Feminine values such as cooperation and sensitivity to the needs of others, Louisa believed, held a higher place in the moral order, in and of themselves, than the ravening male values of survival of the fittest and death to everyone else. As she saw it, it was the duty of the business school to promote these feminine values. "Business education should be a civilizing force," she said, "not a throwback to cavemen clubbing each other on the head." Yet clubbing each other on the head was just what we were being taught.

"Take case discussions," Louisa said. "They're like any male game." If one student gave a wrong answer, ten others would raise their hands to show that they had the right answer. "It's all about competition."

Here I objected. "But, Louisa, markets are based on competition."

"Peter," Louisa said, "you're such a Neanderthal. I want the business school to *change* that. Men have been screwing up the world with testosterone-induced aggression long enough. It's time for a little caring and serenity. If you want to put it in biological terms, it's time for a little less testosterone and a little more estrogen. This school has an obligation to bring that new world about."

I'd estimate that about a third of the women at the business school were feminists like Louisa. The feminists suffered. Since they believed the business school should be radically different, the institution as it was never ceased to pain them. But what galled them most, I think, was that few of their classmates took them seriously. It is a heavy burden to place oneself in open rebellion, then go unnoticed.

The other two thirds of the women at Stanford experienced their own kind of suffering.

"The women here all expect a lot of themselves," Jennifer told me at the O. "We all want to be hotshot executives, but alrnost every woman I know here also wants a family." Career and family weren't completely incompatible, of course. But at the same time, just try putting them together.

"Before we start families, we want to get established in our careers first," Jennifer continued. This meant waiting until at least their early thirties to have children.

"Some of us are beginning to think of that as waiting a really long time," Jennifer said. "I admit it, okay? I want to be a mom. That's not a fashionable thing to say at this place, and some of the women in the class would treat me like some sort of traitor if they heard it. But it's true."

Jennifer was getting good grades and had landed a summer job with a big consumer goods company. There was every indication that when she graduated from Stanford next year, she was going to be able to get a big, demanding, lucrative job.

"But I'm thinking to myself, 'Wait a minute. *My* mom stayed home with me and my brothers, and she always says that raising us was the most rewarding thing she's ever done. Maybe trying to have the big career is the surrender to male values. Maybe treating the idea of motherhood with a little more respect is the really feminist thing to do.' "

Listening to Jennifer I reached a conclusion that I never had any later reason to amend. Business school was a lot harder for the women than for the men. The men only had to worry about getting the work done. True, a poet like me might also agonize about whether coming to business school had been a sensible step, but even

I took it for granted that I wanted as big and demanding a career as I could get, and that even if coming to business school wasn't the best thing I could have done with two years of my life, it couldn't hurt, either.

But for the women in our class, the doubts were of a completely different order. Maybe they *could* be hurt by business school. They didn't know for certain—how could they? They were the first generation of women to attend. Would a Stanford MBA scare off men they might want to date? Would business school imbue them with harsh attributes of aggressiveness or competitiveness? Would it harden them? What about motherhood? Stanford was clearly delaying their chances of becoming moms by two full years, and probably much longer. You didn't take a job with Goldman Sachs, work for six months, then go off on maternity leave.

"I don't want to turn into some hardened career woman going to fertility clinics to try to have her first baby at the age of forty-five," Jennifer said. "I don't know. I like the challenge and the sense of accomplishment I'm getting out of being here, and I'm really looking forward to the opportunities that having an MBA will open up. But sometimes I get so confused that I wonder whether I should have married Don and I end up in tears." Jennifer managed a smile. "If you tell Louisa I said that, I'll kill you."

Just as the second-years had put on a show during winter term, it was the turn of my class, the first-years, to stage a performance during spring term. There were the usual set pieces: a manufacturing skit, skits poking fun at cases. It struck me that two of the skits summed up the differences between business school men and women.

In the first, Sam Barrett, Drew Fisher, and a couple of other jocks had come up with an act in which they all dressed as women. They put on wigs, splotched their faces with lipstick and rouge, and stuck balloons down their shirtfronts. When Sam and the others, all big young men, strutted on stage, tripping over their high heels and swatting each other with handbags, the audience responded with laughter and catcalls. The audience knew that it was supposed to laugh and catcall. This sort of drag act was, after all, a minor part of the culture, a recognized form of good-natured humor—Milton Berle had been doing gags dressed in drag since at least the 1950s. We could all tell before it happened that the skit would end with Sam, Fish, and the others trying to pop each other's balloons.

Later came a sketch put on by women. Shirley Buchanan, one of the black women, strode on stage in a sequined dress and a frizzy wig that made her look like Diana Ross. A moment later, three other women, one of them Louisa Pellegrino, took up positions on stage behind her. Then the band struck up a loud, hot jazz number, and Shirley grabbed her microphone, shouted, "Yeah!" and began to sing as the chorus behind her started to do a choreographed dance like the backup singers in the Supremes. The performers had written the lyrics themselves, and they kept belting out the refrain, "I'm a Stanford woman—*watch* me."

No one in the audience knew quite how to respond. A few students shouted "Right on!" every time Shirley and the chorus got to the refrain. But from the back of the auditorium, where I was sitting, it looked as though many people were just shifting in their seats and waiting for the act to be over. When Shirley and her chorus took their bows they received only confused applause.

In the show as in business school itself, the men were in familiar roles. They knew how to behave and everyone knew how to behave toward them. But the women had to make up their roles for themselves.

TWENTY-ONE

Club Stanford

April 21

I'm pleading with Conor and Professor Healey just below the press box in the Stanford football stadium. "Mercy. Please, have mercy!" I've already run ten sets of stadium steps in the midday sun. Now my vision is blurred. I'm so dehydrated I could faint at any moment and tumble down the steps to my death. I drop to my knees to beg, but Conor and Healey only break into peals of laughter.

"Get up, slug," Conor commands. "You've got another ten pounds of flab to run off." Conor begins to strike bodybuilding poses, flexing his tanned, enormous muscles. How did this happen? Conor used to be skinny.

"You heard him, fatso," Healey barks. "And after you finish the steps, it's off to the weight room." Last term Healey had a middle-aged body that was fifteen pounds overweight. Now he looks incredible, like Johnny Weissmuller or Jack LaLanne. Am I the only man at Stanford with a spare tire? Healey gives a blast on a coach's whistle. "Ten more sets of steps, Robinson," he says. "Let's move."

Then I wake up. It was only a spring term nightmare, and there have been worse. Once I dreamt I drowned playing water polo. Other times I saw myself saying uncool things at dinner parties or burning the shark meat at barbecues. The traumas a business school student suffers once it gets to be spring term.

The pace during spring term remained brisk—there were still ten classes to prepare for and attend every week, and performing the casework for Marketing alone took a good ten hours per class—but by the standards of fall and winter terms, spring term afforded a sense of leisure. The most vivid demonstration of how much the workload dropped took place at midterms, when four out of five exams simply did not take place. In the History of U.S. Business, Professor Font gave us a multiple choice quiz intended only to make certain that we had been keeping up with the reading. (Font said as he handed the quiz out that he would rather have us devoting our time to the research papers due at the end of the term than cramming for a three-hour midterm. As the door swung shut behind him, we chuckled. Devote our free time to research? The very idea.) In Business in the Changing Environment, Strat Man, and Marketing, there were no exams or quizzes at all, just case write-ups to complete. Only in Macro did we have to endure a full, three-hour exam.

Taking advantage of the new spring term regime, students quickly started to behave as though they were at a Club Med. Sam Barrett spent an hour a day at the pool swimming laps. Philippe tried swimming, then switched to volleyball when he found it a better sport for meeting undergraduate women. Jennifer Taylor began tennis lessons. Joe took up golf. Conor and I started meeting Professor Healey a couple of afternoons a week in the weight room, sometimes, as I indicate in the journal entry above, even jogging to the football stadium to run steps. All of us, even Conor and I, went to lots of parties.

While fall and winter terms had both posed daunting questions that every student had had to face—in the fall, Will I flunk or pass?, and in the winter, Will I get the job I want?—spring term at first seemed to present no question of any greater moment than whether to go to a hot tub party or a barbecue on a Friday or Saturday night. Yet precisely because spring term involved so little trauma it afforded students a wider scope for introspection, and although my classmates were not, on the whole, an inward-looking group, every so often one of them would take time out from Club Stanford to wonder.

Business aside, what is happening to the rest of my life?

April 23

Every so often Joe has a moody spell. When he's up he's his old self, but when he's down he mopes, facing the term with nothing better than a kind of grim determination. This makes no sense. Joe is doing what he likes best, net-working. He's out at a party or restaurant almost every night. He's been elected class treasurer and president of the Finance Club. Everybody likes him. He's got a great summer job. So why is he so blue?

Over the next few weeks, I gathered clues.

The first came when Joe's girlfriend, Julie, visited for a weekend, flying in from Hartford, Connecticut, where she worked for an insurance company. On Friday and Saturday, Joe was boyishly happy. He showed Julie the campus, introduced her to his friends, and took her to business school parties both nights. But when Joe got back to the house after dropping Julie off at the airport on Sunday afternoon, he was morose.

"We talked about marriage," Joe told me in the hot tub. "She's all for it, but she wanted me to know two things." The first was that Julie intended to keep her job. This meant that when Joe went back to work for Salomon Brothers he and Julie would have to live in southern Connecticut and both commute an hour or more to their jobs, she to Hartford, he to Manhattan.

The second was that Julie didn't want children.

"Maybe she'll change her mind in a few years," I said.

"Doubt it," Joe said. "She really wants to make it big in her career. I respect that." After a moment of silence he added, "Trouble is, I always wanted to be a dad."

The next clue came when I noticed that Joe appeared uneasy after spending time with Kevin Sumner, the student who had flown to beaches in Southeast Asia in his father's Learjet.

"Last night Kevin and I went to this really fancy French restaurant in San Francisco," Joe told me one day at lunchtime. "We're at our table, right, and who do you think walks in? Charles Schwab. [Schwab, a Stanford business school alumnus who lived in the area, is the founder of a nationwide brokerage house.] Schwab saw Kevin and said, 'Hi, Kevin,' really warmly. Kevin said, 'Hi, Charles,' right back. It just blew me away. Is there a rule that all really rich people are on a first-name basis?"

Joe took a bite of his burger and a gulp of his Coke.

"Sometimes I really want to be a member of that club, you know? Other times I don't know. I guess I'm confused. I want to make all the money I can, just as long as I don't end up rich."

The most important clue came one afternoon while I was upstairs dumping laundry into the washing machine. Down the hall in Joe's office, his phone rang. As I threw in the detergent, I heard Joe's mother leave a message on his answering machine.

"Hi, Joe. Just wanted to know how you're doing. Oh, by the way, I ran into Tony Antonucci's mother after Mass. She says Tony's got three kids now. She was real impressed when I told her where you are. Says you should give Tony a call next time you're home."

Suddenly I understood. Joe had come to business school to do what almost all of us were in one way or another trying to do, move up in life. Only for Joe, it was more of a climb. He was leaving behind a world of big, warm families, nurturing mothers, and fathers whose factory jobs got them home every night in time for dinner. He was about to enter a world in which he would work twelve or more hours a day, travel constantly, associate with people who owned their own jets, and marry a woman who intended to keep her own job and put off having children, if she ever had any. The new yuppie world existed at a higher level of prosperity and prestige than the old, blue-collar world, no doubt about it. But every so often Joe must have wondered whether it was worth it.

May 6

I had been talking to Edita for half an hour tonight when she said she still wasn't sure we should get married.

"But we're engaged," I said. Then I hung up.

Five minutes later, I called back to apologize. Five minutes after that, she called me to apologize herself. Three conversations, an hour on the phone, and all we did was torture each other.

To explain:

During fall term I missed Edita so badly that when we were to-gether during the Christmas break I proposed to her. Before she ac-cepted, she said, we needed to have a talk.

The talk stretched over days, but what it came down to was busi-ness school. In Arizona, Edita had learned that business school changes people, teaching them new methods of thought and afford-ing them new opportunities. How would business school change me? Would the speechwriter turn into a banker? Would he live in New York? L.A.? Chicago? We should not get married, Edita believed, until we knew the answers. On New Year's Eve I put a diamond on Edita's finger, but we agreed not to set a date.

Now, during spring term, Edita and I did what all people in love did during enforced separations: felt miserable. We wrote stilted, self-conscious letters. We ran up phone bills we could not afford. We raided our savings to fly her to California twice. Within the space of a single phone call we could feel close, drift apart, then come together again, and one week was plenty of time for us to break off our engagement, make up and start planning the wedding, then break off the engagement all over again. We had never had trou-ble like this before. *It's business school,* I thought. *Business school is doing this to us.*

I would have liked to believe that the ups and downs between Edita and me were unique, pangs no man and woman in love had ever felt before. But among my classmates romantic woes were com-monplace. I knew of five classmates who had gotten engaged during Christmas vacation only to break off their engagements in the spring. Business school did that to people. It placed students' personalities in flux. It made them wonder how they could decide whom to marry when they could not decide who they were themselves.

Only Gunnar Haakonsen had a relationship that proceeded just as he intended, moving smoothly from the engagement at Christmas to the wedding the following summer (the wedding pictures showed the new Mrs. Haakonsen in a beautiful gown, Gunnar in traditional Scandinavian garb that included hobnailed boots). Gunnar knew what he wanted and got it, as untroubled by doubts or hesitations as a Norseman.

One Friday I took off the entire afternoon to wander around San Francisco with Conor. In the evening we stopped at an Irish pub, and as we sat talking, Conor announced that he was struggling with the whole idea of becoming a businessman.

"You can't imagine what I'm going through," he said.

"What are you talking about? I'm as much of a poet as you are."

"Yes, but you're an *American* poet," Conor said.

"What difference does that make?"

"What difference?" Conor said. "It's obvious. Just look at the American flag. Three colors. Thirteen stripes. Fifty stars. All mathematical and precise. The flag of Eire? A golden harp on a field of green. No numbers at all, just melody.

"You Americans are born to business. Being practical is part of your culture. You conquered a continent. You're makers and doers. For us Irish, it's just the reverse. Our history exalts the dreamers, the mystics, the poets."

Conor took a nip of whiskey, then cradled the glass in his hands.

"Sometimes I think that by becoming an MBA I'm turning my back on my country. This term I'm starting to enjoy spreadsheets and business plans. But that only makes it worse. I feel like a traitor."

Maybe, Conor said, he should have tried to be more like Sam Barrett. Sam had refused to take a conventional MBA job with a big bank or corporation, flying to Hawaii during spring break and landing himself a job designing gear for a little windsurfing outfit instead. Conor argued with a straight face that he should have tried to find a job manufacturing harps or exporting Irish cardigans.

"Conor," I said, "you have a wife and child. You need a career."

Conor nodded in reluctant agreement. "The truth," he said. "The wicked truth."

By now the evening's entertainment, three folk singers, had taken the stage and tuned their guitars. The lights dimmed. One singer stepped forward to announce the first number, "Londonderry Air."

The group struck up, playing the ballad so badly that I turned to Conor to apologize on behalf of all Americans. Conor, however, was too far gone. He sat nursing his drink, smiling sadly, and tapping his foot to the music.

When the lights came up and our bill arrived, Conor refused to let me pay my share. "I may be Irish," he said, "but my MBA still got me a summer job at Apple computer." Then Conor grinned, the businessman in him gloating at the upper hand it had achieved, for the moment, over the poet. "Beats potato famines."

Zen reemerged during spring term, turning up at parties and barbecues (even now he often came late and only stayed an hour or so before leaving to go back to work). One day Zen asked if I would be free for a "typical American evening." I agreed, on the condition that this time he let me pay for dinner. A week later Zen and I went to a restaurant and concert, both of his choosing.

The restaurant was McDonald's. I protested, offering to take Zen to a seafood restaurant or steak house instead.

"But American evening, yes?" Zen said.

"American evening, yes."

"Then Big Mac."

Zen ordered his Big Mac, plus a fish filet, an extra large order of fries, and a strawberry milkshake. As he gobbled them he beamed.

The concert Zen chose was an appearance by Frank Sinatra. Once again I had misgivings. Sinatra was old, and so, it seemed, was his audience; as Zen and I filed into the arena, we found ourselves surrounded by women in their sixties and seventies. But Sinatra was still Sinatra, and the songs were simply marvelous. "That Old Black Magic." "The Lady Is a Tramp." "Love and Marriage." Zen put his elbows on his knees and leaned forward to take in every detail with the eagerness of a child. When Sinatra sang "My Way," Zen and I both joined the ladies in their standing ovation. After the concert, Zen himself started crooning as we wove our way through the giant parking lot. "That ord brack magic has me in its sperr. . . ."

When we got into the car, Zen put his hands on the steering wheel and turned to me, suddenly serious.

"I have written to Paine Webber," he said.

"You want them to help you find an apartment in New York? Joe says the big banks are good about that."

"I have written to Paine Webber to say I cannot accept their summer job."

I was stunned. When he had accepted the offer during winter term, Zen had been thrilled to be joining an American firm. "But why?"

"I am Japanese. I will go back to Mitsui."

Zen popped a Sinatra tape in the cassette and started the car. As we drove south on 101, I realized that Zen must have intended this evening as a ceremonious farewell to his hopes for living in America. Maybe when Zen told his superiors at Mitsui about his plans to leave the company they had pressured him to change his mind. Or maybe Zen had decided that during interview season business school had given him a false, giddy sense of opportunity, robbing him of his judgment, and that now, during spring term, he could see his life more clearly.

Paine Webber was an American company. Zen was Japanese. Some gulfs cannot be bridged.

Conor was finding it difficult to think of himself as a businessman. Zen seemed disappointed that business school had not turned him into an American. And while Joe was struggling to adjust to his new, yuppie world, I was struggling to understand what being an MBA meant to my relationship with the woman I hoped to marry. During spring term it was as though the surgery we had all come to business school to undergo was complete, and while we would still have to engage in a second year of therapy and adaptation, we already had our new identities. Now our bandages came off and we stepped before the mirror. For each of us, as for many of our classmates, what we saw took some getting used to.

It must be said, however, that there were some students for whom Club Stanford involved no angst, just fun. Mr. Cool and Mr. Perfect wore smiles that only grew brighter as their tans grew deeper.

Philippe, too, was as far as I could tell a genuinely happy man. He forgot the ski bunnies he had dated at Tahoe and started dating Stanford undergraduates; when Philippe wasn't with the blonde nineteen-year-old he loved, he loved the blonde nineteen-year-old he was with. Only a single event, later in the term, ever marred Philippe's contented, flawless existence.

May 14

He may have been upset from time to time when a woman failed to respond to his advances, but I never saw Philippe so completely distraught as when he came home this evening with Joe. Philippe had been driving down El Camino in his big Buick, the top down, the engine roaring. Then black oily smoke began to billow from under the hood. When Philippe pulled over, the car burst into flames. A cop called the Palo Alto fire department, which sent a truck that doused the car with foam. Philippe had the Buick towed to the business school parking lot.

"Sorry, buddy," Joe said tonight over dinner, "but the car's a hulk. You might as well get rid of it."

Philippe refused. "I did not come to business school to fall in love with the most magnificent car I 'ave ever seen, only to abandon her. Anyway, the parking sticker is still legible."

Within a week, Philippe had bought a secondhand Volkswagen convertible. But it was a small, boxy, European car, not a big American beauty, and his affection for the charred Buick in the business school parking lot remained strong. "Cars like the 1973 Booeek will never be made again," he would say. "Before we graduate I will 'ave my Boo-eek rebuilt. And when I leave, I will ship 'er back to Europe." He never got the chance. When Gorbachev came to the campus a year later, the Secret Service towed Philippe's car away, along with the heap that Hugh Oglesby had bought for less than the price of a parking sticker.

TWENTY-TWO

We're All Here
to Help the Poor

Stanford business school had a spirit or ethos that I never did figure out. It was completely contradictory. On the one hand, the school had about it a sense of aggressiveness let loose, of what Louisa Pellegrino called an oversupply of testosterone. Students tried to outperform each other in class, struggled to top each other in study groups, even competed fiercely in intramural sports like water polo and tennis that were supposed to be just for fun. It was this aspect of MBA life that Professor Healey was always mocking ("The MBA motto? 'I'll Tread on You.'").

Yet there were lots of circumstances in which my Stanford classmates demonstrated the same help-your-neighbor, do-gooding spirit that you'd expect to find in nuns. During spring term, when students had more time on their hands, the do-gooding became pronounced.

Joe, for example, joined a couple of other members of the Finance Club in organizing a charity called Flights Against Homelessness. Joe figured out that every travel agency on the San Francisco peninsula was lusting after us business school students. Second-year MBAs, after all, often flew thousands of miles to interviews in New York, Los Angeles, Chicago, and elsewhere before deciding on their jobs.

So Joe and his cohorts chose one travel agency, paid a visit to its president, and offered him a deal. If the agency would give Flights

Against Homelessness five percent of the price of every ticket a Stanford business school student booked, Flights Against Homelessness would in turn put up posters in the business school urging MBAs to book all their travel exclusively through the agency. "The guy practically threw himself to the floor and kissed my ankles," Joe said.

These acts of charity were of course commendable. But the do-gooding spirit among my classmates also expressed itself in a very particular sense of propriety or etiquette that could be hard to take. Talking about doing good was good. Talking about making money was not. I know this because I tried it. At one lunchtime conversation during spring term I made the statement, innocent enough to my mind, that after six years on a mediocre government salary I was hoping my summer at Dillon Read would teach me something about making real money. There was a startled, embarrassed silence. I might as well have belched at a tea party.

To an extent, I suppose, this reticence to talk about money was simply good manners. Gifted with intelligence, health, youth, my classmates were the kind of people who probably *would* make lots of money, and they knew it. Talking about money openly would have been too much like gloating.

Yet there were times when the Stanford business school attitude toward money verged on the self-righteous. It is one matter for students seeking graduate degrees in, say, musicology or English literature to look down their noses at profit, but another and sillier matter for MBAs to do so. During spring term, a scandal showed what I mean.

The Reporter was the student-run, weekly business school newspaper. Just after spring midterms, the annual election of the editorial staff took place and the second-years who had been running the paper all year stepped down to make way for the new, first-year staff. Soon after, the first-years found some funny numbers in the paper's accounts. While many students had apparently assumed that putting out *The Reporter* was purely a volunteer effort, it now emerged that the paper had been run for profit. For *profit*, you understand.

To defend themselves, the second-year staff that had just stepped down wrote a memo, placing a copy in every student's mailbox. The memo stressed that $6,000 of the newspaper's revenues had been donated to charity. But the memo went on to admit that, following long-standing practices, the second-year staff had also put some money in its own pockets. Six thousand dollars had been paid as commissions to the dozen students who had sold advertising. Two thousand five hundred dollars apiece had been paid to the business manager, the advertising manager, and each of the two editors. Another five thousand had been blown on *Reporter* dinners. (Even if the other payments were not common knowledge, no one could complain that he hadn't known about *The Reporter*'s dinners, which were famous. The newspaper held a dinner each term for thirty to fifty staffers and their friends. The spring term dinner, just a couple weeks before this scandal broke, had taken place in the back room of a Chinatown restaurant. *The Reporter* had rented a bus to transport its guests to San Francisco and back, providing free booze in both directions.)

"They were ripping us off," Louisa Pellegrino said. "They were only able to sell advertising in the first place because they were connected to the business school. It's just outrageous." Louisa and I were having lunch in Arbuckle Lounge, and judging from what I could overhear of conversations at other tables, many of my classmates shared her outrage.

Joe filled me in on events as they unfolded over the next couple of days. The new first-year staff demanded that their predecessors give the money back. The second-years refused, claiming that they had done nothing wrong and that they had already spent most of the money anyway. Then the deans entered into the action, threatening to bar the second-years from the commencement exercises, only a few weeks away. Events now became unclear, even to Joe and his sources. The best rumors had it that the second-years forced the deans to back off, either hiring or threatening to hire a couple of lawyers. The matter was finally settled, according to the final rumor, when the second-years each agreed to give a couple of hundred dollars back to the newspaper and another couple of hundred dollars to charity. Even at that it took days for all the indignation to die out of lunch table conversation.

I was never able to see that there was much in this episode to get worked up about, let alone to justify a week and a half of dudgeon. The student newspaper I had worked on at Dartmouth had paid students to sell advertising, a practice I had always assumed was standard. Granted, *The Reporter* would have had more the air of an enterprise on the up-and-up if the students running it had made sure everyone knew about their compensation scheme. But they hadn't. So what? They had put scores of hours into producing a newspaper that was given away for free to hundreds of students and alumni every week of the academic year. Was it a surprise that they had asked something in return? This was a business school. We had all come here to get good at doing things for profit.

"Yeah, I know," Joe said when I told him my view, "but you can't blame people for getting upset. Ethics are in, greed is out."

Midway through spring term, Michael Dukakis visited the Stanford campus. As I noted that night in my journal, "my fellow MBAs did everything but shout hosannas."

It was true. Michael Dukakis had carried just ten states and the District of Columbia against George Bush, then returned to Massachusetts to preside as governor over one of the worst budget crises in the history of the commonwealth. But when Governor Dukakis walked through a side door and strode to the stage in Bishop Auditorium, his business school audience greeted him with an ovation.

Dukakis gave a speech that sounded as though he was still running against "eight years," as he put it, "of Reagan-Bush." (Healey, seated next to me, whispered, "That's the way it is with presidential candidates when they lose. Always takes 'em a couple of years to stop campaigning.") Dukakis argued for a government that "cared." He spoke about the economic expansion of the 1980s, which created nineteen million jobs and occasioned a sharp drop in the poverty level, as a decade of greed, out of control and compassionless. Maybe a quarter of the students looked skeptical, but the solid majority wore expressions that ran from respectful to reverential. When Dukakis finished his remarks, he got another standing ovation.

I was baffled. Dukakis was clearly a thoughtful, articulate man who believed in what he said, and a big part of the country undoubtedly shared his views (even though he had lost to Bush, Dukakis had won 46 percent of the vote, three percentage points more than Clinton would carry in defeating Bush four years later). But as I had understood it, the Dukakis campaign platform had been very clear: bigger government and higher taxes, especially on the affluent. It was no surprise that this was anathema to a Reagan man like me, of course. But I would have guessed it to be anathema to the huge majority of my classmates as well. Then before my very eyes the huge majority of my classmates responded to Michael Dukakis as though he were a visionary. I did not begrudge them their opinion. But for a moment I found myself wondering whether I was at Stanford business school or the Kennedy School of Government.

Not long afterward, I mentioned my puzzlement to Milton Friedman, the Nobel Prize–winning economist and probably the smartest man I'll ever meet. (Knowing I would never have another introduction quite like it, I had written to Dr. Friedman, a Fellow at the Hoover Institution, telling him that when I left the White House President Reagan had urged me to look him up.) When I told him about my classmates' politics, Friedman rocked back in his chair for a moment to think.

"No," he finally answered, "I can't explain it." Many people still believed that socialism was based on compassion while capitalism was based on exploitation, even though this notion was patently incorrect. Just look at the difference between life in a mostly capitalist country, like the United States, and life in a mostly socialist country, like Cuba.

"But you'd think," Friedman said, "that at a business school of all places students would understand the importance of low taxes and limited government." If a Nobel Prize winner couldn't explain my classmates' political views, I concluded, I might as well stop trying.

"Aw, c'mon, Peter," Healey said over lunch at a Chinese restaurant still later. "Of course the students here are liberal. They're *students*." Most of my classmates were still in their twenties. More than that, they were MBAs. That meant they expected money to fall into their laps. Since they believed they'd be making good money almost more as a result of luck than of hard work, they wanted to spread the money around.

"But I'm telling you, this is nothing to get steamed up about. When these students graduate, wham, reality rears up and smacks 'em."

A few might be lucky enough to get rich quickly and easily, Healey said, but the rest would have a quite different experience. Even with Stanford MBA degrees, they would have to work for a living. This would lead them to resent paying taxes. "Strange thing. When you work for your money, you get kind of proprietary about it."

Within five or ten years, even my youngest classmates would get married and have children. "Then they'll finally start thinking about doing more with their money than buying fast cars and going on slick vacations." They would want to buy houses. This would introduce them to property taxes. They would want to start putting money aside in stock funds to pay for their children's college educations. This would introduce them to capital gains taxes. In many cases they would want to start their own companies. This would introduce them to the Occupational Safety and Health Administration, the Environmental Protection Agency, the Equal Employment Opportunity Commission, and a dozen other regulatory bodies.

"By the time your class comes back for its tenth reunion," Healey said, "you won't be able to spill a beer without splashing a Republican."

May 19

Tonight there was a big charity auction in Bishop Auditorium. Sam Barrett and Loretta Parker, the woman who used to be in show business, acted as masters of ceremonies. Sam wore a tuxedo jacket and swimsuit, Loretta a black feather boa and a floor-length red dress covered in sequins, a costume from her days as a lounge singer on cruise ships. As Sam and Loretta took bids, a slide of each item appeared on the screen at the front of the auditorium.

Professor van Cleef volunteered to take two students to lunch at the Faculty Club and give them investment advice; the slide showed him seated at his desk, grinning as he counted a huge pile of Monopoly money. Van Cleef's investment advice went for $200. Sam Barrett, Drew Fisher, and several other jocks offered to give a set of windsurfing lessons; they were pictured on the business school lawn in swimsuits, holding a windsurfing board over their heads with one arm each while flexing the biceps of their free arms. A group of five students won the lessons for $150. Marvin Lieberman, the lecturer who teaches entrepreneurship, sold lunch with himself and three of his Silicon Valley venture capitalist friends. After heated bidding, this item went to three students for $300 each. Rupert Dupplin, appearing on the screen in a tail coat, brought in $50 for his services for one evening as an English butler, while three second-year women, appearing in aprons, sold their services as maids for a Saturday afternoon for $150 amid laughing shouts of "Sexist!"

The big event took place at the end of the evening, when a drawing was held for the winner of a prize Joe had persuaded the Flights Against Homelessness travel agency to donate: a ten-day trip for two to Hawaii. Tickets for the drawing had been sold at lunchtime in the courtyard all this week. Sam put the mike to his lips and imitated the sound of a drum roll while Loretta reached into a cardboard box and pulled out a ticket stub.

"Number 242," Loretta announced A second-year woman in the middle of the auditorium shrieked. Then, to wild applause, she walked down the aisle to the stage. Sam asked her to tell us all what it felt like to be the big winner and handed her the mike. The woman waited a moment for the room to quiet down.

"All of us already have plenty of money—or at least we will once we graduate and start our jobs. And since I don't really need this vacation, I'd like to turn it over to Sam and Loretta to auction off for charity." The auditorium exploded in cheers.

The trip to Hawaii sold for $1,000, bringing the evening's total to almost $10,000.

Conor and I left the auction together. "Only in America," Conor said, "would you ever see quite such a mixture of money, high spirits, and do-good-ing."

I corrected him. "Only in business school."

TWENTY-THREE

The Fizzing of the Cheap Champagne

May 26

With two weeks left in the term, students are just sauntering around enjoying themselves as though this first year at business school was no big deal. It was a big deal, and now that it's almost over I want to see some recognition. I want the school to hire a brass band and stage a parade across the campus. I want the Dean to hold a press conference. I want the class president to release a thousand pink and azure doves from the courtyard. We've made it.

We *had* made it. *I* had made it. Marketing, more than any other class, made me see this. I can even remember the precise moment when it dawned on me. Business school, I knew just about halfway through our discussion of the Cinch case, was starting to take.

Cinch was a new product, a liquid dishwashing detergent that Procter & Gamble intended to introduce (the case was set in 1982). P&G was confident Cinch would stand out from other dishwashing detergents because of its secret ingredient, a mysterious agent that would make Cinch powerful enough to take on the cleaning of especially dirty pots and pans. The case assigned us to formulate a promotional scheme for the launch of the new product. How difficult, I figured, could that be? A little advertising, a few coupons in the Sunday newspapers. Then I read the case. It ran to thirty-four pages.

Before the Cinch case, I realized later, I looked down my nose at people who sold soap for a living. After the case, I'd been humbled. Our study group must have spent twenty hours trying to decide how to divide our budget among free-standing insert coupons, TV ads, magazine ads, 30-percent-off prepacks for the twenty-two-, thirty-two-, and forty-eight-ounce bottles, and a big per-case allowance to give to supermarkets in order to win shelf space for the new product. Selling soap, I concluded, was a worthy enterprise for bigger brains than mine.

Professor Dawson turned the case discussion over to the Procter & Gamble executive who had actually been in charge of launching Cinch. A Stanford MBA in his late forties, the executive used the electronic wheel of fortune to call on a study group. As the unlucky group regained its composure and began to present its work, it became clear that their plan was completely defective. To begin with, their plan, like ours, called for a big spending blitz during the product's first. few weeks.

"But what if Unilever does a two-for-one offer on Sunlight at the same time?" the P&G man said.

Sunlight was a leading dishwashing liquid manufactured by Unilever, perhaps Procter & Gamble's chief competitor. A two-for-one offer on Sunlight would cost Unilever $2 or $3 million. In bringing Cinch to market, Procter & Gamble had already spent as much as $10 million.

"You think P&G shareholders would be proud of you if you gave Unilever the right to spend a couple of million bucks in order to kill your product and cost you ten?"

The lead study group had also planned to mail free samples of Cinch to consumers' homes early in the promotional cycle, just as we had.

"You're telling me you want the free samples to be sent out as early as possible, right?" the P&G man said. He had a powerful voice and a combative manner. "So let me ask you, what does the house-wife do if she likes the product?"

"She goes to the store to buy it," the study group leader said.

"And?"

The study group leader hesitated, suddenly embarrassed. "She finds out that Cinch isn't on the shelves yet."

"Correct. Now, how do you suppose that makes her feel?"

"A little angry?"

"Angry is also correct," the P&G man said. "But not a little. A lot. Never, *ever* send out samples before your product is on the shelves."

The P&G man went on for half an hour, tearing the study group's marketing plan apart, before ending the discussion to tell us how P&G had promoted Cinch in reality.

"Let me begin by revealing the secret ingredient," he said. "The essential element in Cinch's new, harder-scrubbing formula was . . . ground seashells."

There was chuckling.

"Don't laugh," the P&G man continued. "The seashells gave the detergent just the right abrasiveness. It worked great on grease but didn't hurt good china. It was a really good formula."

Next came the moment when the executive was supposed to describe how Cinch was a dramatic success. That had been the pattern for Marketing cases all term. Students would offer their flawed solutions, then Professor Dawson or his businessman guest would tell us how the actual businessmen, the big boys, had succeeded where we students would have failed. Instead, the P&G man admitted that Cinch had bombed.

"Even though it failed, I personally learned a lot from the Cinch case," the P&G man said. In the soap business, customers developed deeply ingrained buying habits. It wasn't enough for a new product to be better than other products. It had to be a lot better. It had to be so much better that it reached out and grabbed the customer's attention. "That was something that I just hadn't understood," the P&G man said.

"There was another problem with the product," he continued. "And this is one that you are allowed to laugh at."

When Cinch had moved more slowly than Procter & Gamble had hoped, it began to pile up in warehouses. "We made a disappointing discovery," the P&G man said. "Seashells sink." The seashells had settled at the bottoms of the bottles and stayed there. "You had to shake a bottle like hell for about five minutes to get the seashells mixed back in. Cinch turned out to be better for exercise and weight loss than for cleaning pots and pans. It was a fiasco.

"What can I tell you?" The P&G man shook his head and chuckled. "Even big guys like P&G make mistakes."

Those words were the most exalted I heard uttered at Stanford. They were my MBA epiphany. From then on, everything at business school was different for me.

Probably the best way to explain this is to describe an earlier moment of sudden understanding that I'd had while I was working back in Washington. At the White House, I'd spent my first few years assuming that everyone else knew more than I did, had sharper political instincts, and performed his job with a lot more competence. Then the epiphany had taken place and I'd spent my final few years feeling that I was just about as good as anybody else.

It had begun with a staffer stopping by my office one afternoon to talk over a speech. Before we'd gotten very far, her office forwarded a telephone call to my line. The staffer picked up my phone, asked, "Who is it?," then sat up smartly and said, "Hello, Mr. President." As she listened, she went pale. "Yes, Mr. President," she said. "No—oh, no, sir. I'll be right over to correct that, Mr. President."

As she pulled her papers together to hurry away, the staffer explained what had happened. Working from a list her office had sent to him, the President had been making telephone calls, informing several dozen men and women that he intended to nominate them to federal judgeships. He had become puzzled when he noticed that for one judgeship there were two names listed. "We screwed up," the staffer said. "Somebody sent over the name of the runner-up along with the name of the guy we finally decided to nominate. If the President had made both calls, we'd have been embarrassed across the whole state of North Carolina."

As the door closed behind her, I had understood. The government of the United States was run by human beings. They made mistakes—not just big policy mistakes that affected the course of history and illustrated the tragic nature of earthly existence, but petty, stupid mistakes, stuff like forgetting to cross out the name of the runner-up for a judgeship when sending documents to the Oval Office. High-ranking staffers, even Cabinet officers, were all, I suddenly realized, essentially amateurs, just like me. There was no more of a career track leading to becoming Secretary of Transportation than there was leading to my own job as a speechwriter. We all had to get our training on the job, and I had just as much chance of doing good work as anybody else. I no longer felt intimidated. I felt freed.

But that was back in politics. At business school, I had felt intimidated all over again. Business was *business*, not an amateur effort. My non-poet classmates, with their backgrounds in banking and consulting, had achieved a competence I lacked. They were here at Stanford to polish that competence for a time before graduating and going on to work for companies that as a matter of course would expect them to launch new products, develop new technologies, and engage in dazzling acts of wizardry in the financial markets. How could I ever measure up?

Even big guys like P&G make mistakes.

Now I understood. Even in business, people screwed things up. And, apparently, were permitted to live (the P&G man had gone on after the Cinch failure to become one of the company's leading figures). The best of my classmates were themselves only human. They had their talents, notably skill with numbers, but in matters of business judgment and market acumen perhaps I could develop offsetting abilities and perform almost as well as they did. For the first time since coming to business school, I felt that maybe I could succeed in business—not just not fail, succeed.

Finally I was starting to get the hang of business school. After the Cinch case I started paying some attention in Strat Man, wondering whether Procter & Gamble could have saved itself a lot of trouble by applying concepts like "strategic assets," "isolating mechanisms," "appropriable rents," or "first-mover advantages." I even spent a couple of hours in the library one afternoon looking up financial information on P&G and Southwest Airlines, then trying to apply concepts from Finance and Accounting to the companies' capital structures. I was starting to like this stuff.

But instead of providing an opportunity to celebrate—I pictured myself calling all my classmates and professors together in the business school courtyard, then climbing to the library terrace, one story up, and shouting, "Hey, everybody! I used to be miserable here. Now I'm not!"—spring term in its final weeks just went on as it had before, only faster. Case discussion blurred into case discussion, party into party, temperate, sunny California day into sunny day. I kept thinking of the way sand seems to run through a three-minute egg timer a lot faster during the last thirty seconds than it does during the first couple of minutes. I was, as I've said, just starting to get the hang of business school. Then the year was almost over.

When the registrar's office sent out forms instructing us to sign up for courses for the following fall, I called Steven.

"What's the second year like?" I asked.

"You'll learn a lot of interesting stuff," he said. "But the first year is what counts. When that's over, you're an MBA."

June 3

Sam Barrett and his housemates threw a last party tonight at their house. Conor and his wife, Kate, drove down from San Francisco and stayed until 1:30, drinking beers and dancing. Philippe engaged in a remarkable feat, dancing all night with not one but two blonde undergraduates, while Joe stayed just off the dance floor, talking with one classmate for a moment, then sharing a laugh with another, enjoying himself but working the crowd, too. Rupert Dupplin acted as butler, circulating in the living room with a drinks tray until Jennifer said, "Rupert, put down that tray and dance," then pulled him onto the patio dance floor by his elbow. At midnight, Sam climbed onto a picnic table and had everyone gather around.

"We made it through fall!" Sam shouted. Cheers. "We made it through winter!" More cheers. "And now we've made it through spring!" Still more cheers. "I don't know about you, but I think we deserve some champagne!" Then he jumped down and threw open the lid of a cooler where he had put a

case of cheap champagne on ice. Joe, Conor, Gunnar, and others reached for the bottles and shook them so that when they popped the corks the champagne spumed high into the air to make brief, fizzing, champagne fountains.

Zen was the first to dive into the pool. "Aaaiieee!" he shouted, then disappeared into the water with a huge splash, fully clothed. Sam went next. Then Conor and Kate, Jennifer and Rupert, Joe, Louisa, Mr. Cool and Mr. Perfect, Philippe and his blondes—all of us found ourselves in the pool, splashing and laughing and paddling to the side to get our glasses of champagne.

I'm not writing this down because the party was in any way exceptional; except for the champagne and the swim, it was just like half a dozen I've been to this term. But with classes ending next week, I figure this is the closest we'll come to an official celebration.

Spring term finals proved completely different from fall and winter term finals. I'd say spring term finals were relaxed, except that California usage provides a much more vivid and accurate adjective. Spring term finals were laid back.

In the History of U.S. Business the final exam wasn't even an exam, just a long paper. I chose the question, " 'If American business leaders often seem paranoid, they have good grounds, for they operate in a society which sends them contradictory signals about what is expected from them, what conduct is permissible and what they may expect to receive as their rewards.' Discuss, citing specific examples."

I cited the era of the robber barons. According to the standard theory, when a firm achieved a monopoly it would raise prices on goods, gouging its customers. But virtually none of the robber barons ever did. Carnegie in steel, Rockefeller in oil, Ford in automobiles—each *cut* prices, while steadily improving techniques of production and distribution. By the time these men reached old age, they had transformed the nation. Rockefeller's cheap oil fueled industrialization; Carnegie's cheap steel built America's railroads and cities; Ford's Models T and A gave cars to the common man. Each of these men received his rewards, namely, of course, staggering riches. But each at one time or another ran afoul of public sentiment. Rockefeller even saw his pride, the Standard Oil Company, broken up by government fiat. Given a theme as rich as that, it was easy to go on for a dozen pages. I finished the essay in a day and a half, then trotted over to Professor Font's office and slid it under his door, three days early.

Professor Healey's final in Business in the Changing Environment took a full four hours, like fall and winter term finals, yet only required us to write two essays. Taking this final was a pleasure. At least it was a pleasure for a poet. I wrote, quickly and happily, glancing up from time to time only to enjoy the sight of the engineers and investment bankers biting their pencils and staring at the ceiling as they struggled to find the right words, just as I had struggled to find the right numbers. Vengeance! Reprisal! Business in the Changing Environment would prove the only class during my two years at Stanford in which I would get an H.

In Strat Man, Morris concluded the course by handing out a set of study notes he had written. These notes proved lucid, informative, and a pleasure to read. They discussed the central concepts of the course—strategic assets, isolating mechanisms, appropriable rents, quasi-rents, first-mover advantages, and the rest—in a sophisticated, intelligible way. The study notes were, in short, all that the lectures, readings, and case discussions were not.

"I don't believe this guy," Joe said. "What was he doing, wasting our time all term when he really *did* know what he was talking about?"

Between the study notes Morris handed out and the notes Joe and I had collected from the other professor's Strat Man class, completing the take-home final that Morris assigned was easy.

The Macro final involved a lot of math and forced a poet like me to work as fast as he could during every minute of the four hours the exam lasted. To that extent, it was just like fall and winter term finals. The difference was that by now I knew what I was doing. I worked the problems, applied the formulas, and made certain I completely filled at least one blue book, thereby making a creditable play for partial credit. A typical question:

> According to the theory, an increase in the interest rate motivates people to reduce current consumption relative

to current income. Correspondingly, people increase current saving. Yet although a temporary downward shift of the production function leads to an increase in the interest rate in a closed economy, it does not lead to any change in the ratio of aggregate consumption to aggregate income. . . .

Explain these results.

Looking back on it, I recognize that being able to understand a question like that requires a very particular frame of mind, a kind of temporary psychosis. By spring term I was taking such questions for granted.

The final final: Marketing.

"The exam will give you four hours to analyze three cases," Dawson said during the last class of the term. "Don't give me just words, class, and don't give me just numbers. I want a full analysis. That means both."

"I'm so nervous about this one, I don't know what to do," Jennifer said several days before the exam. "We've spent at least ten hours on every Marketing case all term long. Now he tells us to do three cases in four hours. I just don't see it."

Nobody did see it. Nobody knew how to study for it, either. Conor and I got together one afternoon in the library to do what we could to prepare. We spent half an hour rifling through our class notes, then gave up. "How can you practice running numbers on cases you've never seen?" Conor said.

On the morning of the exam itself we were all tense as we filed into the classroom, took our seats, and arranged our notes. But Dawson, who had always come to class in a suit and tie, stood in the teaching well wearing a polo shirt and jeans. He was smiling, not giving us his usual intense glare. He looked relaxed.

"Class," Dawson said when the room was quiet, "final exams are important for two reasons." One was grading. Dawson, however, already had more than enough material on which to base a grade for every individual in the class. The other was learning. Yet most of the learning occurred as students studied for exams, not as they took them. "By now you've done all the studying you're going to. So I'm canceling the final. Have a great summer, class."

Dawson walked up the aisle and out the door.

The room erupted into cheers. John Lyons and Gunnar Haakonsen slapped each other a high five. Conor and I engaged in a hearty handshake and Jennifer and Sarah embraced.

"Too early for lunch," Conor said in the courtyard a moment later, glancing at his watch. It was still only twenty past eight. "Guess I'll head home. We've rented a house in Tahoe for the weekend and it'll save Kate a lot of effort if I can get the packing started now." I gave him the address of the apartment I'd rented for the summer in New York.

Then I went back to Portola Valley to get started on the packing myself. I spent most of that afternoon making trips to a storage company in Redwood City, half an hour away, where I had rented a garage-like space for the summer with five other students. I jammed in my bike, my stereo, most of my clothes, and eight boxes of textbooks and syllabuses. That night Joe cranked up his stereo so he could hear it while he vacuumed. "Gotta hustle! Can't leave a dirty house!" At midnight Joe, Philippe, and I climbed into the hot tub one last time. When we climbed out, Joe disconnected the motor and pulled the plug to let the water drain.

The next morning the three of us shared a van to the airport.

EPILOGUE

Paradiso (Sort Of)

There are a great many loose ends to my tale, I recognize. But that was the nature of business school. The first year brought together a diverse group of students who underwent an intense, distinctive experience. Then the year ended. That was that.

When we came back for the second year, my classmates and I dispersed ourselves among dozens of elective courses. Those determined to make their fortunes on Wall Street took classes in high finance. I did not follow, instead taking the one truly elementary finance elective, the one that explained, to a class mostly of poets, simple items like the way corporations managed their cash. I was glad not to be in over my head anymore. But I missed hearing Gunnar Haakonsen and John Lyons ask intent questions about aspects of finance I could not begin to grasp. It had been an experience.

Engineers and other quant jocks took courses in computer sciences and business mathematics. They also tended to be the ones who took electives in creativity and personal development. (One of these electives, nicknamed touchy-feely, involved a weekend-long retreat at which the participants swore never to repeat anything they heard, then bared their souls.) Certified Public Accountants took electives in accounting. (In the computer lab one evening I noticed students in a tax accounting course peering at a printout that must have been a dozen feet long. They looked like mandarins examining a scroll.)

Even in the second year I myself felt far too ignorant of business to choose a specialty. So I continued trying out different fields. I took a course in real estate in which every study group had to scour downtown San Francisco for an office building it believed it could purchase and manage at a profit. I took a course in entrepreneurship, another in running small businesses. Under Professor Healey, I studied the economics of the European Community.

Every one of these courses was a lot more interesting to me than most of the first-year core courses had been, just as I'm sure the finance electives were a lot more interesting to the I-bankers and the accounting courses were a lot more interesting to the CPAs. But now the unity of the first-year core had been broken. In the second year, there was no longer a story of business school to tell, just 332 different stories about business school students. (Three weeks after Orientation, one of the 333 members of our class decided that coming to Stanford had been a mistake and went home. He was the only one of us not to graduate. Several of my classmates had to repeat courses in order to get passing grades, but none of us flunked out.)

More and more, our stories were unfolding off the Stanford campus. By winter term of the second year at the latest, most of my classmates and I had stopped leading our lives at Stanford. We were still physically present at the business school, of course, attending classes and even working hard in the courses that interested us. But our minds were elsewhere. They were on jobs.

Students fell into three categories. About a fifth of the class already had jobs by the time the second year began. John Lyons, for example, always intended to return to Leopard Securities, where he had worked for two years before attending Stanford, while Jennifer Taylor had so enjoyed her summer job, working for General Mills back in the midwest, that when the company offered her a permanent position, she accepted on the spot.

The rest of us had to keep looking. Most threw themselves into the second-year interview season. Recruiters put on big receptions at Palo Alto hotels at which they served liver pâté with fancy little crackers and whole platters of big, juicy shrimp, the expensive kind. They flew students all over the country. Philippe got on a plane to New York five times before achieving his goal of joining a first-rate bank by accepting a job with Goldman Sachs, while Joe persuaded Salomon Brothers to fly him to New York twice before he accepted his former employer's offer.

The final category, the last fifth of the class, conducted what the business school's Career Management Center called an "independent job search." The students in this category either could not or would not get a job with the companies that interviewed on campus, so they were on their own, forced to send out résumés, make phone calls, and arrange interviews as best they could. Looking for a job in Dublin, Conor ran up hundreds of dollars of fax and phone bills and then flew back to Ireland for interviews during spring break at his own expense. He finally landed a job with an Irish insurance company. Sam Barrett flew to the Pacific Northwest half a dozen times, again at his own expense, before taking a job with a small Portland design firm.

I fell into this third category myself, and while there were, as I said, 332 different stories, the one I can tell best is of course my own. My job hunt proved one of the more colorful in our class. I'm not taking credit for it, though. It just happened.

The starting point was the Dillon Read office in Manhattan where I worked for the summer. The recruiters who interviewed me at Stanford were right to worry that I'd find investment banking less exciting than politics. But it wasn't in contrast to politics alone that I found investment banking dull, it was in contrast to *anything*. I would sit at my computer screen from 7:00 in the morning until 11:00 or midnight, creating huge, complicated spreadsheets that told how a client could save an eighth of a cent per share when he launched his takeover bid for Amalgamated Acme. I suppose most of my classmates at Stanford would have thought it all fascinating. But as I glared at the scores of tiny numbers on the screen, I would find myself daydreaming about riding aimlessly for hours on the New York City subways or sitting on the curb in front of my apartment building long enough to discover how many sticks of bubble gum I could fit in my mouth before my jaw locked up. Anything—anything but numbers. I reminded myself that investment banking was the best shot I was ever likely to have at getting rich. I should feel grateful, I said to myself, not bored. But I felt bored. By the time my ten-week summer job ended I knew (as did everyone at Dillon Read) that I could not turn myself into an I-banker no matter how hard I thought about money.

I was hesitant to admit this to Edita. I guessed that after my hysterics during so much of the first year, Edita would want me to begin demonstrating at least a rudimentary emotional stability together with some minimal capacity for earning a living. In a word, I thought Edita was waiting for me to grow up. Pretending I liked investment banking seemed the mature, responsible thing to do. My father hadn't always liked the jobs he'd held, after all, but he'd done them. When toward the end of the summer I told Edita the truth, she astounded me.

"Good," she said.

It had been obvious to her for weeks that I wasn't going to be happy as a banker. "Now you can stop trying to be something you're not."

Back at Stanford the following autumn, I puzzled over my problem. How could I combine an interest in business with the work experience I had gained at the White House? I concluded that a job in the media made sense. That was where people dealt with words and ideas, not numbers, for profit. I asked a journalist friend who knew Robert Maxwell, the British media baron, to write him a letter on my behalf. Another friend agreed to mention me to someone he knew who worked for Rupert Murdoch, the Australian media baron. Later, Steve Jobs, the American computer baron, heard about me from still another acquaintance and asked me to interview for a position in his company. My interviews with these three showed that while a business degree opens doors, they might not always be doors an MBA will want to step through.

When I presented myself at the London offices of Robert Maxwell in March, I was told that Mr. Maxwell wanted me to introduce myself to an American employee of his named Matthew Wilkes.

Wilkes, in his mid-thirties, greeted me nervously. He spent twenty minutes describing the marvelously enticing jobs he could make available in finance, marketing, or programming. Then he told me what a wonderful man Robert Maxwell was. "He's a genius," Wilkes said, looking anxious. "You'd love working for him. I do." All this struck me as peculiar. I was the one who needed a job, but Wilkes was the one doing the selling. He seemed as overeager as a car salesman struggling to make his quota. Maxwell, I began to suspect, must have told Wilkes to hire me no matter what.

Forty minutes into Wilkes's pitch, the windows in his office began to tremble with a sudden, deafening *whup, whup, whup.* "Helicopter's landing," Wilkes shouted. "We'll give him five minutes, then go up and meet the great man."

When Wilkes and I got off the elevator on the top floor we found ourselves in a vast hallway with huge, art deco chandeliers. On one wall hung the Maxwell logo, a gigantic M superimposed on a map of the world. Two secretaries sat outside a tall door. One looked at Wilkes and nodded curtly. "He's waiting for you," she said. Wilkes adjusted his necktie, shrugged his shoulders to straighten his jacket, and opened the door.

Robert Maxwell was seated at a massive desk a good forty feet away. Windows ten feet high looked out onto the London rooftops. Maxwell stood, slowly strode to a huge conference table, then gestured us to join him. He looked over six feet tall. He must have weighed 300 pounds. His hair and eyebrows were jet black—too black, clearly dyed—and he wore a suit and shirt of electric blue with a bow tie of hot pink. My first impression was of a circus bear.

"Mr. Robinson," Maxwell rumbled. He took my hand in his paw and gave it a pump. "Take a seat."

I sat as Maxwell settled his own bulk into a chair, easing himself down like a man entering a bath. Wilkes remained on his feet until Maxwell impatiently waved him to a seat.

"Well?" Maxwell asked Wilkes. "What are we to do with this young man?"

Wilkes seemed to swallow hard.

"Peter and I have talked about his career interests at great length," Wilkes said—this was of course untrue—"and we've decided that Peter would be happiest working for me in electronic media." Wilkes discussed the need he'd felt for a long time now for someone just like me to help him with the finances and marketing of Maxwell's television properties in Europe. "I could keep a close eye on Peter and help him learn the business quickly. Then after a year or two we could give Peter a piece of the business to run on his own."

Run a piece of the business after a year or two? My own estimate of my abilities was that after twice that time I might be qualified to man the switchboard. Maxwell brooded for a moment in silence.

"No," Maxwell said at last. "Quite wrong. That would be the wrong use to make of Mr. Robinson entirely."

Maxwell laid down the correct use to make of Mr. Robinson.

"Mr. Robinson will act as my personal assistant. He will sit with me at the negotiating table. This weekend, for example, when I fly to Moscow, you will come with me. But once Mr. Robinson joins us, he will make such trips instead. He will report back to you on the decisions that have been taken and on the actions you and others in this organization will need to effect as a result. After six or eight months I will know Mr. Robinson well enough to decide what use to make of him next."

Wilkes had turned pale.

"Your assistant?" Wilkes asked. "But Peter doesn't know the business yet—"

Maxwell waved his hand. "I have decided," he said. "You need only find out whether Mr. Robinson accepts my offer. If he does, negotiate a salary and starting date. If he does not—" Maxwell produced another dismissive wave of his hand.

A secretary put her head in the door. "Ariel Sharon on the line for you, Mr. Maxwell."

"That is all," Maxwell told Wilkes. Maxwell strode heavily back to his desk and picked up the telephone to speak to the Israeli cabinet minister. "Arik!" he boomed as Wilkes and I left his office.

"What is the weather in Tel Aviv?" Throughout the meeting, I had not uttered a word.

Wilkes shut the giant door behind us and took me a few paces down the hall, out of the secretaries' hearing. Then he looked me directly in the eyes and said, "You don't want this job." Wilkes looked badly shaken, but even so it crossed my mind that he was joking. Why else would he try to talk me out of a job just moments after his own boss had offered it to me? But Wilkes repeated himself. "You don't want this. Don't come here." Wilkes was clearly serious. For reasons I did not understand, Robert Maxwell had flown me from California to London, spoken precisely five words to me ("Mr. Robinson. Take a seat."), then used me to belittle one of his managers. It must have been bad enough for Wilkes to have been told to hire me. But Wilkes had probably been under the impression that at least I would report to him. Now Maxwell had told Wilkes, in effect, that instead Wilkes would report to me.

Wilkes took me back to his office. He sat behind his desk, bending and unbending a paper clip while he took back everything he had told me about Robert Maxwell just an hour before. Maxwell threw tantrums. He was cruel to his subordinates. I wouldn't have any job security. Personal assistant? One day Maxwell would lose his temper, fire me, and leave me standing on a runway in Moscow.

"Why don't you just tell me right now that you don't want this job?" Wilkes said. "Go ahead, say it. 'I don't want this job.' "

I told Wilkes I would think it over. But as I left Wilkes's office, I felt no more inclination to go to work for Robert Maxwell than to indenture myself to Jabba the Hut.

One evening three weeks later, I drove to the headquarters of NeXT, Steven Jobs's company in Redwood City, just ten minutes from Stanford. While Maxwell's offices had been a gigantic, art deco suite that looked like a set from a 1930s movie, Jobs's headquarters looked like a museum of modern art, clean, simple, functional, sleek. Down one hallway I noticed a bed of gravel set under a stairway, and I slipped past the receptionist for a closer look.

"Japanese rock garden," a voice behind me said. I turned to meet

Steve Jobs. "Zen Buddhist. To inspire serenity." Still in his early thirties, Steve (he was so young it was impossible to think of him as "Mr. Jobs") had already made tens of millions and secured a place in history as one of the seminal figures in the development of the personal computer. He was dressed in a black turtleneck, faded jeans, and running shoes.

After showing me around his headquarters, Steve drove me to a restaurant in downtown Palo Alto, and over dinner he posed questions about where I'd grown up and what it had been like to work in Washington. It was a relaxed, enjoyable conversation, and I had to keep reminding myself that Steve was an important figure, not just an intent, friendly guy my age. "Let's keep this going," he said as we shook hands good night. "There are some people at NeXT I want you to meet."

A week later I found myself back at NeXT. A receptionist seated me in a conference room with a can of Pepsi. Then Steve's senior staff began filing in one after another to interview me. The Director of Personnel, a businesslike man in his forties, came first. He told me about the position Steve had in mind.

Jobs's only assistant, the Director of Personnel said, was a secretary. She could handle Steve's phone calls and correspondence. But she lacked the clout to manage his time.

"Give you an example," he said. "Ross Perot is one of the biggest investors in this company. Just last week, Ross called to talk to Steve. Steve's secretary glanced into Steve's office, saw that Steve was eating lunch, and told Ross that Steve was busy. So Ross called Kristen, a vice president here, and screamed at her for about twenty minutes, making the very good point that when he wanted to talk to Steve, Steve's secretary should damn well put Steve on the line."

For weeks the staff had been telling Steve he needed to hire a chief of staff. "Yesterday Steve came in and told us that if we all liked you, he'd give the job to you."

For the next couple of hours I heard a lot about the senior staff's frustrations with Steve. The top manufacturing guy saw me. The woman in charge of sales came in. The chief designer. The head of marketing and advertising. All of them told me the same story. Steve

Jobs was a brilliant young man who commanded their affection and loyalty, but he missed important meetings and was lousy at returning phone calls. In the words of one vice president, "It's vital for somebody to be around who can *force* Steve to focus on things when we need him to."

The nature of the job thus became clear. I would find myself between the senior staff, a group of intelligent, determined individuals, who would demand that I deliver Steve to them whenever they wanted him, and Steve himself, a brilliant and evidently stubborn young business titan to whom, I gathered, I would not exactly be in a position to issue orders.

"Everything going okay?" Steve said, walking in while I was talking to one of his vice presidents. "Listen, I've got to run to catch a plane, but we'll get together again when I get back." He wished me good luck and left.

The vice president scowled. "Why's he catching a plane? He was supposed to be here all week." Then she made a face that said, "See what I mean?"

I liked Steve. I liked every member of his senior staff. What I disliked was the sound of the job.

When the secretary in Rupert Murdoch's New York headquarters opened the door to his office one month later, Murdoch, a spare, wiry man, ambled over from his desk to shake my hand, then gestured me to a sofa while he picked up a phone on a side table and took a call. It was only 8:00 in the morning, but Murdoch looked as though he had already put in a full day. His shirt was wrinkled. His hair needed combing.

While Murdoch talked, I noticed the five televisions set into the wall facing Murdoch's desk. Each was tuned to a different network, and the display reminded me of the special cabinet a Director of Communications had had at the White House so he could watch all the newscasts at the same time every evening. This was in the early 1980s, and the cabinet had held three television screens, one each for ABC, NBC, and CBS. Now, at the beginning of the 1990s, Murdoch needed five television screens—a fourth for CNN and a fifth for

Fox, the network Murdoch himself owned. Murdoch had founded Fox by combining a chain of TV stations around the country with the old 20th Century-Fox production company in Hollywood. Murdoch also owned Sky Television, a satellite broadcasting venture he had founded in Britain, and newspapers and magazines in Britain, the United States, Australia, Canada, and Hong Kong.

Murdoch hung up the phone and sat in a sofa across from me. "I've seen your résumé," Murdoch said. "We'd love to have you come to work for us." Murdoch spoke with such a heavy Aussie accent ("We'd lave to 'ave yer come to wick ferris") that it took me a moment to decipher what he was saying. I looked at him blankly before blurting, "I'm honored."

"Given your background I'm tempted to make you my personal assistant, but that would be a dead end." Instead, Murdoch wanted me to learn the television industry, especially television news. He envisioned my spending six months to a year at WNYW, the Fox station in New York, where I would learn how to schedule a news show, how to write for TV, and how to produce and shoot a story. After this basic training, Murdoch would probably send me to London, where he intended to launch his own twenty-four-hour TV news channel, in direct competition with CNN. "But first you need to put in your time here in New York. How does that sound?"

"It sounds good," I said. "When do I start?"

In late May, three weeks before business school ended, I had a job.

I graduated in June. Over the next fourteen months events happened fast.

September: Edita and I get married.

October: I start work for Murdoch. Edita and I learn that she is pregnant.

November: I find out that Murdoch is in financial trouble.

June: Our daughter is born.

August: I lose my job.

As my experience in so quickly being both welcomed into and then thrown out of the Murdoch empire indicates, what happened to the fresh crop of Stanford MBAs was, for many of us, unpleasant. At

Stanford, we had spent two years watching big, important companies coax us to join them. We could be forgiven for concluding that we were really something. The business world loved us. The business world *needed* us. We were surfing on the eighties, the biggest flood tide of economic expansion the peacetime United States had ever seen.

Then the tide went out.

By the time we graduated in the spring of 1990 a recession was well under way. A good many of us were, so to speak, left on the beach, high, dry, and—after spending two years of our lives and a great deal of our money getting ready for the fun—terribly embarrassed.

More than a dozen of my classmates still hadn't found jobs when we graduated. One friend, the student who studied in Leningrad before coming to business school and described "capitalist encirclement" as his hobby, was out of work for more than a year. Another few dozen classmates joined me in landing a job only to lose it. Several students who accepted offers with Bain and Company, a leading consulting firm, were told shortly after they reported to work in the fall that their services would not be needed after all.

Even the members of our class who managed to land and hold big impressive jobs with big, impressive firms experienced a good deal of anxiety and uncertainty. Philippe, as I've said, got a job with Goldman Sachs—precisely as he had planned. But when he got to New York to join the Mergers and Acquisitions department, he learned that there were no mergers or acquisitions taking place; in the face of a faltering economy and new government regulations, the takeover movement of the 1980s had collapsed. Philippe spent months sitting at his desk with nothing to do. After hours, he enjoyed the Manhattan restaurants and the chance to meet new women. At least he tried to. Worries that he might lose his job took a lot of the *joie* out of his *vivre*.

Goldman Sachs did finally find a use for Philippe, but in Europe, not New York. Based in Goldman's London office, Philippe began spending almost all his time on the road, touring Eastern European factories that the Communists had mismanaged and Western investors were now hoping to revamp. "The work is interesting enough," Philippe told me nine months after we graduated. "But you must not even try to imagine the nightlife in Dresden or Krakow."

Joe went back to work for Salomon Brothers, just as he too had planned. Ten months later Salomon Brothers suddenly found itself consumed in scandal, admitting that it had broken the rules in U.S. Treasury auctions. Salomon's stock price plummeted, and within days Salomon's three most senior executives resigned. Other executives soon departed, including Joe's boss. For the better part of a year, Salomon Brothers continued to be buffeted by controversy, the firm's business was erratic, and Joe worried every morning that when he got to his office he would find a pink slip on his desk.

In Dublin, Conor's Irish insurance company assigned him to a branch office—in Frankfurt. The company led Conor to believe that after ten months it would give him a permanent position back home. What it gave him instead was a fond farewell. Conor spent almost a year looking for another job.

I myself thought that by going to work for Rupert Murdoch instead of Robert Maxwell or Steven Jobs I was choosing stability over one or another form of chaos. This proved naive. With recession striking all three of his markets, North America, Britain, and Australia, Murdoch found himself losing millions of dollars a week. To stanch his losses he sold $600 million of magazine properties, cut back on unprofitable operations in Australia and England, and let go hundreds of employees. All the young MBAs Murdoch had hired were dismissed. It consoled me that I was one of the last to go, but for that, along with some extra severance pay, I probably had Murdoch's sympathies toward me as a recent father to thank, not my skills.

Today I'm back to being what I was before I went to business school, a writer. Edita is delighted. She thinks I've grown up.

After almost a year out of work, Conor now has a job in Dublin with an Asian bank, operating the bank's first office in the European Community. He and his wife have had two more children, and although they've bought a roomy house in Dublin, Conor is keeping his eyes open for jobs in New York or San Francisco. "It's the Irish disease," Conor says. "When we're in the States we cry big tears because we're not home. When we're home we long for the States."

Philippe has become one of Goldman Sach's recognized experts on Eastern Europe. He balances spending Monday through Friday in Bratislava or Budapest against spending as many weekends as he can in Paris. "I still miss the California women," Philippe says. "But the French women—well, life could be worse."

Although still with Salomon Brothers, now once again one of the leading firms on Wall Street, Joe is looking for a small company to buy near Hartford so that he and his wife can start leading a more settled home life. "Julie's still not sure," Joe says, "but she thinks that after another year or two we might even think about starting a family."

Jennifer Taylor, still with General Mills, is dating a vice president of Northwest Airlines, another big Minneapolis company. "I'm pretty sure he's the one," she says. "Now what do I do? Keep working or stay home and have five kids like my mom?"

Sam Barrett operates a windsurfing shop on Maui.

Sam's old house mate, Louisa Pellegrino, works for the Environmental Protection Agency in Washington.

Rupert Dupplin works for McKinsey. He spent his first year in L.A., then moved back to London. "Funnily enough," he says, "I actually started to miss the fog."

Zen is back in Osaka, still with Mitsui, as he expects to be for the rest of his working life. "Good news!" his last postcard read. "Maybe next year promotion! Maybe move to Australia!"

Gunnar Haakonsen is in New York, working for Morgan Stanley in the Latin America group, one of the most prestigious and profitable of Morgan's divisions. Mr. Cool has made his quantum leap.

Since we graduated, the old dean of the business school has retired and a new dean, Michael Spence, has made a number of changes, both in the staff and the curriculum. By and large, Professor Healey informs me, Spence is attempting to make the school more practical. "But it ain't easy. He keeps running smack into the guys on the faculty who think the school exists to let them do their research."

I still consider it one of the minor outrages of American higher education that Stanford sends students into the business world without even attempting to teach them the intellectual underpinnings of free markets—without insisting, for example, that students read the principal theorists of free markets, including Adam Smith and Friedrich von Hayek, or, for that matter, the principal opponents of free markets, including Karl Marx. Yet it sounds as though on the whole Stanford is a better business school today. (In its two most recent surveys, *U.S. News* ranked Stanford the best business school in the country one year, second-best the next. *BusinessWeek*, on the other hand, recently published a survey that ranked Stanford seventh.) It also sounds as though the warfare at Stanford between the applied and the theoretical, the practical and the academic, rages on.

So was business school worth it?

Not as a straight and easy road to riches. In the couple of years since we've graduated, so far as I know only one of my classmates, John Lyons, Mr. Perfect, has made it really big. After Stanford, John went back to Leopard Securities. In his second year, at the age of twenty-nine, he made $5 million. No other member of our class has made anything like that kind of money, and even in John's case it is unclear that business school was responsible for his success. Steven notes that John worked for the same securities firm *before* going to Stanford. "Instead of teaching him how to make $5 million," Steven says, "it's quite conceivable that two years of business school cost him $10 million."

As the Clinton administration raises taxes on "the rich," however, most of my classmates certainly qualify, making, I would estimate, an average of $100,000 a year, while perhaps a quarter of the class, chiefly the investment bankers, earn more than $150,000 a year. Yet most of these young men and women were probably headed for the upper reaches of the middle class even before they went to Stanford. "This business school admits proven performers," Professor Healey once said, "lets them play around for two years in a sunny setting, then takes credit for everything they do afterward."

What am I *certain* that Stanford gave us?

To begin with, a credential. Neither Steven Jobs, Robert Maxwell, nor Rupert Murdoch would have offered me a job if I had not been about to graduate from a business school program. (In the case of Rupert Murdoch, I can make this assertion with certitude. A couple of years before going to business school I wrote to Murdoch asking for work, but I never got so much as a postcard in reply.) Call an MBA a signaling device or, as Professor Healey would have it, a yuppie union card. It works.

For as many as half the members of our class, business school was also a chance to make a basic change in their professional lives, an opportunity for poets, the medical doctors, and the engineers among us to launch themselves into entirely new fields. Business school enabled Philippe to switch from law to banking. It got Conor out of the civil service and into finance. Even though I returned to writing, I, too, was able to make a transition, equipping myself to write not only about politics, my whole background before Stanford, but also about business.

For the half of our class that went back to the banks or consulting firms they had come from, Stanford provided an education that was to at least some extent broadening. Gunnar Haakonsen would no doubt have spent every waking hour studying finance if he could have. Stanford forced him to acquire at least a smattering of learning about manufacturing, marketing, and other disciplines.

A number of students found that Stanford gave them poise and self-confidence. "I used to feel intimidated by people with advanced degrees," Jennifer Taylor said just before graduation. "With an MBA of my own, I won't." All of us, I think, found that Stanford made our thinking more rigorous. Today I can still scrutinize a corporate annual report or a mutual fund prospectus with a fair degree of skill, and for this I have no choice but to credit Stanford's insistence on numbers, numbers, numbers.

For many of my classmates, the people they got to know at Stanford now represent an economic benefit, just as Joe predicted they would. During my ten months with Rupert Murdoch, for instance, I got several calls from classmates at investment banks who needed information about Murdoch's plans, and in a couple of cases I was able to help. That kind of legal, informal sharing of information is of immense value to those active in the business world, especially on Wall Street. So Stanford gave us contacts.

It also gave us friends. Conor and I still make occasional long phone calls between Dublin and the States just like the long calls we made between his apartment in San Francisco and my house in Portola Valley. I see Joe when I get to New York. Edita and I exchange Christmas cards with Philippe, Jennifer, Sam, and two dozen others. My Stanford classmates continue to strike me as the most impressive group of people I have ever encountered, and I treasure these Stanford friendships.

Yet to describe what was, for me, the chief benefit of business school, I need to return for a moment to the fortieth President.

During my first-year spring break I spent a few days with a friend in Los Angeles, and while I was there I stopped by the suite of offices that had just been set up for former President Reagan and his staff.

As he stood to greet me, Reagan had the same twinkle and shine in his eyes and the same knowing nod that he had shown me in the Rose Garden more than a year before. "Just doing a little writing," he said, gesturing to the pad of paper on his desk. "Now that I'm out of office, I have time to get back to writing my speeches myself."

After a moment of small talk, the former President frowned and asked if I had seen the morning newspaper. I had, noticing over breakfast that the *Los Angeles Times* referred to Reagan in two front-page stories. "Saw Risk of Reagan Impeachment, Meese Says," one headline read, while the other stated, " 'Star Wars' Was Oversold, Cheney says."

"I just don't understand it," Reagan said.

"Neither do I, Mr. President."

"How can a *judge* decide the outcome of a sporting event?"

It took me a moment to realize Reagan was not talking about his administration. He was commenting on the America's Cup. A judge in New York had just awarded the cup to the boat from New Zealand, even though the American boat had put in a faster time. "San Diego Loses America's Cup," the headline stated. "Conner's Use of Catamaran Ruled to Be Violation of Governing Deed."

"Well," the former President said, the twinkle returning to his eye, "at least it wasn't a judge *I* appointed."

When I left, I was disappointed at first that the former President had not even mentioned world events, let alone imparted any secrets or insights of historical moment. I felt like the young man in the joke about the dying rabbi. "Rabbi," says the young man, "before you leave this world, tell me, what is the meaning of life?" The rabbi opens his eyes with an effort, then croaks, "Life, my son, is a fountain." The young man blinks for a moment in confusion. Then he gathers his courage. "Rabbi, what do you mean, 'Life is a *fountain?*'" The rabbi opens his eyes once again, looks startled, and asks, "Life *isn't* a fountain?"

I had had my moment with the man who won the Cold War, and all I had managed to come away with was some talk about a boat race. How could Reagan have done that to me?

But by the time I was back in traffic on the Santa Monica Freeway, I recognized that the former President had given me a very good example of the wisdom and simplicity of spirit that I had always cherished in him. For eight years he had been the most powerful man in the world. He had accomplished what he had set out to accomplish, or at least as much as he could. Then he had set it all down and gone back to being as ordinary an American as a former President can be. When Reagan looked at the newspaper, he read about sports. Power wasn't everything.

Likewise business school. I arrived at Stanford determined to learn how to make just as much money as I could. While I had not taken a vow of poverty by the time I graduated, I *had* decided that it made more sense to do work I liked than to earn five or ten times more as an investment banker but feel miserable every day. Business school, in other words, helped me to put gain for the sake of gain in its proper place. I still see money as terribly important, even more so now that I am the father of two (our second child, a son, was born a year and a half after our daughter). But I also value doing work that suits my talents, getting home early enough to help Edita put the children to bed, and spending time with my family on weekends. Money isn't everything.

Had I done the right thing? Sure.

Stanford heightened my appreciation of the brains and talent and sheer creativity required in business. It permitted me to mingle for two years with bright, business-minded classmates and to give serious thought to all kinds of business careers. Stanford even let me *try* being a banker, and get paid for it, and try working in a gigantic communications empire, and get paid for that, too. Most of my classmates learned where they fit in business. I learned that I fit best outside, writing about business rather than participating in it directly.

Did business school lead us into paradise? Business school taught us that there *isn't* any paradise. It assigned cases like Cleveland Twist Drill, Pringles, and Cinch, in which capable, intelligent people worked hard but still failed. It presented us with the spectacle of gifted classmates graduating from Stanford, starting impressive, remunerative jobs, then getting fired.

Even among the richest and most powerful, business school taught us, there is no such thing as an ideal state of ease and success. Just look at the people with whom I interviewed. As news was about to break in 1991 that he had stolen nearly a billion dollars from his companies' pension funds to offset his gigantic debts, Robert Maxwell took a cruise on his yacht, and, in the middle of the night, flung himself into the sea. At NeXT, Steve Jobs was forced in early 1993 to dismiss several hundred employees and stop manufacturing computers, struggling to turn NeXT into a software company instead. Today Rupert Murdoch's properties are once again profitable, and he has just expanded his operations into Asia, making him arguably the most important figure in communications in the world. Yet just three years ago Murdoch nearly lost his entire empire to his creditors.

If even Maxwell, Jobs, and Murdoch were subject to such vagaries, all a lesser mortal can do is work hard, try to be smart, and hope for luck. Business school wasn't able to assist my classmates and me with luck, of course. But it did help to make us smarter, giving us an extensive, rigorous training. And who knows? Maybe even the sheer hellishness of business school had its uses. Getting fired by Murdoch would certainly have been a lot worse if I hadn't been able to say to myself, *I'll make it through this. I made it through Stanford.*

The reader will have to check in with me again in twenty or so years to learn how my classmates and I stand, but it's my belief that after a bumpy start, all of us are going to do just fine. Business school did not, as I've said, deliver us into paradise. But it did equip us all to lead pretty interesting lives here below.

ACKNOWLEDGMENTS

I wish to thank two friends, Steven Manacek and Joshua Gilder, whose friendship I sorely tested. Steven (the same who appears in these pages) called in his suggestions, all of them invaluable, from New York, London, Chicago, Dallas, and, on one occasion, an Alfa-Romeo convertible he was navigating through Los Angeles. This says something about the life of a consultant. And about Steven's generosity with his time. Josh, who was working on his own book, put his remarkable talents at my disposal by commenting on mine. Josh also exchanged writers' agonies with me over the phone, an exercise that was more helpful than it sounds.

I am grateful to Clark Judge, John Podhoretz, and Robert Bork, Jr., colleagues during the 1980s, now members of the White House Writers Group, for their encouragement. I am likewise grateful to the youngest member of the group, Everett Wallace, who checked my facts, suggested changes, proofread the manuscript, and then proofread the galleys—all with unfailing intelligence, diligence, and good humor.

Tony Dolan offered advice on early chapters with the same zest he exhibited when he was Ronald Reagan's chief speechwriter and my boss. Jay French, Javier Piedra, Keith and Elizabeth Pratt, and

Konstantin Graf von Schweinitz, all valued friends, read the complete manuscript and offered detailed suggestions. Two other good friends, José Meseguer and Michael Lucia, helped me with my math. I am grateful to them all.

I would also like to thank Cynthia Cannell, my literary agent, for leading me to Warner Books, where Jamie Raab, my editor, deserves my profound gratitude for the intelligence, tact, and wit she employed in bringing this volume into being.

Finally I wish to thank my parents, Theodore and Alice Robinson, and my wife, Edita. Since we got married, Edita has given birth to our two children, overseen our move across the country to California, and begun teaching Romance languages. All I've managed to do is write this book. I offer that as a handy guide to our relative merits.